WITHDRAWN

FROM
HUMBLE
PETITION
TO
MILITANT
ACTION

A HISTORY OF THE
CIVIL AND PUBLIC SERVICES ASSOCIATION
1903–1978

FROM HUMBLE PETITION
TO MILITANT ACTION

BY ERIC WIGHAM

Paperback Edition   ISBN 0 901411 05 1
Hardcase Edition   ISBN 0 901411 06 X
Limited Edition   ISBN 0 901411 07 8

Published 1980 by The Civil and Public Services Association
© 1980 The Civil and Public Services Association

Edited, designed and produced by Youé and Spooner Ltd
Filmset, printed and bound in Great Britain by Hazell Watson & Viney Ltd

Contents

Foreword

The Civil and Public Services Association, today the largest Civil Service union, has grown considerably from the few hundred civil servants who came together in 1903 to try and improve their way of life. The National Executive Committee of the CPSA decided two years ago to commission a new history of the Association to mark its 75th anniversary in 1978. In a union as controversial as ours, there will probably be many items in this history which some people, particularly those involved, would want to put differently, or at least with a different emphasis. We felt that having carefully chosen an author, we would leave him completely free to handle the story in his own way. For the job we chose Eric Wigham, labour correspondent of *The Times* for more than 20 years, who has written several books on trade unions and related subjects. But while we are looking back on the struggles and triumphs of the past 75 years, we must not forget that we are looking forward to a new era for the Civil and Public Services Association, and realise that the Association will probably change as much in the next 75 years as it has in the past.

Kenneth Thomas
General Secretary

INTRODUCTION
On the Combative Character
of Civil Service Clerks

The Civil and Public Services Association (CPSA), with its 225,000 members the largest union in the Civil Service, had its origin in the formation of the Assistant Clerks' Association, with less than 400 members, on March 2, 1903. Great national lock-outs and strikes, such as those which mark the history of big industrial unions, are not to be found in its 75 years, but few organisations have been so constantly engaged in external and internal conflict and few have produced such brilliantly aggressive personalities.

From the beginning it faced the apparently insurmountable task of extracting concessions from the most powerful monopoly of all, the Government of the country. The members felt themselves ill-paid and down-trodden, but the weapons at their disposal were pitiably weak. Their only right was to send a memorial or petition, couched in the most humble terms, to departmental heads, who might reply or not as they wished. They were unrecognised and had no negotiating rights.

For long they could not turn to the last resort of industrial unions, the strike. This was never illegal but was regarded as a breach of discipline which could be penalised by dismissal, suspension or withdrawal of pension rights. They were servants of the Crown, through ministers and an elected House of Commons, and it was commonly held that there was no right to challenge the decisions of Parliament. In its most extreme form the view was put by a commentator when there was a threatened Post Office strike in 1912: 'Men who are employed by the public cannot strike. They can, and sometimes do, mutiny. Then they should be treated not as strikers but as mutineers.' In any case, the Civil Service unions, at the beginning of the century, were too weak to have any hope of success. There was talk of strikes in the hectic days of industrial strife after the First World War, but by then the Association believed there was more to be gained by arbitration.

The Association eventually adopted a strike policy in 1969, and since then minor strikes or overtime bans have not been unusual, but even today there is argument, within the union as well as outside it, as to whether, protest though they may, members have the right to resist a Government decision, which incidentally goes against their interests.

The story of the CPSA is that of how, by ingenuity, courage and perseverance, it developed an effective means of pursuing the interests of its members in spite of the formidable obstacles. It found friends in Parliament to air grievances. It once secured a Government defeat. It organised great public demonstrations. It made the utmost use of the media, in the knowledge that governments were always sensitive to public criticism of their treatment of their employees. When, after the First World War, the Whitley System of joint committees and independent arbitration was established, the Association, more than any other Civil Service union, displayed a remarkable ability to make use of it.

The prestige gained by victories over the Treasury and the Government helped it in this period to swallow up, by fair means or foul, most of the rivals which sought to represent sections of the clerical class until it grew to a size which enabled it to provide unrivalled services to its members and to compel attention. Under the able and uncompromising leadership of W J Brown, from before the end of the

First World War to the beginning of the Second, it held an outstanding position among the country's white-collar unions.

Brown fought internal as well as external battles. More than a decade of struggle with Association President Ross Wyld of the Post Office Section of the union, culminated in a special conference to decide which of them should go. It was partly a political battle, partly a personal one and partly an example of the conflict between permanent officials and elected executives which is not uncommon in trade unions.

Since the Second World War, internal struggle has been almost continuous, with great emphasis on political differences between the moderates and the left. It has led to several lawsuits and one inquiry by a Commons Committee on Privileges. Top full-time officers have seldom been appointed without one or more appeals to the annual conference against the Executive's choice.

In the 1970s, rival factions each started their own publications, printing their own list of candidates for election to the National Executive Committee and other offices, chosen at their factional meetings or conferences. Control of the Executive changed four times in four years. In 1978 alone it changed twice. In 1977, members took part in a sit-down protest in the union headquarters. In 1978, full-time officers and staff picketed an Executive meeting, and allegations of election infringements resulted in a Vice-President being unseated and the Association having to do without an Executive while a new ballot took place.

The abrasive character of Association life is probably in part a reaction to the humdrum routine of many of its members' jobs. When the Association came into existence, members' work as assistant clerks was largely routine. Their responsibilities have been expanded since and increased social legislation has resulted in more and more becoming involved in the problems of ordinary people, but there remain large blocks of Clerical Officers engaged in monotonous tasks. Moreover, only about half the membership consists of Clerical Officers. About a third are Clerical Assistants, employed on such things as routine filing, and most of the remaining members are typists, data processing staff, etc.

There is as much apathy in the CPSA as elsewhere, but it is not surprising that many of the more energetic young members seek to develop in union work a freedom of expression they cannot find in their daily tasks. It is an increasingly youthful union, and there are no longer special examinations to give the successful ones a sense of status and self-confidence. Five 'O' levels for a Clerical Officer and two for a Clerical Assistant are the main requirements for a boy or girl seeking to enter the Service. After an average of seven years, the abler ones are promoted to the executive class and join the Society of Civil and Public Servants. They are no longer brought from every corner of the British Isles to work in London at the heart of the Government machine. When the Assistant Clerks' Association was formed, 85 per cent of clerical staff worked in London. The proportion is now no more than 25 per cent.

This is partly a result of the spread of work resulting from increased legislation, and partly the deliberate policy of dispersal adopted by governments during the past 30 years. Many officers are now recruited locally for work near their homes.

Youth is impatient. Association work offers an escape from the restraints and inhibitions of Civil Service life. Conferences and meetings give members an opportunity to let their hair down. Certainly on these occasions they bear little resemblance to the image of tea-drinking, rubber-stamping, buck-passing plodders which seems to be imprinted on the public mind. Veterans recall the conferences at Corton Holiday Camp, near Lowestoft, between the wars, where after long hours of debate they would link arms and walk singing through country lanes. They once set the bells of the village church ringing, to the bewilderment of the local inhabitants, before settling down to the night's drinking and talking. Many more remember the hectic social life at Prestatyn Holiday Camp where several conferences were held after the Second World War. The cheering and jeering youngsters at the conferences of today, some with tangled beards, jeans and tee-shirts, seem to have little in common with their bowler-hatted predecessors in striped trousers.

Union work provides something more for the talented than an opportunity to let their hair down. As active members they can take some part in organisational work, throw themselves into personal and political conflicts which give a zest to life and take part in struggles for power at branch, sectional or national level. It is not unusual for an active member to refuse promotion so he can continue his work in the Association. Others accept promotion and continue their conflicts in the less open battlefields of the Society of Civil and Public Servants, where many have risen to high office.

For those who stay there are other opportunities. Even the full-time officers are young by comparison with those of other unions because of a rule making retirement at 55 compulsory, which opens the possibility of a union career earlier than elsewhere.

Most rank and file members, many of whom have no strong partisan views, probably dislike the factional conflicts. They would prefer to see their leaders working amicably together to improve pay and conditions. A considerable number are probably Conservatives, but their voice is only heard when they are shocked by some major political decision, for instance in relation to the General Strike in the 1920s, the Spanish Civil War in the 1930s, proposed affiliation with the Labour Party in the 1940s and the Anglo-French Suez adventure in the 1950s. It is something for which the leaders of the Association have to watch out.

In 1971, the conference adopted an amendment to the constitution to rule out the circulation of election lists. For a time the factions went underground but this did not last long. It has been questioned whether so many active spirits would be attracted to union work without the stimulus of battle, but there are a good many who think it has gone too far. It will be hard to stop, however, so long as conflicting idealisms lie behind the petty squabbles.

For many, the internal battles are much more than an opportunity to find release for cloistered talents. There are moderates who believe intensely they are taking part in a nationwide struggle to preserve traditional freedoms. There are those on the left who believe no less intensely they are helping to lead the workers towards a happier, more equal society. There are those who believe the only hope of progress is to mobilise support for the Labour Party leadership, and those who believe that little can be done without revolutionary change in the leadership of the workers.

Revolt within the Association has always become particularly fierce when one faction or another obtains a dominating position; the Post Office – Admiralty caucus in the 1930s, the Communists and their allies in the 1940s and the moderate Group in the 1960s.

It would be a mistake to suppose that internal struggles have prevented the CPSA from making progress towards its objectives. Though the elected leaders tend to be pre-occupied with the struggles and they attract much public attention, most time is spent on the basic union job of improving or defending the interests of the member-ship. Each faction must have achievements of which it can boast.

A Civil Service staff association is very much a part of the Civil Service, the characteristics of which the Association reflects in many ways. Changes in departmental responsibilities necessitate changes in the pattern of union branches and the union sections which bring together all the branches of members employed by one department. The pay of CPSA officers and staff is related to the grade structure of the Service. The right of appeal against rejection of an application for promotion is comparable to the right of appeal in the Service. After the last war the Association was operating a bar against the employment of married women even when it was urging the Treasury to stop the marriage bar.

Many of its major problems have always been special Civil Service problems, unfamiliar to other trade unionists and sometimes difficult for them to understand; superannuation, the employment and rights of temporary workers, incremental scales, promotion procedures, dispersal, the position of departmental classes, provincial differentiation, representative capacity, civilianisation, open reporting, security measures in sensitive departments and the exercise by state servants of political and civil rights.

In many of these matters, substantial progress has been made since the war, often through the Staff Side of the National Whitley Council, on which all the main unions are represented, but with the CPSA playing an active part. Landmarks have included the gradual introduction of equal pay for women which began in 1955, an agreement on superannuation in 1972 which met many of the claims the Association had been making for 50 years and the Facilities Agreement of 1974.

The special position of Civil Service unions as representatives of government employees continued to have a major influence on their history. It has been impossible for them to pursue forms of industrial democracy which have been advocated in outside industry in recent years. The Whitley System, as operated in the Civil Service, was for a time among the most advanced developments of industrial relations in the country and the CPSA aims to develop it further. It is, however, widely accepted that civil service unions cannot expect representation on the controlling bodies, Parliament and the Cabinet.

Governments have always been in a dilemma over pay, liable to be accused on the one hand of being mean or unjust and on the other of wasting the taxpayer's money. A serious attempt was made in 1956, on the recommendation of the Priestley Royal Commission, to remove pay claims from the area of conflict by relating their settlement to the movements of pay in comparable employments outside with the help of the Pay Research Unit. Successive governments, intermittently operating incomes policies, felt they must set an example in their treatment of their own employees and repeatedly broke away from the system. The result each time has been a renewal of conflict, which continued in 1978 and was threatened for 1979. How far are government employees justified in fighting against economic policy? The relationship between governments and their employees has still to be settled. So far as pay is concerned, it perhaps never can be unless and until there is national acceptance of a general incomes policy within which the Civil Service can find its place.

PART ONE
THE HARD ROAD TO RECOGNITION 1903-1919

CHAPTER ONE
Threadbare Beginnings

The economy responsible for the institution of the Assistant Clerk Class results in the passage from youth to manhood of a large number of boys, educationally well-equipped and specially selected, being made in poverty-stricken circumstances. Forced to exist amid the dismal environment obtaining amongst that section of the community which, in large cities, has to preserve respectability of appearance under the most trying economic conditions, what real happiness in life can be theirs? Unable to marry at a proper age, and when married unable to bring up a family under decent conditions, the course of time brings little relief. Such economy is not worthy of the dignity of the State.

That was how the Assistant Clerks' Association described the plight of its members in the first years of this century.

The preceding 50 years had seen the development of the modern Civil Service, in the recruitment of which nepotism and patronage had been largely replaced by competitive examinations, and which at the same time had undergone rapid expansion to fulfil new responsibilities in the Post Office and elsewhere. From 39,000 in 1851, the number of employees grew to 116,000 in 1901 (about three-quarters in the Post Office) and by 1914 had reached 281,000.

The Treasury and the heads of departments were under constant pressure to reduce the resultant growth in costs. By 1870, some departments were beginning to use boy clerks and women. The 1875 Playfair Commission on the Civil Service approved both innovations. A very ordinary boy, the Commission said, could do more than half a man's work, while he could be got for less than half a man's wages, and the best boys could do more than the average man's work. As for female clerks, who had been recruited by the Post Office, the Commission saw no reason why their employment should not be extended to other departments as 'they are well qualified for clerical work of a less important character and are satisfied with a lower rate of pay than is expected by men similarly employed.' Another advantage pointed out by the Postmaster-General was that 'they are less disposed than men to combine for the purpose of extorting higher wages.' There was also the point that women were not entitled to pensions.

A Lower Division of permanent Civil Service clerks was set up as a result of the Commission's report, but departments were anxious to get cheaper labour for **A hunt for 'less-than-lower' clerks** the more routine work. Boys and women could help in this, but boys had to be promoted or sacked after a few years and the introduction of women, including the first 'typewriters' (typists), involved administrative and social problems which daunted many departments. A hunt continued for unestablished men at rates of pay below those of the Lower (later Second) Division clerks. These less-than-lower clerks might be called 'writers', 'copyists' or 'abstractors'. None of the departmental experiments proved wholly satisfactory.

In 1897, the Treasury cut the knot by setting up a new all-Service class of Assistant Clerks who were permanent, pensionable civil servants to be recruited exclusively from boy clerks to do routine work less onerous than that of the Second

Division clerks for substantially lower pay. The fact that the new class was to be pensionable may perhaps be explained by the observation of the Playfair Commission that superannuation was a means of securing cheaper labour. 'In all employment of labour, security has an element of reduction in the settlement of wages.' Moreover, pensions were not a firm entitlement and while normally paid according to an accepted scale, there was always a possibility of using the threat of their withdrawal as a means of enforcing discipline.

The creation of this new Treasury, or all-Service class, in addition to the First Division of top civil servants and the Second Division of more senior clerks, was of vital importance for future trade union organisation. Such a class, with members on common pay scales and conditions in different departments, could form a basis for the formation of unions of substantial size which could reasonably expect to represent their members in all departments to the Treasury rather than, as previously, being restricted to claims within single departments. The Treasury was conscious of the danger of this to management control, however, and it was a long time before it came about. The new class also provided a way to a permanent career in the Civil Service for the growing number of boy clerks, though it proved to be inadequate.

Inadequate career prospects for boy clerks

Lasting Civil Service unions had begun to appear, before the formation of the new class, in the comparatively prosperous years following 1887; the period in which dockers and gas workers laid the foundations of the great general unions and white-collar workers such as teachers, clerks and shop assistants began to organise. Civil servants had had their temporary committees and associations for many years, mostly set up to give evidence to commissions or committees of inquiry, or to present petitions to departmental heads, but, except among the Post Office manipulative grades, who had more in common with industrial workers than clerks, almost all had been short-lived. The small Court Officers' Association, which merged with the CPSA in 1974, traced its origins back to the County Courts (Clerks and Officers) Association formed in 1881, but this was exceptional. The developments of the 1890s included the formation in 1890 of the Second Division Clerks' Association, predecessor of the Society of Civil and Public Servants; in 1892 of the Association of Tax Clerks, predecessor of the Inland Revenue Staff Federation and in 1893 and 1894, of the Customs federations.

Before the turn of the century, the tide of trade had turned. Employers had been victorious in great lock-outs in engineering and other industries. A series of legal judgements took away from unions the rights which everyone believed had been established in the 1870s. There was a period of unhappy industrial peace, the unions concentrating their resources on a political campaign to restore their rights. The ending of the Boer War in 1902 accentuated a new cyclical trade depression. Unemployment and the cost of living were going up but wages were not. In this difficult period of trade union history, the formation of Civil Service associations continued unabated. The Association of Women Clerks in the Post Office appeared in 1901 and the Senior Clerks (Abstractor Class) Association in the same year; the Civil Service Writers' Guild followed in 1902, and in 1903, besides the Assistant Clerks' Association, the Civil Service Typists' Association and the Association of Tax Surveying Officers were started. There were numerous others, and it is estimated there were 80 by 1914.

More and more Civil Service Associations

The creation of the Assistant Clerks' Association was prompted by a circular from clerks in Dublin enclosing a memorial (memorandum) they had prepared to petition for increased pay. It came into the hands of James Maxwell, an assistant clerk in the Post Office Savings Bank, where work was particularly hard and discipline particularly strict. Action there by the Second Division clerks had been severely repressed ten years earlier.

Maxwell, who may be regarded as the founder of the CPSA, contacted colleagues in other London departments and a provisional committee was formed, which called the inaugural meeting of March 2, 1903. *The Civilian*, a weekly journal for civil servants, reported that representatives of all the principal London offices were present and two resolutions were passed. The first declared support for an association 'since united effort is necessary to secure further improvement in the pay and status of the class.' The second resolution authorised the members of the representative committee to take what steps were necessary to secure public interest in the grievances of the class and incur any legitimate expenditure in attaining that object. To meet this blanket authorisation it was agreed there should be a voluntary contribution of one shilling (5p) a member. James Maxwell was elected honorary secretary.

James Maxwell in uniform during the First World War

The contribution, which later became an annual one, proved adequate for a long time because of a steady rise in membership from 383 in 1903, to 534 from 22 departments in 1904, and to 2,223 from 52 departments in 1912, when there was a potential membership of 2,400. Accounts for the period from October 1903 to September 1904 show a contribution income of £32 9s (£32.45), of which the largest amount (£6) came from the Savings Bank, with the Board of Education and the Admiralty not far behind. Cash in hand amounted to more than £25, which suggests a careful hand on the purse-strings. The highest single item of expenditure was an honorarium of £10 for the secretary.

The Assistant Clerks were initially on a salary scale rising, from £55 a year at 19, by annual increments of £2 10s (£2.50) to £70, and then by £5 increments to £150, with an efficiency bar at £100. They were established civil servants but career prospects were poor. After working for an open examination to become boy clerks they had to take another, covering English (with handwriting and spelling), arithmetic, precis writing and indexing, digesting returns into summaries and bookkeeping or shorthand, to advance into the Assistant Clerk class. Having achieved that, further promotion depended on yet another examination to enter the Second Division. This was an open examination and success was arbitrarily restricted to protect the interests of candidates, normally with higher educational qualifications, from outside the Service. In all these examinations, there were many more candidates than openings.

Compared with outside manual workers, most of whom were still working a 53 or 54 hour week, hours were short: seven a day including a lunch break. This made study for examinations possible except for those doing much overtime or forced by circumstances to what is now called moonlighting, taking a second job to supplement pay. One man recalled how he kept the accounts of a Smithfield meat firm from 5 to 8 a.m., worked all day at his office and then went to a hosiery firm to work on its books.

The overriding grievance was over pay, which at the lowest level of the scale the Assistant Clerks found insufficient to maintain the respectability required of them, and by the time they reached marrying age, insufficient to maintain a wife. They wanted a living wage, a marriageable salary. The Association petitioned for improvements immediately after its formation, addressing its memorial directly to the Treasury, and received no reply. It was encouraged, however, by the report in 1904 of a committee which inquired into Post Office wages. This committee not only recommended substantial increases but accepted the principle that when a man reached marriageable age (taken as 26) he should earn enough to maintain a wife in reasonable comfort. The Association resubmitted its memorial and this time the Treasury considered it. It was an important gain that the Treasury dealt with it directly, instead of rejecting it, as it had done on occasion with such memorials in the past, on the grounds that they should have been presented to individual departments. However, the recommendations of the Post Office inquiry were largely rejected and the Association obtained only minor improvements in the scale.

The Savings Bank Assistant Clerks were growing increasingly resentful and towards the end of 1904 became the first members of the Association to take industrial action, a ban on overtime. 'Ever since the introduction of Assistant Clerks,' recorded *The Civilian*, in January 1905, 'much of the economy shown in the estimates is due to the fact that this class has been doing the work at 9d (4p) an hour, or half what their more fortunate colleagues of equal age were getting. Petitions have been addressed to the Treasury without avail, and at last the assistant clerks resolved on action. The great majority of the 110 assistant clerks of the Savings Banks declined to perform overtime; and as they are free agents the department has lost their services. Attempts were made to alter their decision by bringing pressure to bear upon them individually; but the recalcitrants remained obdurate, and there the matter rests at present. We trust that their courageous action will be met by the authorities in the right spirit.' But nothing was achieved.

The growth in the number of Civil Service unions and falling real salaries resulted in a multiplicity of memorials reaching the Government. The Post Office alone received 45 in 1905, 130 in 1906 and 630 in 1911. Most were ignored or curtly rejected. The Assistant Clerks' Association decided its only course was to appeal to Parliament over the head of the Treasury. They set to work to canvass support for a petition to the Prime Minister, Sir Henry Campbell-Bannerman, requesting the appointment of a small parliamentary committee to inquire into the conditions of service of the class. The 1906 general election gave them their opportunity. Candidates could be made aware of their grievances and many were induced to promise their support. Maxwell, a popular and respected figure, worked indefatig-

First industrial action by Association members

A 'Red Tape' cartoon envisages 'the petition-rejecting branch' of the Treasury

ably and was released from his duties as secretary to concentrate on parliamentary work. A member from the Admiralty, R McC Beamish, took over as honorary secretary.

When the new Parliament was returned, with its huge Liberal majority and substantial Labour group, 376 members signed the petition and numerous questions were asked in the House, notably by Philip Snowden, later to become Chancellor of the Exchequer in the first two Labour Governments. In spite of all the Association's efforts, the Prime Minister rejected the petition. The pay and prospects of assistant clerks had repeatedly been considered by the Treasury during the past few years, he said, and no useful purpose could be served by holding an inquiry. The Association's efforts were not wasted, however. It had gained valuable political friends who continued their efforts on its behalf in the following years.

The Treasury receives deputations – a new step on the road to recognition

The Association presented another memorial to the Treasury, and this time the Financial Secretary consented to receive a deputation, which presented a mass of evidence in support of its contentions. The Financial Secretary promised sympathetic and earnest consideration. During the ensuing year or two, the Treasury several times received deputations, a new step on the road to recognition as it is now understood.

After an irritating delay, the Treasury announced some changes in the Assistant Clerk Class, including reducing the age of entry to 17 and the starting salary to £45. It also made small improvements in the scale, the third in a dozen years, which was now to rise by £5 a year to £85 and then by £7 10s (£7.50) a year, but the maximum remained at £150 except for increases for men of special merit after a further five and ten years, which would eventually give them £174.

The Association was considering efforts to improve this in detail when it ran into the first internal crisis of the many in CPSA history. A resolution was received from the Office Committee of the Board of Education requiring the suspension of action on all the proposed salary items until a maximum salary of £200 had been secured. The National Executive considered the position very grave and decided to hold a referendum. Opponents angrily insisted that the salaries of junior men should not be set aside in this way and the Board of Education resolution was defeated by 670 votes to 510.

The Executive compromised by an agreement that, in future, claims for a £200 maximum and for improvements in the salaries of junior men should be given equal prominence. Another memorial to the Treasury was drawn up but in April 1911 the Treasury informed heads of departments that: 'My Lords are satisfied that the pay of the class, which was considerably improved in 1909, is adequate.'

The Association sent copies of its memorial to the Prime Minister and Chancellor of the Exchequer, who replied in the same words as the Treasury. Yet pressures on the Government were building up. In industry generally, resentment at declining living standards had resulted in a wave of strikes from 1910 onwards, more menacing than ever before in the country's history. In 1910 there were fierce clashes between miners, police and soldiers in South Wales. The following year, a national strike by seamen was followed by stoppages by dockers and road transport workers in one great port after another, with outbreaks of arson and looting. Then, while Liverpool was almost paralysed, the railway unions called their first national strike. It only lasted a few days but shook the Government. There were big strikes in engineering and shipbuilding and a lock-out of cotton weavers. In the Civil Service itself, postal workers were threatening to go out on strike. Prominent union leaders were talking about syndicalism, a socialist doctrine advocating industrial ownership and control by workers.

When major industrial assault is threatened, governments feel they must secure their rear. They cannot afford restlessness and the danger of revolt among their own people. Weakened by the 1910 general election, the Government was also beset by violent struggles over Irish home rule, women's suffrage and the powers of the House of Lords. Perhaps the last straw was public outcry about a revival of patronage in the Service. Minor examples were found in the Admiralty and other departments. When employment exchanges were set up under Winston Churchill's Act of 1909, large numbers of staff were wanted quickly and were appointed as temporary clerks by committees.

A campaign of protest was launched by the *Civil Service Gazette* and in April 1911 Philip Snowden asked the Prime Minister in the House whether he was prepared to appoint a commission or committee of inquiry to look into Civil Service appointments and promotion. Asked for further information, Snowden, in conjunction with the Assistant Clerks' Association and the Second Division Association, prepared a memorial which was signed by 406 MPs.

The young Philip Snowden, a friend of the Civil Service associations

About the same time, a storm was aroused by publication of a confidential memorial from E G A Holmes, the Chief Inspector of Elementary Schools, to the Board of Education, after he found that of 123 junior inspectors, 104 were former elementary school teachers. The qualifications looked for, wrote Holmes, were most readily obtainable in Oxford and Cambridge undergraduates. Elementary teachers, as a rule, were uncultured and imperfectly educated, many of them creatures of tradition and routine.

Civil servants joined with teachers in a protest meeting in the Royal Albert Hall. Meanwhile, the threat of a Post Office strike was gathering force and it was announced that a select committee (the Holt Committee) would be appointed to inquire into the grievances of postal staff. Finally, in December 1911, Prime Minister Asquith gave way and promised, in a letter to Snowden, to set up a Royal Commission to look into the Civil Service.

CHAPTER TWO
Victory Snatched Away

> *'There are great and good times coming,'*
> *Says the young assistant clerk,*
> *'And I think it very likely*
> *We shall soon be men of mark!*
> *Our grievances abolished*
> *With joy we'll be amazed;*
> *All in the happy future*
> *When our maximum is raised.*
>
> *'We'll all wear shiny "toppers",*
> *And sport spats on our feet,*
> *And drop into Frascati's*
> *When we feel inclined to eat;*
> *The "fiz" will flow like water,*
> *And our chiefs will think we're craz'd*
> *All in the merry future*
> *When our maximum is raised.'*

These verses poke a little fun at the euphoria produced by the promise of a Royal Commission, but jubilation was understandable. 'The long prayed for has happened,' wrote L E de St Paër, the Association secretary. 'A continuous representation of grievances, much spilling of printers' ink and the spending of wearisome months in the lobby of the House of Commons have at length achieved what will prove, we all hope, the first step towards a contented Civil Service. To all Assistant Clerks, this news is good news.'

After nearly a decade of dashing their heads against the Treasury wall, the Assistant Clerks would have a chance, for the first time, to explain their troubles to an independent committee. They were so convinced of the justice of their cause that they could not envisage any impartial group of men failing to see it. The announcement was the climax of a year in which events had combined to make them feel that at last things were moving. In April, 22 associations had agreed to form the Civil Service Federation, so that it seemed the Assistant Clerks would never again be compelled to fight lone battles. October had seen the first issue of their own journal, *Red Tape*, which was an immediate success and ever since has been the medium through which members and officials talk to each other and the outside world.

The first Civil Service federation

The formation of the Federation had its origins in the urgent desire of many associations for an independent body to hear their grievances. An initial move came from the Inland Revenue associations in 1906, at the same time as the Assistant Clerks were presenting their petition to the Prime Minister. The Inland Revenue people were agitating for a court of appeal in the form of a standing committee of the House of Commons, composed of members of all parties and representatives of rank and file civil servants. Half a dozen other associations, including that of the Assistant Clerks, gave their support and in 1909 formed the Civil Service Court of

Appeal Committee. In the next two years support grew until in the spring of 1911 a conference representing the great mass of organised civil servants, more than 100,000, agreed to set up the federation. Its objectives were wider than those of the Court of Appeal Committee: 'To watch over and advance, by all legitimate and constitutional means, the interest of civil servants', and the display of unity must have added to the pressures on the Government to set up a commission. The unity did not last long. There was much dispute as to whether associations of temporary employees should be admitted. Old differences between manipulative grades in the Post Office and clerical workers were revived. The Second Division Association decided not to affiliate and was much criticised by the Assistant Clerks' Association for not doing so.

The arrival of *Red Tape* in October must also have impressed the Government with the determination and ability of even the lowly assistant clerks. Produced on a budget of £15 from an upper room in The Clarence, a Whitehall public house, it sold for a penny and obtained an immediate circulation of 5,000, which showed that it was widely read, as was intended, by civil servants outside the Association. It was something quite different from the few existing association journals, which were dull in format and prosaic in matter, and from independent publications like *The Civilian* and *The Civil Service Gazette*. Edited by F W Saunderson of the Savings Bank, the editorials, headed *The Tape Machine*, often discussed the moral and philosophical background to events. The journal mixed hard-hitting attacks on the Treasury with light verse and satirical sketches and parodies, had a lively correspondence column and was illustrated with cartoons, notably some of the highest quality by Henry Sayers. He also, using his wife as a model, was responsible for a figure of justice, in classical robes and carrying scales and sword, which

The famous cover of 'Red Tape', the Association's journal, and F W Saunderson, its first editor

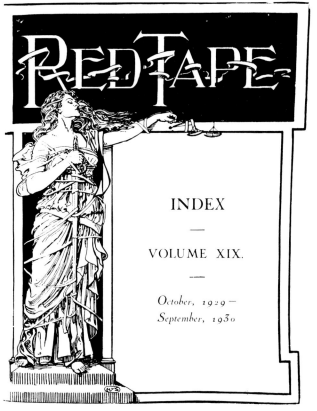

INDEX

—

VOLUME XIX.

—

October, 1929 —
September, 1930

appeared on the cover for many years. The figure was bound round and round with the red tape then used for official files.

For the historian, *Red Tape* fills out to some degree the life of Assistant Clerks in that period. In spite of their penury, civil servants managed to take part in a wide variety of leisure pursuits. There were reports of dinners, concerts, dances, athletic and swimming meetings, cricket matches and civil service football league games. A civil service unit in the territorial army seems to have been active. The Assistant Clerks' Association organised an annual Bohemian concert in the Pillar Hall, Victoria Station, which one year aroused the ire of a senior member by concluding the proceedings with *Auld Lang Syne* instead of the national anthem.

There were many advertisements in *Red Tape* for correspondence colleges, often boasting of the successes of students in Civil Service examinations. W & G Foyle offered the books students needed. Discounts were promised for civil servants at retail shops. There were small ads of apartments to let 'for Civil Service gentlemen' in London and for seaside holidays. One firm offered 'West End tailoring at City prices'.

There were parliamentary notes and in January 1913 the journal made a regular feature of reports from the Federation. Space was allowed from time to time to other associations, for instance those of the Second Division and typists. However, for nearly three years, the journal's overriding preoccupation was with the activities of the Royal Commission.

A Royal Commission nightmare, as drawn by Henry Sayers for 'Red Tape'. The chairman peers down from high above the diminutive witnesses, but Snowden regards them sympathetically over his shoulder

The initial euphoria soon gave way to uncertainties and doubt. Who would be the members of the Commission? How comprehensive would be the terms of reference? It was not until March 1912 that these anxieties were set at rest. The names of the commissioners announced by the Prime Minister surpassed all expectations. 'We regard the composition of the Royal Commission as a matter on which Mr Asquith may well be congratulated and for which he should be thanked,' said *Red Tape*.

The choice of Lord MacDonnell as chairman was considered a guarantee that the procedure of the Commission would be scrupulously impartial. MacDonnell, then 68, had made a name for himself in the Indian Civil Service when he was Lieutenant Governor of the North-West Provinces. From 1902 to 1908 he had the thankless job of Parliamentary Under-secretary for Ireland and tried vainly to lift the old quarrels above the bitterness of party warfare. Among those with him was the Assistant Clerks' old friend, Philip Snowden; S J G Hoare, another friendly MP; Professor Graham Wallas; Arthur Boutwood, a former higher grade clerk in the Charity Commission, and J R Clynes, a leading trade unionist, and also a duke and a bishop.

Sang a *Red Tape* contributor:

> *What a Commission! What a Commission!!*
> *Carol their praises without intermission,*
> > *See represented the Law and the Church*
> > *(Why should the stage have been left in the lurch?*
> > *Did the nobility collar their perch?)*
> > > *What a Commission!*

> *What a Commission! What a Commission!!*
> *Carol their praises without intermission,*
> > *One or two dons and a Labour MP,*
> > *Throw in a title and then you will see*
> > *What Civil Service commissions should be.*
> > > *What a Commission!*

The Commission was asked to report on methods of appointment and promotion, the system of competitive examination and whether the existing organisation met the requirements of the public service. Asquith gave an assurance to the House of Commons that it was not intended to exclude salaries from the scope of the inquiry.

The associations hurried to put the finishing touches to their submissions on which they had been working since the beginning of the year. In the Assistant Clerks' Association, much of the burden fell on L E de St Paër of the Board of Education, who was honorary Secretary from 1910 to 1913, when he left to take a post at the new University of Leeds. *Red Tape* described his work on the Commission statement as brilliant and energetic and congratulated him on 'the recognition now given to such ability and individuality as government departments neither recognise nor reward.'

Among the first witnesses to give oral evidence to the Commission was Sir Robert Chalmers, Permanent Secretary to the Treasury, who adopted a curiously off-hand attitude to staff associations, as this exchange with Snowden shows:

Snowden: *Do you at the Treasury recognise associations of civil servants?*
Chalmers: *I do not know what associations you mean. I know the National Excise Federation. . . .*
Snowden: *Have you not heard of the Association of Second Division Clerks?*
Chalmers: *Yes, we have received deputations from the Second Division Clerks' Association and corresponded directly with them.*
Snowden: *Do you know of the Association of Assistant Clerks?*
Chalmers: *No, I have no knowledge of that.*
Snowden: *You are not aware that memorials have been sent to the Treasury in recent*

L E de St Paër

years by the associations?

Chalmers: *Yes, I am aware that the abstractors, for instance, and the Second Division clerks have sent a memorial through the head of their office asking for this, that and the other improvement of their conditions.*

Snowden: *You do not object to recognise associations of clerks?*

Chalmers: *Oh, no.*

But the Second Division Association said in its evidence that in 1911 it had petitioned for the right of corresponding with the Treasury on matters affecting general conditions and had been refused.

The Assistant Clerks' Association, in its written statement, urged that the class of Assistant Clerks should be abolished and recruitment of boy clerks should cease. There should be a system of recruiting for clerical duties, excluding pure copying but including supervision, by one external entrance examination. Copying could be done by female typists and simple routine duties by entrants in their first years. The Treasury did not define the duties of assistant clerks until 1910, when an Order in Council described them as copying and routine duties. After referring to the wide range of subjects covered by the boy clerks' and Assistant Clerks' examinations and giving figures to show how difficult it was to get through, the Association observed: 'It is obviously impossible, short of cast iron rules, to keep a body of men so educated, and trained in the Service, on those "copying and simple" duties which have been so light-heartedly assigned to them.'

In practice, continued the Association, assistant clerks were rarely if ever put on copying work and usually got more than routine duties. After seven or eight years they were frequently doing responsible and intricate work similar to that of Second Division Clerks.

The main theme of its evidence, however, was the impossibility of making ends meet on a scale rising from £1 1s (£1.05) weekly at age 20 to £2 17s 10d (£2.90) at 35, when an Assistant Clerk reached the maximum. It was particularly hard for the majority who were recruited from the provinces and had to live in lodgings which offered 'the greatest available maximum of cleanliness and respectability of neighbourhood with the minimum of cost.' Such lodgings would cost at least 15s (75p) for a single man for board and breakfast and full board on Sundays. Add to that 6s (30p) for dinners, 4s (20p) for clothes, 2s (10p) for fares and 1s (5p) for washing, and how could a man with £1 1s a week live? Some got help from their parents and some got evening jobs but, without such aids, any kind of amusement could only be had by saving on food and clothing.

The Association contended that the Government was failing to act as a model employer. The wages paid 'ought to be considered with the question of the income below which efficiency and decent family life can be maintained. For the Government to pay less than this is actually to create the poverty and social demoralisation which it is elsewhere combating.'

Oral evidence for the Association was given by David Milne, the President, who was closely questioned about his day-to-day work to find out whether it was purely routine or involved any exercise of judgement. What happened to a communication which arrived at the Patent Office, where Milne worked? Who decided how to deal with it, what reply to give, where to file it and so on? It did not appear from his replies that Assistant Clerks exercised much responsibility, but he remarked at one point that the Patent Office was exceptional because of the specialised nature of the work.

Milne made a strong point of the lack of career prospects. 'As things are at the

David Milne

moment,' suggested the Bishop of Southwark, 'you think that when a young man enters the Service he has a certain amount of vague and undefined hopes, and the longer he goes on the more those hopes are deadened and he finds that really the avenues to which he looked are only blind alleys?' Milne wholeheartedly agreed.

Milne said much more routine work could be done by mechanical means. There were still many offices which had not introduced typewriters. The Board of Trade was the only department, so far as he knew, which had a calculating machine and he knew of none with franking machines for stamping letters.

Another point made by Milne was that a great taint of caste ran through all government departments and people in subordinate positions felt it very keenly. References to the caste system in the Service often appeared in *Red Tape*. This was, of course, the period of *Upstairs, Downstairs*, when class distinctions were still widely accepted and it was natural for the Oxford and Cambridge men in the First Division to think of Assistant Clerks, many of whom came from poor families and had not completed secondary education, as belonging to a different order.

A 'taint of caste' in government departments

Milne was also strongly critical of the treatment of boy clerks, who were employed for two or three years and were then, except for the minority who became Assistant Clerks, thrown on the labour market. Originally they were recruited from the age of 14 and discharged at 20. They were paid 4d (2p) an hour with an annual increment of ½d an hour. It seems to have been assumed that a few years in the Civil Service would commend them to outside employers, but outside employers did not see it that way. In 1909 the age of entry was raised to 15 or 16 and the age of departure dropped from 20 to 18, to give them a chance of finding other employment while still in their teens. Sir Robert Chalmers appeared to think that this had resolved the problem, but there was a mass of evidence to the contrary.

One who certainly did not agree was Edmund Phipps, an Assistant Secretary at the Board of Education, who was honorary Secretary of the Boy Clerks' Friendly Society. This organisation was founded in 1903 by senior civil servants, shocked at the plight of the boys, to help them find suitable lodgings when they arrived in London and to find jobs when they were thrown out of the Service. Altogether 1,287 boys appealed to them and 507 were found work.

Examinations were advertised throughout the United Kingdom but neither parents nor boys realised that success did not guarantee employment of a permanent kind. Few had considered the possibility of being discarded by the age of 18 or so or what they could do if it happened. They might have no one to help them except perhaps a parent in the West Coast of Ireland.

The point of view of the boys themselves was put to the Commission by a slightly-built, fair-haired, self-composed youth of 18 named William John Brown, who was to become the most successful and controversial Civil Service union leader throughout the inter-war period. He had been made an Assistant Clerk a month before he gave evidence, and was now at the Ministry of Works, but had spent his years as a boy clerk at the Savings Bank, where James Maxwell had become his mentor.

Evidence from a self-composed youth of 18 named William John Brown

When the decision to appoint a Royal Commission was announced, he had contacted boy clerks in other departments and formed the Boy Clerks' Association in order to give evidence. He was accompanied before the Commission by Maxwell, now promoted to the Second Division, and another Second Division clerk, but he alone acted as spokesman.

Lord MacDonnell was evidently intrigued by the appearance of this seemingly confident youth but incredulous that the boys could have produced unaided the well phrased and prepared document. He said it was a remarkable document to be written by a boy, with the obvious implication that Brown had had help from his Second Division friends. Brown, always sensitive to any slight, was touched on the raw, and insisted it was his own work. 'That statement of case was very intimately and personally my own,' he wrote later. 'Maxwell had helped only by pruning some of the more extreme expressions.'

The statement pointed out that the boy clerk system was at variance with practice in commercial undertakings, where boys were retained without further examinations. The Civil Service system deprived the State of many of its servants at a time when their experience was beginning to prove of value, so causing unnecessary waste to the taxpayer. The Assistant Clerks' examination ought to be abolished. Boy clerks, who had entered the Service after a stiff competitive examination, should not be liable to discharge at 18 but should continue in employment on the basis of proved efficiency. Brown suggested sweeping away the three grades of clerk – boy, Assistant and Second Division – and replacing them by one class into which the boys would go.

In reply to sympathetic questioning by Philip Snowden and Graham Wallas, Brown described how, having succeeded in the boy clerks' examination, he had worked all day in the Savings Bank and studied in the evenings for the Assistant Clerks' examination and having passed that hurdle, was now studying for the Second Division. His wages did not permit paying for coaching and there was nobody to guide boys about text books and so on; they had to pick it up by themselves. The position of Assistant Clerk, when they reached it, was only a stepping stone. The pay was a scandal. All the boys were aiming at the Second Division. Their life was not living at all, but merely existing.

The day after he had given evidence, Brown, worrying over the way he had handled his case, found a letter from Snowden waiting for him when he arrived at the Office of Works. It congratulated him on a remarkable performance and said he had made a deep impression on the Commission as a whole.

The Assistant Clerks become critical of the Commission

As witness succeeded witness and the months passed, the Assistant Clerks became more and more critical of the Commission and its chairman; particularly in reference to the class distinctions, as it seemed to them, drawn between the university men and the ordinary clerks. Addressing the Association's annual meeting in 1912, David Milne referred to veiled antagonism to the lower grades which could only be the outcome of prejudice, and because of it, he said, the Association would be ill-advised to centre all its hopes on the Commission.

'Never an opportunity is missed,' complained a *Red Tape* editorial in March 1913, 'by which the education, the social standard and the work performed by the main body of civil servants may be minimised, never a chance is lost whereby the qualities which legend attaches to the privileged may be lauded. Patronage, that filthy thing, but the real matter at issue, is swiftly and deliberately hurried out of sight. University education, which all admire and prize, and about which there is no question, is lingered over and defended *ad nauseam*.' A couple of months later, referring to reports of a hostile reception given by the Commission to Board of Education clerks, Milne wrote that the idea that self-control, justice and courtesy were to be exercised in dealing with the lower orders was a sentiment which the upper classes found little difficulty in waving aside. In July 1913, when the GPO Assistant Clerks were refused a hearing because they applied too late, Milne returned to the attack: 'Where all the witnesses for the defence are called and recalled and evidence for the prosecution suppressed, we are entitled to say – as we say now of the Royal Commission – that all claim to justice, impartiality and authority must frankly be abandoned.'

But when the Commission at last reported in April 1914, Milne greeted the report as a good one from which the Assistant Clerks had more to gain than any other class. It had recommended that they should have more leave, more opportunities for promotion, an increased maximum reached by increased increments and an immediate increment on the scale. Milne gloated that all the pretty excuses and petty arguments of the superior persons who received the deputations had been torn to shreds and the inspired authority for meanness had been overthrown. 'But we will not rub it in,' he added.

W J Brown was delighted because of a recommendation that the boy clerks' class should be abolished. For days, he said later, he carried the report about with him and almost literally hugged it to his bosom. The proposal was that boy clerks and Assistant Clerks should be replaced by an established Junior Clerical Class examined for entry at about 16, on completion of the intermediate stage of secondary education. A Senior Clerical Class, recruited at 18, would replace the Second Division and intermediate grades which had grown up in some departments and the First Division should be renamed 'Administrative Class'. The vital principle was laid down that when temporary staff were found to be employed on permanent work, they should be either established or dismissed. The possibility of further integration of departmental grades into all-Service classes should be considered. Further special inquiries were suggested into the civil rights of civil servants and into the possibility of creating new machinery for considering grievances.

But Brown hugs the Commission's report to his bosom

The Association waited impatiently, but with great expectations, for the Treasury to act on the recommendations. The Secretary to the Treasury (the Hon E S Montagu) declared in the House of Commons that civil servants were entitled to an early, detailed and reasoned reply to their allegations. With the report still being considered by the Treasury, the Association President W R Dayton, and Milne, now the Honorary Secretary, had a meeting with Montagu and were impressed by his courtesy, directness and candour. A few days later, Montagu telegraphed to Milne to say he hoped an announcement would be possible before the end of August. But that was just two or three weeks too far away.

On August 4 war was declared. The Treasury notified the Association that further consideration of pay and conditions would have to be suspended. And that was that.

CHAPTER THREE
The Strains of War

We agree to sink our differences in the face of the common danger, and to support the Government in all the many ways we can. We shall see to it that whatever duties come to our hands shall be done to the very utmost of our ability. We shall insist on doing more than our share so that those of our colleagues who have been trained to bear arms may be free to serve, and that others whose services are called for by other departments may be free to go, and if in addition we can help by service and money those who most need, we shall not be found lacking.

Thus David Milne, now the Honorary Secretary, responded on behalf of the Assistant Clerks' Association to the call to war. Perhaps the *Red Tape* editorial reflected even more closely the emotional response aroused in the country as a whole: 'Already as at a trumpet's call the old heroisms are waking, the old ideals of manhood and of womanhood come back once more, the old forgotten loves of country and of place are reasserting themselves, the fear of God, the honour of the King.'

Everywhere there was the same mixture of exhilaration and determined patriotism. The joint board of the Labour Party, the TUC and the General Federation of Trade Unions urged trade unions to terminate all disputes. Up and down the country strikes and lock-outs were called off, for the time being. Many people thought it would be a short war, perhaps over by Christmas. Young Civil Service Assistant Clerks flocked to the colours. In less than a year some 1,500 had joined the forces.

There were, of course, a few left-wingers who opposed the war, and among them was W J Brown, the young man who had distinguished himself by his evidence to the MacDonnell Commission. The independent Labour Party, of which he was a member, was bitterly divided. Such leaders as Keir Hardie, Ramsay MacDonald and Philip Snowden broke away from the majority and there was a violent split in Brown's local Clapham branch. To him, it seemed, as he put it in his autobiography years later, that the whole world had gone unanimously mad. Believing with Marx that war was the expression, in its final form, of the capitalist struggle for markets, he determined to have no part in it.

He described in detail in his autobiography how, by an ingenious rearguard action, he succeeded in evading the call-up when conscription was introduced in 1916. He was then on the establishment of the Office of Works, but had been placed on loan to the War Office and loaned from there to the Board of Trade. When told by his chief at the Board that he was to be released for military service, he pointed out that his chief had no power to do that but only to return him to the War Office. In due course he was returned to the War Office, where the same thing happened and after further delay he found himself back at the Office of Works. There he was welcomed because of the shortage of trained men and made First Assistant to the head of the furniture section, which enabled him to claim a special allowance of first £30 and then £60 a year.

Eventually his chief at the Office of Works said he could keep Brown no longer, but Brown had found a clause in the Military Service Act which gave exemption to

Brown as a young man

full-time national trade union officers and part-time branch secretaries. He was now Assistant Secretary of the Assistant Clerks' Association and he wrote to the Ministry of National Service claiming that he was morally covered by the clause. The Ministry pondered some time and replied that the Assistant Clerks' Association was not a trade union. Brown retorted by quoting the 1913 Trade Union Act which defined a trade union as 'any combination of employees or employed designed to regulate wages and conditions of employment.' Another long pause followed before Brown received a further letter agreeing that the Association was a trade union but pointing out that the exemption clause did not mention part-time national officials. Brown then expressed the intention of informing every part-time Branch Secretary in the Association and other associations that they were exempted under the Act. Nothing happened for several months until his department took the matter up with the Ministry of National Service, only to be informed that the papers relating to the case were lost. So it all had to be gone through again, but before this was completed the war came to an end. Brown had escaped the call-up without pleading conscientious objection, which he did not do because his opposition to the war was on political and social, not religious, grounds.

His ingenuity in avoiding the call-up

The curious story is worth repeating partly because it illustrates so well Brown's qualities of resource and persistence, and because it resulted in this remarkable man free-wheeling to the leadership of the Association instead of being engulfed in the mud of Flanders. Many of the active workers had volunteered and others were so overworked that few could find time for the Association.

After his evidence to the Commission, Brown was made Assistant Secretary of the Office of Works branch and when the Secretary joined up, he became Secretary, which entitled him to a seat on the Council of the Assistant Clerks' Association. When Milne was criticised for his handling of the Assistant Clerks' case before the Commission, Brown defended him in an able speech and was elected to the Executive and in 1914 made Assistant Secretary. In 1916, Milne was promoted to the Second Division and Brown, at the age of 22, became Secretary of the Association. It was, however, a narrow decision. Both the Executive and Council recommended his appointment, but at the annual general meeting, which all members could attend, the Savings Bank put up a surprise rival candidate named Hough and attempted to pack the meeting. Brown scraped home by one vote. 'It was my first experience of the "caucus" type of mind which all my life I have cordially hated and despised,' Brown wrote later.

Milne and Brown made an almost ideal team for the back-to-the-wall job of holding the Association together and fighting off Treasury encroachments during the four years of war. Brown was young, impulsive and tremendously energetic. Milne, more experienced and ten years Brown's senior, was as Brown described him: 'Very tall and always immaculately dressed in black coat and waistcoat and striped trousers. He had a long, angular face and the high dome of his head was prematurely bald. He was a Scot and spoke with a delightful Edinburgh accent. What I liked about him was his urbanity and sense of humour. He was always in the battle but always, somehow, ahead of it, and again and again his dry but infinitely gentle humour would resolve a dispute, reconcile opposing points of view and produce an agreed line of policy.' Before long, Brown left his lodgings in Balham and went to live with Milne and his family in Hounslow. He found it an intensive education because Milne was a stickler for accuracy and would not tolerate overstatement.

Struggle to hold the Association together during the war

Milne and Brown had a hard struggle. The rush of volunteers to the forces in the first year was followed by a steady stream which removed many active

Women crowded into the Civil Service to replace men called to the Services. Here, they prepare sugar rationing cards in the food control office

Association members, branch secretaries and contributors to *Red Tape*. The journal managed to maintain its existence, although by the end it was reduced to eight pages, much of it written by Saunderson and the officers.

Membership of the Association, which reached a peak of 2,837 in 1914, fell to 1,449 in 1916 and to 609 the following year. It was estimated that 94 per cent of Assistant Clerks, including volunteers and those called up, went into the forces. More than 400 were killed in action. Among these was James Maxwell, founder of the Association, who became a lieutenant in the Finsbury Rifles and lost his life at the Dardanelles. Saunderson wrote this elegy on him:

Jim

Hail and farewell, good friend of all the years;
In a far land 'neath skies for ever blue,
Your grave is set, and through the prideful tears
There comes a vision of the man we knew –

Jim.

Careless, light-hearted, friend of all the world,
But most the friend of those whose need you knew,
Who, helpless, feckless, in the vortex whirled,
Knew, when the rest had failed, there still was you –

Jim.

A thousand kindly deeds without a name,
A thousand fights 'gainst tyranny in power;
No cause so hopeless but its need might claim
The knightly service of your waking hour –

Jim.

So to your death you passed, the death you'd choose,
A fighter ever and a patriot true;
And England, living in the life men lose,
Thanks God, in hours of need, for men like you –

Jim.

The Assistant Clerks found their first promises of patient sacrifice grew hard to maintain. The cost of living index which the Board of Trade had started at 100 in July 1914, reached 110 by the end of the year, 135 by the end of 1915, 165 by the end of 1916, 185 by the end of 1917, and topped 220 when the war ended. The value of the clerks' salaries, which the MacDonnell Commission had found so inadequate before the war, diminished continually. As more and more went into the forces and were transferred to the new and expanding wartime departments, those that remained found themselves working even longer hours. At the same time they had to guide the hands of a growing multitude of temporaries.

Many of these were girls, usually no longer segregated from the men as they had been previously in the few departments which employed them, but working, many in short skirts and sleeveless jumpers, side by side with the weary but excited young males. *Red Tape* versifiers had a field day. For instance:

To a Sweet Substitute

Maiden fair, you're bright and smiling,
As the moments you're beguiling,
For statistics you're compiling
  Of your country's trade.
Cares in me you're oft confiding
And each day your feet I'm guiding,
Knotty points for you deciding,
  When you need my aid.

Now, alas, there's news surprising
That your rate of payment's rising,
So no more I'm supervising,
  Though you sadly sigh.
Ne'er you'll see old days returning
Though to help you I'll be yearning,
For I fear you'll soon be earning
  More per week than I!

'Red Tape' begs to introduce itself to the ladies of the Service

She must have been an unusual 'maiden fair', however, for most of the girls were very cheap labour and there were serious anxieties lest many would be kept as cheap labour after the war, replacing men. In 1914 there were about 65,000 female civil servants, about 58,000 of them in Post Office non-clerical grades, but by the end of the war there were 225,000, the majority temporary clerks. Though many of the established clerks were guiding the feet of the newcomers, male and female, most got no financial reward for it, even when doing Second Division work, and promotion was almost at a stand-still because of the policy of keeping posts open for ex-servicemen returning after the war.

Although the Treasury had said that consideration of the MacDonnell Commission recommendations must be shelved, Milne and Brown saw no reason why the immediate increase of one increment in the pay scale should not be implemented, and in April 1915 they succeeded in getting this concession. But since it meant only £5 a year for some, and £7 10s (£7·50) for others higher in the scale, it was nothing like enough to compensate for rising prices.

There were hopes of war bonuses such as were awarded in outside industry by the Committee on Production, which acted as an arbitration tribunal after strikes were made illegal, and dealt particularly with claims for pay increases to compensate for increased living costs. When a claim by postal unions for a war bonus was rejected, therefore, they asked for arbitration, arguing that if this was right for outside employees it must also be right for government employees. The Post Office unions were strong and well organised and the Government gave way. An independent arbitrator was appointed and in July 1915 awarded small bonuses to employees earning £3 a week or less.

However, when the Civil Service Federation asked for arbitration on a similar claim for their other affiliates, including the Assistant Clerks' Association, the Government instead referred it to the Committee on Retrenchment and accepted its view that claims should be considered on their merits, department by department. The object, it appeared, was to break the wage-price spiral. The associations concerned filed grade claims and were all informed that a case had not been made out for throwing such a heavy burden on the taxpayer. It was not until October 1916, after Brown had led a deputation to the Financial Secretary to the Treasury, that the Association secured a bonus slightly higher than that awarded to the postal workers 15 months earlier.

Milne and Brown had become increasingly angry not only with the Treasury but also with the postal unions and the Federation. Milne wrote an article entitled *The Failure of the Federation* in which he said: 'The Postal Associations, knowing all the time that the Federation was taking action, destroyed the Federation's strength by taking an independent line of their own, gained a war bonus for themselves, and undoubtedly helped to lose it for the rest of the Civil Service. When it is realised that postal associations account for nine-tenths of the Federation's membership, the seriousness of their defection can be realised.'

The ill feeling between the postal unions and the Assistant Clerks' Association may well have been accentuated by a personal antagonism felt by Brown for G H Stuart-Bunning, the postmen's Secretary. In more than one of his later books Brown described the origins of this. It began with their first contact at a meeting

G H Stuart-Bunning, the postmen's leader for whom Brown felt a personal antagonism

of the Council of the Civil Service Federation of which Stuart-Bunning was chairman. Brown, only 20 years old and attending his first Federation meeting, seconded a motion put forward by Milne. 'I dare say what I said was immature enough,' ran Brown's account, 'but the remarkable thing was not my immaturity but the ferocity with which Bunning, over 20 years my senior, the leading figure in Civil Service Association work and shortly to be President of the Trades Union Congress, dealt with me. He took my poor little speech and tore it to shreds like a schoolboy dismembering a helpless fly. I suffered an extreme sense of outrage. I went home and analysed as best I could how he had done it, and resolved to return to the attack at the first opportunity. I did so again and again, with pretty much the same results. But each time I learnt something, and ultimately the time came when my judgement, which for all my youth was superior to his, was sustained by a dialectical capacity greater than his own.' Brown claimed he had never in his life fought anybody except on the merit of an issue, but confessed that in Stuart-Bunning's case personal feeling lent zest to the battles.

Whatever the relevance of this, the Association turned to new allies. On March 30, 1916, the Treasury had issued a circular stating that it proposed to apply for an Order in Council providing for an eight-hour day (instead of seven) throughout the Service with a half-holiday on Saturdays. The announcement heated the already bitter feelings in the clerical associations to boiling point. Since most civil servants were working more than eight hours, the immediate effect would be to deprive them of an hour's overtime pay. But the civil servants saw the proposal as something more serious than that; an attempt to use the war situation to establish a permanently longer working day when the war was over. The Assistant Clerks' Association immediately got in touch with the Second Division Association and at a meeting on April 7 they agreed on a full-scale campaign. A petition was to be sent to the King praying him to withhold his assent to the proposed order until vital representations had been made and considered; that an all-grade memorial should be signed in each department, that arrangements should be made for a mass protest meeting in Central Hall, in Westminster; that the sympathy of MPs should be enlisted, and that the co-operation of all grades of civil servants affected should be sought. By the following evening, the associations of female clerks, female typists and intermediate clerks had agreed to join with them. The petition to the King was signed and delivered and memorials were being signed in all departments. On April 11 the mass meeting announcement was circulated. On April 12 the Treasury capitulated. The mass meeting was cancelled.

Associations combine to thwart the Treasury's attempt to introduce an eight-hour day

It was an example of rapid concerted action rare in the Civil Service, but the postal unions were not impressed. The *Postman's Gazette* accused the promoters of the movement of 'intellectual incapacity, meanness and disloyalty' because the Federation was not asked to organise the campaign.

Exhilarated by the campaign's success, however, Milne and Brown retorted suitably and joined the Second Division Association, which had never been a member of the Federation, in calling a meeting, also attended by representatives of the women's organisations, at which the Civil Service Clerical Alliance was formed. By the time of its first semi-annual conference in April 1917, the Alliance had seven affiliated associations with a membership of 15,000. David Milne, now in the Second Division, became its first Secretary and continued to work closely with Brown. The Association formally withdrew from the Civil Service Federation in December 1916.

The Government apparently wearied of the alternating pressure from the Post Office and clerical unions and in November the Prime Minister announced it had been decided to set up a standing arbitration tribunal 'to decide during the war questions of wages arising between the Government and its civil employees', and early in 1917 the Conciliation and Arbitration Board was established. The title chosen was significant. Starting with experiments half a century earlier, such boards had become recognised as the best means of resolving disputes in outside industry and their formation had been vigorously encouraged in the report of the Royal Commission on Labour in 1894. There were 64 boards then, but by 1913 there were 325. They varied in detail but all laid more emphasis on collective bargaining and conciliation than on arbitration, which was seldom provided for except as a last resort.

The procedure laid down for the Civil Service Board was that: 'in the first instance the official representatives and the employees' representatives shall endeavour to arrange the difference by mutual agreement, but should they fail to settle the matter by conciliation, the case will at once be referred to the Board acting as arbitrators.'

The Treasury is obliged to negotiate with Civil Service associations

The Treasury was thus obliged for the first time to enter into negotiations with employees. The board consisted of three members under the chairmanship of Sir William Collins, MP, an experienced arbitrator. With him were Harry Gosling of the Transport Workers' Federation, a well-known figure after his leadership of a big dock strike in 1912, and Sir A Kaye Butterworth, general manager of the North-Eastern Railway. The Assistant Clerks' Association considered the selection 'almost unusually happy'. It was particularly pleased with the employers' member because his railway company had granted war bonuses as high as those the clerks were seeking. The tribunal's jurisdiction was restricted to differences over pay, but it could deal with claims for permanent improvements as well as for improved war bonuses. The Chancellor of the Exchequer gave an undertaking to honour the board's awards.

It was immediately inundated with claims, nearly all for a 30 per cent bonus increase and all got slightly less than that, backdated to the beginning of the year. After that there was claim after claim. From 1917 to 1919 the board allowed 13 small general increases, but at the end the bonuses were still too small to compensate for the rise in prices.

In addition to the war bonus claim, handled by the Civil Service Clerical Alliance, the Assistant Clerks' Association asked for the increases recommended by the MacDonnell Commission. The board urged further negotiations and a series of meetings with the Treasury followed. The result was the first negotiated agreement to be reached by an all-Service class of employees. The clerks still did not get the £200 maximum for which they had struggled so long but the settlement provided for higher increments after £130 to a maximum of £170. The settlement was accepted as provisional, leaving the claim for a £200 maximum for settlement when the Service was reorganised after the war.

Thus, when fighting ended on November 11, 1918, Treasury and Association representatives knew and probably understood each other better than they had ever done. This was not saying very much but it was at least some preparation for the new relationships of the post-war era.

CHAPTER FOUR
Pushing the Treasury into Whitleyism

It has been a good year. Last October there were but a few hundred of us in effective membership. Now there are as many thousand. A year ago our colleagues were scattered over Europe and Asia. Now they have returned to us, bringing into Association life a new vigour, a wider outlook and a determination deepened by what they have endured. Then our organisation was scrappy and disjointed. Now it is strong and well-knit, and the promise of greater strength is with us. Materially, too, we have prospered. There was never a year in which we have achieved so much . . . Spiritually we have grown out of recognition. The dispirited weariness which grew upon us towards the end of the war has given place to a new life. The demeanour of the class has undergone a striking and significant change which our rulers would do well not to ignore.

That was Bill (W J) Brown, writing in *Red Tape* in October 1919, nearly a year after the end of the war, and there was justification for his satisfaction. During the year, the Assistant Clerks' Association had laid the foundations of its future by appointing him as full-time secretary, the first in any Civil Service clerical association. And Civil Service associations, led by G H Stuart-Bunning and for once united, had put through a plan for a National Joint Council.

The impact of peace on the Association was dramatic. The release of civil servants from the forces was given a high priority and almost at once the Assistant Clerks began to flood back to a country which did not seem to them fit for heroes. They found themselves more badly off in real terms than they had been before the war. The cost of living was still rising and, in a hectic boom period, continued to do so until the end of 1920. Membership of the Association rose from 623 in 1918 to 3,500 in 1919 and 5,368 in 1920.

Outside the Service, the country entered upon the worst period of industrial strife in its history. The number of trade unionists had doubled and in industry after industry pre-war hostilities were resumed. The triple alliance of miners, railwaymen and transport workers, talking of direct action to gain political ends, was an unprecedented menace to the Government. Strikes by the police shook public confidence.

In this atmosphere, the returning assistant clerks wanted action from their Association and Brown was ready for them. At the Annual General Meeting on November 28, 1918, little more than a fortnight after the end of hostilities, he presented plans for a campaign for abolition of the Assistant Clerk class and its incorporation in the Second Division, for the appointment of a full-time Secretary and for an increase in contributions to 1s 6d (7½p) a month. A special general meeting would be called to examine these proposals. Everything was carried unanimously. The meeting, declared *Red Tape*, was unique in point of numbers and enthusiasm and of the boldness of the view which found expression.

Month by month, the numbers and militancy of the returning Assistant Clerks grew. *Red Tape* stoked the flames. 'Today, five years after the Royal Commission

Action is demanded by Assistant Clerks returning from the Services

recommended a scale of £50–£200 for the Class, the scale remains at £50–£170. What do the discharged men think of that? Are they content to return to these conditions? The Treasury has maintained its cynical callousness to every canon of decency and fair treatment. Argument, reason, persuasion are wasted upon it. During the war the associations, with a sadly depleted membership, hampered by lack of funds and by the administrative difficulties of the war period, have done their best and they have failed. The Service is the old, bad service. The conditions to which the men return are the old, bad conditions. We confess our failure.

'To the discharged men we turn. It may be that they, who have spent the last four years away from the subtleties and bitterness of our life, who have been at grips with the primitive and elemental things, may find a straighter, directer method of setting wrongs right than the Service has yet experienced.'

At the end of January 1919, Brown put in one more claim for the £200 maximum the Association had sought so long, but in terms very different from those of past years. 'My Council,' he wrote to the Treasury, 'anticipate that they will be confronted with unrest of serious dimensions in the class unless their conditions are ameliorated. This is particularly true of the discharged men, who feel that all that they have undergone entitles them at any rate to a wage which will permit them to live . . . The Council feel that unless something is done to improve the lot of the class, for the first time in its history a strike of the men concerned is not outside the range of probability.'

Brown warns the Treasury of the possibility of a strike unless the conditions of Assistant Clerks are improved

Almost by return post, the Treasury at last conceded the £200 maximum. As before the war, the general unrest, no doubt, made the Government feel it necessary to pacify its own employees. But a few months later the Association prepared a new claim for a scale with a maximum of £350.

In the same month that the £200 maximum was obtained, February 1919, the Association held its special general meeting to consider reorganisation. It took place in a crowded Central Hall since nothing smaller was now adequate for such meetings. Brown reported that the Council had offered him the post of full-time Secretary, but he had been unable to accept and a suitable man had not been found. It soon became very clear, said the *Red Tape* report, that the meeting had definitely made up its mind as to who the Secretary should be. In the first five minutes of the debate one man said very emphatically that if the meeting broke up without securing Mr Brown's services it might as well never have been held and there were similar speeches from all parts of the hall.

Brown initially rejected the job because he considered it insecure. He had married in 1916 (with Milne as best man) and both his mother and father had died, leaving him with two young sisters and a young brother to support. He had no confidence that the Association would continue to maintain a full-time secretary and he told those at the meeting so with extreme bluntness. The past record of the Association did not suggest that members had been in earnest about the business, he said. If they were prepared to put the organisation on a really sound basis then, subject to the settlement of details, he was prepared to reconsider. There were loud cheers and the Council was instructed to fix it. In the meantime W B Bird, Saunderson's successor as editor of *Red Tape*, and Ross Wyld of the Post Office Savings Bank were appointed to help him. The meeting then turned down the Council's proposal that the subscription should be 1s 6d (7½p) a month and made it 2s (10p) instead. In a single year, subscriptions income increased from £73 to £2,417 and the number of branches doubled. The Council settled with Brown that members should be invited to subscribe to a guarantee fund to protect his position, in addition to their 2s subscription, and in 12 months raised about £2,000.

The first headquarters of the Association (above) were in a small room above this shop. The staff consisted of W J Brown and his secretary, Jean Cormack, shown here 20 years later, still together

Brown thus became full-time Secretary and set up an office in the box room of his flat above a second-hand furniture dealer's shop in Penge in south-east London. The Association's first office was about 10 by 6 feet, contained a table, an old typewriter and a duplicator, and often had to be shared with a pram. He brought with him from the Office of Works a shorthand-typist named Jean Cormack. Jean was a monosyllabic little Scotswoman from a village near Aberdeen, whose father, sisters and brothers were all teachers, except one who entered a bank. She had worked in a solicitor's office in Peterhead (Aberdeenshire), which she rather liked, but had reluctantly obeyed her father's behest to go into the Civil Service. She readily accepted Brown's offer to take her away from it because she could not endure the tedium of typing the same document over and over again 50 times and because Brown, so full of his ideals and ambitions, was like no one she had met before. She found life with the Association more varied and lively and remained in it for 30 years, always quietly efficient, the one stable element in its turbulent history, until Brown left, taking her with him. He often described 'faithful Jean' as the perfect secretary.

Central Hall mass meetings continued. One, called by the Civil Service Alliance in March to demand improvements in salaries, passed a resolution pledging support, if nothing was done in three months, for 'any steps considered necessary to enforce such a demand'. Delegates openly spoke of the possibility of strikes and the shocked *Civilian* afterwards referred to 'Bolshevism in the Service'.

Even Brown was finding the membership getting out of control. The Service, he wrote in the next issue of *Red Tape*, seemed to be divided into those who wanted a strike immediately and those to whom the word was synonymous with Bolshevism. Both were wrong. The strike used as a last resort was a perfectly legitimate weapon but it was a boomerang which could hit the users as hard as the men against whom it was directed. This was particularly so when the users were not adequately prepared and that was the position in the Service. There was no organisation of the salaried classes with sufficient resources at that time. It might be different later.

Brown was militant enough at another crowded Central Hall meeting in June,

37

this time called by the Assistant Clerks' Association, described in *Red Tape* as 'the most impressive demonstration against the oppressors of Whitehall that the Service has yet witnessed.' The purpose this time was to endorse the £350 claim and repudiate the report of the Gladstone Committee on organisation and staffing of government offices which, as the clerks interpreted it, proposed that Second Division work should be done by Assistant Clerks for less money and clerical work transferred to women at even lower rates of pay.

Brown said the claim would be pressed by all the means in the Association's power. 'But, if we find in the Treasury neither the bowels of compassion nor the instincts of justice, if the claim is treated as previous claims have been, then we promise them war – fierce, persistent, relentless war until Treasury control as we know it, Treasury control and the abominable things for which it stands, is swept utterly and for ever away.'

According to *Red Tape*, his speech was received not only with a storm of applause but also with low, angry cheering. The conference unanimously endorsed the claim, instructed the Council to approach the Treasury, the Prime Minister, the Chancellor of the Exchequer, the Labour Party and the Minister of Labour, and gave a pledge to support any action necessary. By this time, however, such reports and wage claims, except for bonus increases, were being left over for the National Whitley Council, when formed. Perhaps Brown's strong words were an attempt to frighten the Government into accepting Whitleyism as the associations wanted it. The plan was to be considered by the Cabinet a week later.

The associations had been compaigning for the application of Whitley principles to the Civil Service ever since the Whitley Committee had first reported in March 1917. Set up under the chairmanship of J H Whitley, Deputy Speaker of the House of Commons, to make suggestions for a permanent improvement in relations between employers and employed, the Committee had recommended the establishment of joint councils in every industry to consider regularly the progress and well-being of the trade and 'to give opportunities for satisfying the growing demands made by trade unions for a share in industrial control.' But it had made no specific reference to public employees. The associations, however, immediately saw their chance. Such councils could give them the opportunity to play a part in the control of their affairs going far beyond anything they had known or probably hoped for. 'It is inevitable,' wrote Brown, 'that if the scheme is adopted for industries, the Government will have to adopt it in some form or other for the Civil Service and it is extremely necessary that associations should be alive to the opportunity.' The Treasury, however, did not regard it as inevitable.

The Associations campaign for Whitleyism in the Civil Service

The story of the associations' successful campaign has been told in some detail by Dr Henry Parris in his history of the first 50 years of Whitleyism. Within a few weeks of the publication of the report, the Civil Service Alliance raised the matter with the Ministry of Labour. 'It is not contemplated,' replied the Permanent Secretary, 'that its application should be extended to occupations of a purely commercial or clerical nature.' Then the Civil Service Federation took the matter up with the Chancellor of the Exchequer, assuming the principles of the report would be applicable to government servants and suggesting that he should appoint three or four of his officers to consult with the Federation Executive in order to arrive at smooth and easy working of the scheme.

Getting a reply similar to that given to the Alliance by the Ministry of Labour, the Federation expressed surprise at the statement that the report was not intended for application to occupations of a commercial or clerical character and, having found nothing in it to justify this conclusion, reminded the Chancellor that many of the classes in the Service did not come under either designation. The Federation was no doubt thinking of the Post Office manipulative grades which made up the largest part of its membership. The Chancellor's private secretary now replied: 'I am desired by the Chancellor of the Exchequer to say he would certainly deny that the Civil Service could be regarded as an "industry" or as being included in the "main industries of the country" to which reference is made in paragraph 3 of the report in question.'

The Treasury obviously hoped that this would be the last word but it was only the beginning. The Government had accepted the report in October 1917 and organised a campaign led by the Minister of Labour to persuade industries to accept it. Scores of meetings were held and, according to Brown: 'Wherever a government speaker appeared to commend the scheme to employers and employed, there was a pertinacious civil servant blandly inquiring why, if the idea was so good, the Government, which was the biggest employer of all, did not apply it in its own house.' As *Red Tape* succinctly put it: 'Obviously co-operation between employer and employee should, like charity, begin at home.'

Stuart-Bunning went to see Whitley himself at the House of Commons and asked him whether it was intended to leave the Service outside the scheme. Whitley, according to his account, indignantly denied it and denounced the action of the Ministry, adding that at one time the Committee had considered an experimental period, and one of the members, Beatrice Webb, had suggested the Civil Service was the ideal body for experiment. The Committee unanimously supported its Chairman and its next report made it clear that the expression 'employers and workmen' was intended to cover state and municipal authorities and their employees.

The Government gave way and in December accepted that it was up to them to set an example. The first Government Joint Councils were established for employees in their workshops without much difficulty. It was not for a year, however, that the Government got down to consideration of how the plan could be applied to the non-industrial Civil Service.

The Government gives way at last

In the meantime, the associations had been busy formulating their own ideas on the subject. They had, of course, worked out plans for changes in Civil Service organisation before, always aimed at ending domination by the hated Treasury. The Civil Service Federation had from the beginning advocated the use of Commons select committees to exercise overall supervision. They were to hold inquiries into the whole Service and into groups of departments every five years.

Saunderson had used *Red Tape* editorials to expound the ideas of guild socialism, an advanced theory of joint control which G D H Cole was persuasively advocating at that time. Brown found much to be said for a plan put forward by Fred Jowett, MP, under which each department would be controlled by a committee of MPs. Since the Treasury dealt with establishments, its committee would include employee representatives.

The Whitley Committee proposals concentrated union leaders' minds on turning speculative ideas into practical propositions. Whitley was concerned with the establishment of machinery for co-operation between employers and employed, but in the Civil Service it was far from clear who was the employer for practical purposes. The chairman of the Civil Service Alliance, J C Monahan, posed the question at an Alliance conference on the subject in November 1917. 'In reality,' he answered himself, 'the State. In form, no doubt, the Crown; but in flesh and blood who is he? Neither the Government nor Parliament gives, or can give, that assiduous attention to the needs of the Service that ought to be given in the 20th century by a responsible employer. Heads of department, it is true, discharge some of the functions of employers, but their powers are limited, their responsibilities divided, and the most vital modifications of conditions of service can be effected against their will. The Treasury claims neither to be the employer nor to represent him, it washes its hands of responsibility.'

The Alliance decided to recommend the creation of an employer in the shape of a board, under the chairmanship of a member of the Ministry of Labour, composed of equal numbers of people appointed by the Government and representatives of associations.

'We must be very emphatic in our demand,' urged Monahan, 'that the management of the Civil Service shall not, in any way, be connected with the Treasury. The Treasury is the guardian of the public purse, and to approach these questions from a purely financial point of view is to be certain of mischief.'

Brown put this view about the Treasury with characteristic vigour in *Red Tape* shortly after the Government announcement was made. 'Most of the good results which might be expected to result from the application of the report to the Service will be lost if the system of Service control remains what it is. Treasury control is archaic, inefficient and offensive, and it must go if the Service is to be made a place worth living in.'

In October 1918, a committee was set up, under the chairmanship of Sir Thomas Heath, Joint Permanent Secretary to the Treasury, to consider the possible application of the Whitley principle to the non-industrial Civil Service, but its report did not appear until March 1919, when it infuriated Association leaders. It recommended a National Joint Council, with Joint Committees in the departments and at local level, all very much according to the Whitley plan, but the National Council was to be merely consultative and advisory. The State, the report said, was the ultimate employer of Government servants through the heads of departments, who consequently had not the freedom of decision enjoyed by the private employer. Ministerial responsibility presupposed that a minister should be free to accept or reject the conclusions of any joint body. Functions of an advisory and consultative nature must therefore take the place of the executive functions exercised by joint councils in outside industry.

Combined tactics by the associations outwit the government

The recent stormy meetings at London's Central Hall made it apparent that the membership would be in no mood to accept this watering down of Whitley, but the Association leaders adopted skilful tactics to deal with it when Austen Chamberlain, the monocled Chancellor of the Exchequer, met them on April 8 at Caxton Hall, Westminster. He was flanked, according to Stuart-Bunning, by a galaxy of high officials such as had never before been seen. The Treasury in full force and heads and sub-heads of departments crowded the platform.

After Chamberlain had introduced the report, Stuart-Bunning thanked the Government for accepting the Whitley principle but regretted that it had departed from its spirit of equality in that associations had not been represented on the Committee. He then moved the adoption of one clause only of the report which provided for the appointment of a Joint Committee to work out details of the scheme. This Committee was to consider all reports, not only that of the Heath Committee, and report back by the end of May. After the motion had been seconded, there was a period of silence. By pre-arrangement, no one spoke for fear of clouding the issue. At last, after twice inviting further speakers without result, Chamberlain said that the platform gladly accepted the motion, it was adopted unanimously and a Joint Committee was set up, consisting of an Official Side and a Staff Side, each with 15 members.

Austen Chamberlain

The Joint Committee quickly produced a unanimous report which differed from that of the Heath Committee mainly in the definition of the Council's functions. It was to determine rather than consider the general principles governing conditions of service, and: 'The decisions of the Council shall be arrived at by agreement between the two sides, shall be signed by the chairman and vice-chairman, shall be reported to the Cabinet, and thereupon shall become operative.' The report was accepted by the War Cabinet on June 13. Sir Malcolm Ramsay, first Controller of Establishments in a newly created Treasury office, then had the task of selling the scheme to the heads of departments. Some had misgivings but Ramsay warned them that if the system did not succeed 'we shall find ourselves embarked upon a sea of troubles far more stormy than we have yet had to navigate.' They agreed to give it a trial. On July 3, Chamberlain again met the staff associations at a Caxton Hall meeting packed to the doors, with Ramsay on one side of him and Stuart-Bunning on the other, and the revised scheme was enthusiastically given the go ahead.

The first meeting of the Civil Service National Whitley Council took place on July 23, 1919.

23 CU
IO YE
IS THIS
SACRIF

PART TWO
ELBOWING A WAY UP
1919–1942

CHAPTER FIVE
Bill Brown

He soon made his mark in the House. He was, in my opinion, head and shoulders in ability above all the back bench Labour members. There were few members in the House who were his superiors in logical and incisive speech and in knowledge of the subject upon which he spoke. I regret to have to add that his influence was impaired by an unnecessary aggressiveness. If he returns to the House, as he probably will, there will be a great future for him if he will cultivate the art of making friends instead of alienating people.

That was Lord Snowden's impression of W J Brown after watching him for the two years of the second Labour Government. But Brown never did cultivate the art of making friends, whether among politicians or trade union colleagues. This was how he was summed up in a *Red Tape* obituary by Douglas (Lord) Houghton who was General Secretary of the Inland Revenue Staff Federation in the inter-war years: 'Brown was an exhibitionist, he was ruthless and on occasion unscrupulous and he had few loyalties. But his great ability, his powers of oratory and advocacy, and his engaging personality made him the most loved and disliked of men in our movement.'

Houghton frequently clashed with Brown in the inter-war years and his assessment may not err on the side of charity, but it is a balanced assessment from outside which is a useful corrective to the memories of Association members who were dazzled and bemused by his oratory, his self-confidence and his long succession of unprecedented victories, in the battles with the Government and other unions, which made the Civil Service Clerical Association (CSCA), as it became, the most powerful Association on the clerical side of the Service.

Those who recall Brown in his youthful prime can still picture in their minds 'the formidable little man with the white face, the blue eyes opened aggressively and the decisive set of the jaw,' standing on the platform in front of them. They speak of 'the soft, husky voice, laden with all the gravity and emphasis of an Old Testament prophet, coming through the pursed lips with an incisive style of speech – quiet, intimidating with the force of the organised mind and the will to break down all opposition to the course of action which he is so sure is the one to be adopted.'

He made a commercially shrewd appraisal of the balance of advantage in different possible courses of action. He had an almost religious conviction of his own infallibility, a remarkable clarity of exposition, a readiness to exploit tactical opportunities and a melodramatic talent for staging explosions at the right moment.

Brown was always ready for battle and often invited it

Brown was always ready for battle and often invited it – with the Government, the Treasury, the Labour Party, the TUC, the Post Office unions and the Post Office section of his own union. Management representatives often hated and feared him, regarding him as an unscrupulous opponent, but he could almost always surpass them in the clear and convincing exposition of an intricate argument. In one case before the Civil Service Arbitration Tribunal he so demolished an opponent's case that the spokesman for the Official Side was reduced to tears.

National Staff Side colleagues found him a partner given to dispute. He had a gift for biting sarcasm and sometimes abuse. Houghton has recalled how he and Brown nearly came to blows at one meeting. Henry Parris, in his book on the history of Whitleyism, quotes accounts of other occasions when words almost turned to blows. Brown, it seems, once threatened to throw his old enemy, Stuart-Bunning, out of the window and the two men had to be held in their chairs. Later, Brown had similar rows with J W Bowen, also from the Post Office, notably when Brown accused him of being a ponderous mediocrity and other members had to intervene between them.

J W Bowen, whom Brown called 'a ponderous mediocrity'

Even within the Association, Brown had bitter disputes with the Post Office Section and the Executive. In later years there was an occasion when Brown, exasperated by Executive opposition on some point related to his parliamentary position, picked up his papers and said, with perfect precision and seriousness: 'You are a contumacious set of swine!' He then left the room with his chin thrust in the air, just as depicted by the bronze bust now in the CPSA boardroom. Hater of others' tyranny as he was, Brown himself became something of a tyrant in his later years. He was always ambitious and he had the ability to nourish any amount of ambition. But he also had a temperament which made it difficult for others to collaborate with him on terms of equality.

Whatever his faults, he made the Civil Service Clerical Association the power it became. Of his ability there can be no question. He had tremendous energy and an exceptional command of the spoken and written word. The former he had developed as a speaker at Methodist open air meetings – at one time pressure was put on him to train for the Ministry – and at meetings of the Independent Labour Party. The latter he attributed, at least in part, to writing two essays a week in preparation for the Assistant Clerks' examination. He was a master in the marshalling of facts. He defended himself in a libel case after the General Strike and afterwards Lord Chief Justice Hewart complimented him on one of the most able lay defences he had heard.

Brown was a many-sided man. The autobiography which he published in 1943 dwells at length on his struggle with youthful religious doubts from which he emerged with a highly individual faith. 'The great issue in the world today is not an economic one but a religious one. It is whether the individual is to be treated as a thing of no account, whose life is to be ordered at all points from the cradle to the grave in the interests of a huge impersonal State machine, in whose direction the individual is to have no effective "say" at all, or whether the function of the State is to subserve and promote the interests of the individual soul.'

For a period after he became General Secretary, he turned to poetry as a relief, he said, from the problems and difficulties of his union life. He produced two slim volumes of verse in the early 1920s, many of them expressing emotions inspired by his mother, his young son or his religious convictions.

Brown's slim volumes of verse

But he had in him more of the extrovert than the introvert. He was exuberant company and the life and soul of the social occasions which followed weekend schools and days in conference. He would contribute songs at the least provocation; often negro spirituals or folk songs delivered in a pleasant tenor. In spite of a casualness of dress and tobacco-stained fingers (he was the only man ever allowed to smoke at arbitration tribunal hearings), his youthful good looks, self-confidence and assured dominance made him immensely attractive to women. 'High tributes have been paid to my capacity as a lover', he boasted in one of his books. This was an aspect of his behaviour which some of his contemporaries recall with disapproval, some perhaps with nostalgia.

There was also a severely practical side to Brown's character and in later years, according to drinking companions, this developed into parsimony. The conditions he laid down for accepting the job of full-time Secretary were an example of his careful eye to the financial future. A year or two later he had the idea of starting a holiday camp. He tried to get his Executive to finance it, but they were unwilling to risk the union's money on such a project. He appealed to the branches but they were equally cautious. So he invited members, friends and acquaintances to take up shares and, with contributions from several Permanent Secretaries, at last got enough to make a start. The Civil Service Holiday Camp at Corton, near Lowestoft, opened in the spring of 1924 and proved a great success, setting a pattern which was later developed by Sir William Butlin and others. The Association held some of its annual conferences there, which was cheaper than going to a seaside resort and assured the camp of a week's business outside the most popular holiday season. It was not long before he opened a second camp on Hayling Island, Hampshire.

Another Brown venture was the publication of the Civil Service Compendium, which summarised the history and existing regulations and agreements on all staff matters. Again the Executive was unwilling to take responsibility but it proved a success. First compiled and issued by Brown in 1921, it was revised every few years and was later taken over by the Association.

He was an eager socialist in his early days. This was natural in a man of exceptional ability and brought up in the poverty-stricken home of a plumber with six children. Brown was particularly sensitive to slights or the assumption of superiority in others in a period when class distinctions were more marked than today. He won a scholarship to a grammar school, but even there the scholarship boys were treated as an inferior class to the paying boys though some, including Brown, were more successful scholastically. As a boy clerk and then Assistant Clerk, he experienced the caste system in the Government machine and from first holding union office knew the supercilious patronage of the Treasury. He was opposed to the system which kept good people like his parents in poverty and valued people according to their social class rather than their merits.

The Association affiliates to the TUC and Labour Party

Brown took his Association into the Labour Party and the TUC with large ballot vote majorities in 1920. But beneath his socialism there was an inherent individualism always straining to get out and in the end it took complete control. As he came to know the leaders of the Labour movement at conference and congress he was disillusioned by the self-seeking attitudes and back-biting of party politicians and the bureaucracy of the TUC.

Nevertheless, he could still enthuse over socialist ideals. In 1927 he went to Russia for three months at the invitation of the Union of Soviet Employees. On his return appeared the first of the books he became accustomed to write every time he travelled to distant countries, mixing personal reflections on anything which came into his mind with vivid pieces of description. In Russia he saw the dark side clearly enough but was inspired by what the people were trying to do. 'The most striking impression of all was that here at any rate, in contrast to Europe, society was not just drifting dully and helplessly from crisis to crisis, without rudder or compass, and with no clear vision of where it was going, if indeed it was going anywhere at all. Here in Russia was direction and purpose. Here men were in charge who knew, at least, what they were attempting to do, and were going about their business with energy and with hope, and getting an immense satisfaction from their efforts.'

The turning point was his experience as a Member of Parliament in the second

Labour Government from 1929–31. After its affiliation with the Labour Party, the Association started a political fund and decided to sponsor Brown as a parliamentary candidate. 'My merits as a candidate were considerable,' Brown wrote later, 'I had youth and relatively good looks. I was good on the platform, sure of myself in answering questions, and a good hand at repartee.' He was unsuccessful at Uxbridge in 1923 and at Wolverhampton West in 1923 and 1924, but he lost by only about 300 votes in 1924 and in 1929 he won the seat. The 1927 Act which forbade political action by Civil Service unions was easily evaded by collecting voluntary subscriptions to support his candidacy.

'The two-and-a-half years I spent in this Parliament represented the greatest period of disillusionment of my life,' Brown wrote. 'I emerged from it as an Independent, disillusioned not merely with the Labour Party but with the whole political set-up at Westminster, and especially with the domination of the parties by the party caucuses; of which ever since I have been, and am still, an unrelenting foe.'

Brown is disillusioned by his experience of Parliament.

He put his frustration into a long succession of quatrains after the manner of Omar Khayyam, of which these were three:

> 'Tis all a foolish game of 'Ayes' and 'Noes',
> And Right or Left, the Private Member goes
>   As they, the mighty ones, the whips, direct,
> And what it matters, heaven only knows!
>
> We 'Socialists' defend the bills we draft
> By what the Tories said (the while we laughed)
>   A year or so ago; and later on
> The Tories will apply the self-same craft!
>
> And this I know, whene'er the one True Light
> Seen sober, or when absolutely tight,
>   In Temple or in Tavern has been caught,
> In this abode of lies 'tis lost outright.

At first Brown gravitated to the left of James Maxton, Aneurin Bevan and their followers, and was often in trouble with the Whips. He was suspended for making a scene in the House about the bonus issue. He was expelled from the trade union group for attacking Snowden's financial policy. He became increasingly exasperated by the 'half-hearted' policies of the Government and when Sir Oswald Mosley resigned from office, Brown became one of the impatient young men who clustered around him. They planned to resign from the Parliamentary Labour Party and form the New Party. Brown was one of the few who carried out their agreement to resign but at the last minute he held back from joining the New Party, which later developed into the British Union of Fascists. It was widely assumed he had not joined the New Party because of pressure within his Association, but he explained later that what stopped him was a Mosley interview in *The Observer* which gave the New Party a quasi-Fascist complexion. From then on he fulfilled his natural political role of highly independent Independent. In his letter of resignation to the Prime Minister, Ramsay MacDonald, in March 1931, Brown reiterated his faith in socialism and accused the Labour Party of having ceased to be a socialist party and of having failed to defend trade union interests. 'The Party is tied to the caucus, the caucus is bound by the decisions of the ministers, and the ministers appear to be guided by the sole principle of "when in doubt, say no". The result is negation where positiveness is necessary, drift when determined action is necessary, surrender where resistance is necessary,

He becomes a highly independent Independent

and a situation in which the nation slides steadily into greater crisis with Parliament reduced to a position of almost complete irrelevance to what is happening in the country.'

Brown lost his seat in the crisis election of 1931, when he was an Independent Labour candidate, and in the next few years produced several pamphlets to explain himself to his constituents, his Association members and the world in general. Divorced from the Labour Party, hating Fascism, condemning the existing social system, he still proclaimed his socialism, and a socialism more extreme than before. 'I am a socialist. I stand for a new order of society based upon the communal ownership of the means of life – the land, the factories, the means of transport.' But the Labour Party, he wrote, had ceased to be the party of socialism or even of social reform and had become 'the caretakers of capitalism'. The present system could not be successfully opposed, Brown wrote, without facing the necessity of bringing down the capitalist structure and being prepared to establish a new social order in its place.

In the summer of 1937, after a famous victory over the Treasury in the Industrial Court and establishing undisputed dominance over the Association at a special conference and concluding his struggles with other associations, Brown began to look for wider fields of battle. Opportunity seemed to offer itself when the local Labour and Liberal parties in Stroud, Gloucestershire, jointly adopted him as People's Front Parliamentary candidate for the division. 'If the National Government is to be defeated it can only be defeated by a combination of the parties of the left,' said Brown. 'The movement to this end must come from below. If, in 30 or 40 constituencies, the local Liberal and Labour parties adopted People's Front candidates, the position of Labour Party headquarters would be impossible to maintain. Then a People's Front, national in scope, would emerge. Its emergency would transform the political situation overnight. Apathy would give place to interest, despair to enthusiasm, and the next general election would see a Progressive People's National Government in power.' Before the end of the year these dreams were crushed. Under heavy pressure from the national Labour Party, the Stroud party twice reaffirmed its decision to back Brown but in the end had to withdraw its support.

Since the General Strike of 1926, Brown had become no less disillusioned with the national trade union leadership than with the Labour Party and in 1937 he challenged the anger of the most powerful of them all, Ernest Bevin. Following the 'Coronation Strike' of London busmen a number of their leaders had been expelled by the Transport and General Workers' Union which Brown considered an industrial octopus rather than a union. He thought the expulsions vicious and vindicative and helped the victims to form a breakaway organisation, the National Passenger Workers' Union, of which he was made honorary President. Bevin wrote to the Civil Service Clerical Association demanding that it should discipline Brown. The Association replied that it was nothing to do with it, since Brown was acting in a purely personal capacity, and declined to interfere. Transport and General threats to attack the Association were ignored.

Brown's feud with the trade union establishment

Brown's feud with the union establishment continued. Though the 1927 Act prevented the Association from sending delegates to the Trades Union Congress, it usually had observers there. In 1938 Min Jackson, the first female president of the Association, was an observer and was severely critical when she reported to the 1939 Association Conference. Walter Citrine, the TUC General Secretary, wrote to Brown to complain that she had been guilty of gross misrepresentation.

In his reply, Brown said that if he had reported on the Congress, his criticism

Walter Citrine (left) and Ernest Bevin – objects of Brown's attacks

would have been much more fundamental. 'It would have been that the Trades Union Congress is about the most undemocratic and reactionary piece of machinery in Britain; that by the failure to provide anything but a nominal opposition to the Government on any point of major importance for years past, it has come to be little more than a convenient "cover" for the policies of the National Government; that as an instrument for the protection of working class interests it is about as effective as a sticking plaster on a wooden leg; that if it did not exist it would be necessary for the employers to invent it; and that if Fascism ever comes to Britain, the TUC might easily be converted into a "Labour Front" overnight without anybody noticing any marked change.' The Labour Front was, of course, the Nazi organisation in Germany.

Towards the end of the 1930s, Brown visited Australia and wrote a new book, *Very Free Speech*, during the voyages there and back, even more bitter about the Labour movement. 'A rebel against the rebels', he called himself. 'They embody in their outlook, their teaching and their practice precisely those evils against which they are nominally in revolt.' The Labour Party 'so far from being a democratic party in which great spirits can live, is the most illiberal and undemocratic party in politics. In the Labour Party, only mediocrity can rise to the top.

'I speak as a trade union leader, but I am inclined to say sometimes that it would be better for the working masses of Britain if there were no trade union movement. So far from being the spearhead of the working class urge to a fuller and freer life, the trade union movement serves in the main to canalise into harmless channels and to sterilise that very urge. The General Council of the trade union movement exhibits all those qualities of repression and persecution which we have come to associate with the Fascist outlook.'

A year or two later he wrote that, except in a general sense, he would no longer describe himself as a socialist. He claimed, however, to be no less radical than in the past.

During the Second World War Brown gives a series of broadcasts and undertakes a lecture tour of the United States

In the Second World War, in contrast to the First, Brown immediately offered his services to the Government and shortly after the Churchill Government was formed he went on speaking tours in the factories and at public meetings in support of the war effort. Later he gave a series of broadcasts which made him known to millions who previously knew nothing of him. In the summer of 1941 he undertook a speaking and lecture tour of the United States, which resulted in yet another collision with the TUC. A statement by the TUC General Council said they had found it necessary to inform the American Federation of Labour that the British trade union movement was in no sense associated with Brown's visit to the United States. 'The Trades Union Congress was not consulted about Mr Brown's visit and, if it had been, it would have made it clear that Mr Brown had neither the standing, experience, nor connections which would entitled him to act as spokesman for the British workers.'

Brown jumped at the opportunity to have another go at the TUC. Statements by Len White, the Association Deputy General Secretary, in London and cables from Brown in the United States followed in rapid succession. White said it had been made perfectly clear that Brown's visit was an unofficial one. 'The TUC was not consulted about his visit,' he added, 'but I am not aware that their approval is necessary before prominent people who are doing their best to help the war effort can visit America or anywhere else. Months ago the Civil Service Clerical Association was presented with the alternative by Sir Walter Citrine of getting rid of W J Brown or forgoing co-operation with the TUC. Sir Walter emerged a very bad second on that occasion, and there is not the slightest reason to assume that his position has improved since.' Brown cabled: 'I have never claimed to be sent by the TUC or to represent it or to speak for Sir Walter Citrine – as if I would. As to whether I represent British labour as distinct from Sir Walter Citrine and company, if I do not, so much the worse for British labour.'

The TUC statement also announced that, because of the failure of the CSCA to control Brown's 'obnoxious' activities, the Association would not be invited to discussions about the amendment of the 1927 Trade Unions and Trade Disputes Act. Because of this the National Staff Side refused to take part in the talks but some individual unions did.

Another cable from Brown said that his 'obnoxious' activities consisted of following the view that trade unionism was meant to serve the workers' interests and not those of a trade union clique. 'I am doing good work here for Anglo-American relations and it is characteristic of Sir Walter Citrine and company that they appear not to care what damage they do if thereby they can injure me. That is quite unforgivable.'

In 1942 Brown was returned to the House of Commons in a by-election at Rugby. There was a war-time truce between the main parties which prevented them from putting up candidates for seats previously held by another party. This let in a number of leftish independents who ignored the truce. His secretary, Jean Cormack, went to Rugby with him to organise the committee rooms. Churchill sent a letter of support to Brown's Conservative opponent and the National Council of Labour published a resolution condemning Brown's 'disruptionist record' and declaring that he was not a fit and proper person to represent Labour in the House of Commons. Even the Communists, whom Brown had vigorously attacked for their changing attitudes to the war, opposed him. But he swept away the Tory majority of 8,000 and was returned with a margin of 700.

The Association made him Parliamentary General Secretary, to release him from his general duties, and Len White became General Secretary.

(Opposite) Brown during his successful campaign in the 1942 Rugby by-election

CHAPTER SIX
Swallowing the Small Ones, Wearing Away the Big Ones

You have got to put strength behind Whitleyism. Now strength means many things. It means money. There are over 250 organisations in the Service and hardly one of them pays a decent subscription. Strength means numbers. Do you wonder these people (the Treasury) are not impressed when they know there is one organisation for every thousand civil servants.

That was Brown addressing civil servants of all grades at a Royal Albert Hall meeting in July 1920 attended by more than 8,000 men and women. He moved a resolution, which was carried unanimously, calling upon all Civil Service organisations to improve their organisations and resources. He himself was determined to increase the numbers in his own organisation, and did so with tremendous energy and success.

It was a time of opportunity. Civil Service trade union organisation was in the melting pot. The National Whitley Council had set up a Joint Reorganisation Committee, the recommendations of which, drawing partly on the MacDonnell Report, shaped the Service along lines which have remained basically unchanged. There was to be an Administrative Class of top men concerned with the formation of policy, an Executive Class broadly corresponding to the old Second Division, a broadened Clerical Class, an all-women class of Writing (later Clerical) Assistants for simple routine work, and two separate grades of typists and shorthand-typists. The boy clerks at last disappeared. The assistant clerks were absorbed into the new Clerical Class.

A special meeting of the Assistant Clerks' Association to consider the Reorganisation Committee's report became a kind of wake for their class. Only members and close associates were invited and Monahan, who had been leader of the Staff Side of the Committee, came dressed in black because, he said, the occasion was, in its way, a sad one. But, he confessed that he was very glad to see the dear departed decently coffined at last. Brown said it was the proudest achievement of the Assistant Clerks' Association that it took a name which was despised and rejected of men and made it the proudest name in the Civil Service.

Scrambling for membership in this remodelled Civil Service were, even if Brown was exaggerating somewhat, more than 200 organisations. Many new ones had been formed during the war to take advantage of the arbitration facilities and many more had been created afterwards to seek protection for their members through the national and departmental Whitley councils. They catered for civil servants at all levels from messengers to permanent secretaries. A few represented Treasury classes, many departmental grades. Some were restricted to established civil servants, some to temporaries and some included both. Some were 'sex unions', confined to women or men. At least one aimed at a single union for the whole Service.

In 1920, there were 370,000 non-industrial civil servants. The Assistant Clerks' Association had a membership of 5,000. The creation of the Clerical Class, with a possible membership of 40,000, provided a tempting opportunity and Brown

A scramble for members in the Civil Service

staked out a claim to represent the Clerical Class as a whole. Before long he widened his sights to cover what he called the general clerical field, including the writing assistants and typists as well as departmental clerical grades. His successes were rapid and numerous. By 1925 he had raised the membership to 20,000, by 1930 to 29,000 and by 1935 to 43,000. With the flood of new war-time recruits, the membership jumped to 85,000 in 1940, and 130,000 in 1942, when he passed over the general secretaryship to Len White. In 22 years, membership had been multiplied 26 times.

The foundation for this phenomenal growth was constructed in two years. After an amalgamation with the (Post Office) Clerical Assistants' Association, the Assistant Clerks' Association changed its name to Clerical Officers' Association (COA). Mergers then followed thick and fast. Most departmental clerical associations came in without difficulty. The leaders of one small Post Office group stood out so Brown appealed to the members over their head and a whirlwind raiding campaign left them without a following. The only other serious difficulty with departmental grades, one which was to have long repercussions, was the Employment Exchange Clerks, who entered into negotiations and then withdrew, partly because of the COA's decision to affiliate with the Labour Party.

Brown next started talks with the Civil Service Union, a more formidable proposition since its membership appears to have been larger than that of the COA. It had a history, going back to 1906, as the Admiralty and Outports Clerical Association, but in 1919 had opened its ranks to clerical civil servants generally, both temporary and established. Both unions aimed at one organisation for the clerical class, however, and eventually they agreed on a merger with Brown retained as full-time General Secretary. The COA still did not admit temporaries but agreed to take in those who were already members of the Civil Service Union. (This union had, of course, nothing to do with the present body of that name.) The merged organisation became the Civil Service Clerical Association, which, with about 16,500 members, was a relatively powerful body. Among other groups absorbed shortly after its formation were four small War Office associations who went in together.

The Civil Service Clerical Association is formed

The progress involved a complicated series of manoeuvres, but the essentials were neatly wrapped up by a *Red Tape* contributor:

> *There once was a youthful A.C.,*
> *Who pondered what answer might be*
>   *if the term 'C.A.A.',*
>   *Plus the term 'A.C.A.',*
> *Were joined mathematically.*
>
> *After delegates all had their say,*
> *And the ballots had pointed the way,*
>   *An undoubted 'progression'*
>   *Disclosed the expression*
> *Described by the term 'C.O.A.'*
>
> *Such success has attended that day,*
> *That the formula named 'C.O.A.',*
>   *Did amalgamate too*
>   *With the old 'C.S.U.',*
> *And the answer is C.S.C.A.*

The initials CSCA quickly earned the admiration, envy and verbal abuse of

Norah James, the Association's first female officer, addressing a meeting in Trafalgar Square

Douglas Houghton (left) and Reg Crook, general secretaries of two departmental clerical associations which defied Brown's efforts to swallow them

the Civil Service trade unions. They remained familiar to the union movement for nearly half a century until, after the splitting off of the Post Office from the Civil Service, they were replaced by CPSA.

Simultaneously with its expansion among Clerical Officers, the COA absorbed for the first time a number of organisations of women, mostly in the sub-clerical field, such as the Association of Writing Assistants, in 1920, and the Civil Service Typists' Association and the Civil Service Branch of the Association of Women Clerks and Secretaries, an outside union, in 1921. Norah James, Secretary and Treasurer of the last-named, became the first full-time female Assistant Secretary of the COA. She later left to become a novelist.

Brown did not get all he wanted, however. There were still four organisations in particular which made big gaps in his ideal of a single Association for the clerical field. The CSCA was involved in long periods of open warfare with three of these, and a cold war with the fourth.

Two were important departmental organisations which had retained their independence, the Association of Officers of Taxes, which in 1936 became the Inland Revenue Staff Federation; and the National Association of Employment and Clerical Officers, which in 1925 became the Ministry of Labour Staff Association. Both had followed the Assistant Clerks' example in appointing full-time general secretaries: Douglas Houghton in 1922 for the tax officers, and Reginald Crook in 1925 for the Ministry of Labour staff. Houghton retained his position until 1960, Crook until 1951. Both held high public office after the war and received life peerages. Crook was the first serving trade union leader to be made a peer and had a long stretch as chairman of the National Dock Labour Board. Houghton was on the TUC General Council from 1952–60, to the exclusion of the CSCA. He was an

MP in 1949, held junior office in the 1964 Labour Government, was chairman of the Parliamentary Labour Party during the Government-TUC crisis of 1969 arising out of Barbara Castle's *In Place of Strife* and received his peerage not long afterwards. Both were young, energetic and able men in the 1920s and '30s. Both became full-time officers at the age of 24. While a few years younger and less experienced than Bill Brown, they were able to stand up to him on the Civil Service Confederation and the Staff Side of the National Whitley Council, where they had numerous set-tos in the inter-war years. Houghton christened them the 'Three Bears' of the Civil Service (perhaps implying that the Treasury was the Goldilocks who ate their porridge while they were otherwise engaged). Both Houghton and Crook kept their organisations out of the CSCA's clutches. Houghton, indeed, was in too strong a position ever to face a serious assault, though he was several times invited to amalgamate. The taxmen, because of their special responsibilities, were able in the early 1930s to negotiate somewhat better terms than those obtained by Brown for Clerical Officers generally. Their tax association was the first in the clerical field to affiliate with the TUC, in 1911, but never affiliated with the Labour Party. It had also been active in the Civil Service Alliance. In 1929 Brown agreed to leave it alone on condition that it would recruit writing assistants and shorthand-typists in its department and pass them automatically to the CSCA.

The position of the Ministry of Labour Staff Association was very different. After it broke away from the amalgamation talks with the Clerical Assistants' Association in 1920, it was subject to intermittent attack. Brown was furious with it for making its own terms, inferior to those he was negotiating, for assimilation into the new Clerical Class, particularly when other departments adopted the Ministry of Labour model.

The CSCA had recruited headquarters Clerical Officers at the Ministry, but the staff association represented those at the employment exchanges, including women and temporaries. It had begun before the war with the formation of several regional associations which had come together in a loose federation and there was a constant struggle between the regions and the London Executive. When Reg Crook became General Secretary, he recognised the disadvantages of the Ministry of Labour agreement on assimilation but efforts to change it, in consultation with Brown and Houghton, were unsuccessful. In the *Red Tape* of November 1932, after another offer of amalgamation had been rejected, the CSCA declared open war and started a recruitment campaign among staff at the exchanges which lasted more than five years. At one point Len White, Brown's deputy, was sued for libel but won the case. Crook's defence was passive resistance. Instead of meeting attacks with counter-attacks, in which Brown would be certain to come off best, he concentrated on holding his membership together, and in fact increased it.

The CSCA declares war on the Ministry of Labour Staff Association

As a consequence, Brown's unanswered onslaught tended to create antagonism. Yet he showed a surprising ability to remain on good terms with his victims. Crook says he rather liked Brown. On one occasion, Crook was in hospital and Brown went to see him. 'Why didn't you tell me you were ill,' he demanded, 'I would have laid off for a bit.' Relations with Houghton, who was friendly with Crook, tended to be more strained. In the first year Crook estimated his losses were limited to 19 members. During the whole campaign Brown won little more than a thousand.

The Civil Service Confederation, a merger of the Federation and the Alliance, realised the conflict was weakening the position of Clerical Officers generally and proposed an amalgamation of all the clerical associations, but Houghton thought

ASSOCIATION OF EX-SERVICE CIVIL SERVANTS

FIT FOR HEROES

**NO WORK
NO MONEY
NO FOOD**

YET Men and Women of
INDEPENDENT MEANS
WORK IN
DEPARTMENTS

ASSOCIATION OF EX-SERVICE CIVIL SERVANTS

A FITTING WAR MEMORIAL

**HUNDREDS OF
DISABLED MEN**
DISABLED BY THE GOVERNMENT

**HUNDREDS OF
CONSCIENTIOUS OBJECTORS**
REINSTATED

A GRAVE SCANDAL

*Ex-service Civil Servants
parade down Whitehall*

there must be a period of cooling off between the two main antagonists before negotiations would be profitable. He kept in touch with both in the ensuing years, however, and in 1937 wrote to the CSCA, suggesting a federation of the three unions and the small County Court Officers' Association, which had also remained independent. The CSCA instructed its branches to cease activities directed against the Ministry of Labour Staff Association (MLSA). Brown left the negotiations to his deputy, Len White, and the President and it was agreed to set up a new Civil Service Alliance, comprising the four organisations, to co-ordinate their activities. The Alliance was established in 1939 and maintained peaceful working relationships between the four organisations until the early 1970s, when the MLSA and the Court Officers merged with the CPSA.

The other two unions to offer determined and long-drawn-out resistance to the CSCA embrace were the National Union of Ex-Service Temporary Civil Servants, formed after the war to try to secure improved pay and press upon the authorities the claims of ex-Servicemen, as against temporary women and non-Service men, to permanent positions in the Service, and the Federation of Women Civil Servants, pressing the claims of women.

The former had considerable success but as soon as the men became permanent the CSCA, which did not admit temporaries, snapped them up. The union, which had built up a membership much larger than that of the CSCA, changed its name in 1921 to Association of Ex-Service Civil Servants, bringing in other ex-Service associations and dropping the word temporary so it could retain in membership the men who got permanent jobs. *Red Tape* published an indignant editorial, in the style of W J Brown: 'While it may be good policy, when rival claims to permanent posts are under discussion, for ex-Servicemen to organise on the basis of past military service, it is ludicrous to perpetuate that form of organisation after establishment has been won. After establishment they became Clerical Officers and are treated as such. The Government does not lay down one scale of pay for ex-Service Clerical Officers and another for non-Service Clerical Officers. Any organisation which is to remedy the grievances of the Clerical Class must be able to speak for the whole class, ex-Servicemen, non-ex-Servicemen and women . . . he who attempts to divide the Service, he who would raise artificial barriers between one man and another, prevents unity against the common enemy and deserves the condemnation of all save that enemy whose work he does.'

The size of the goliath ex-Service association made it a serious threat. If it had retained its members it might have become the recognised association for the Clerical Class to the exclusion of the CSCA. After mutual raiding campaigns, the two organisations made an agreement not to coerce each other's members, but it did not last and open war followed. 'This war lasted some years,' wrote Brown 20 years later, 'and it was a very lively one indeed. I wrote and circulated leaflets and pamphlets by the dozen. The AECS replied with counter-leaflets and pamphlets, which afforded me material for yet further leaflets. And since my argumentation and literary capacity were vastly greater than those of my opponents, every such exchange brought members over. We organised branch meetings in every department. Whenever we could contrive it, we would engaged AECS speakers in debate. In this ding-dong battle we won steadily. Whenever their numbers shrunk, we challenged their "representative capacity" and got recognition withdrawn from them. This resulted in still further shrinkage. The upshot was that we drove the AECS from the Clerical Class field altogether. It diminished and diminished until it became what it is today, a tiny organisation of some 3,000 strong confined, for practical purposes, to minor and messengerial grades.

'This battle was vital to us and I fought it with great vigour and determination but – I must admit – a good deal of somewhat unholy glee in the struggle.'

In 1938 the AECS and the National Association of Women Civil Servants formed the Federation of Civil Servants but failed to obtain any general recognition. The AECS had a temporary increase of members during the Second World War but by then the recognised associations were too strong to allow any repetition of what happened after the First World War. In 1954 it changed its name to the National Guild of Civil Servants and opened its ranks to the whole Civil Service. It was sometimes consulted on ex-Service problems and represented some individual members.

The clerical officers were handicapped in the early stages of the battle by the fact that they did not admit temporaries into membership except for a few who came in through mergers. It is understandable that in the hectic struggles to bring established associations into their net from 1920 to 1923, they were hesitant to assume the very different problems of the unestablished, especially as it would have been hard to avoid becoming involved in the battle going on between the ex-Servicemen and the women's federation, each fighting to get as many of its members established as possible. It was not until 1929 that the Clerical Association admitted male temporaries, and two years later female temporaries.

The struggle with the Federation of Women Civil Servants, which became the National Association of Women Civil Servants in 1932, followed a similar course but Brown seems to have found less glee in it. Women's associations had developed early because of their special grievances and they had federated early. The Federation had been active in the formation of the war-time Civil Service Alliance and worked with the men's unions in the campaigns for arbitration and Whitley councils.

The reorganisation of 1920, however, created common classes for men and women in the clerical and executive fields and later the administrative field, so that to many people sex-based associations no longer seemed necessary. As has been mentioned, the writing assistants were among the first to enter the COA and the Typists' Association, which had been affiliated to the Women's Federation, transferred to the COA soon afterwards. The Women's Federation, however, which represented female clerks, was upset by the failure of the Civil Service Alliance to hold out for equal pay in the reorganisation negotiations. It withdrew from the Alliance and thus lost its representation on the National Staff Side.

Repeated offers of amalgamation by Brown were either rejected or ignored. Brown attributed their attitude to an anti-man complex dating from the early days when many male civil servants resented the recruitment of women as cheap labour. Even his 'bright eyes and good looks', he confessed, could not overcome this deeply-rooted instinct. So he had to fight and, as with the AECS, gradually wore the women down until they had lost practically all recognition rights. The Women's Federation remained in existence until the agreement for the gradual introduction of equal pay was reached in 1955, when it dissolved itself.

'Anti-man' women's federation rejects Brown's overtures

By the end of 1934 the number of female members of the CSCA was 12,850 (out of a total of 35,360) and was growing considerably more rapidly than the number of men. The proportion of women was thus about 27 per cent, as compared with 70 per cent in 1978, but at that time women had to leave the Service when they married. The result was a very low average age. Some 44 per cent of writing assistants were from 16 to 20 years old. Almost 70 per cent of writing assistants, and 56 per cent of copying typists, were 25 or younger.

CHAPTER SEVEN
Taking on the Government

The establishment of Whitley Councils cannot relieve the Government of any part of its responsibility to Parliament, and ministers and heads of departments acting under the general or specific authority of ministers, must take such action as may be required in any case in the public interest . . . It follows that, while the acceptance by the Government of the Whitley System as regards the Civil Service implies an intention to make the fullest possible use of Whitley procedure, the Government has not surrendered, and cannot surrender its liberty of action in the exercise of its authority.

While the wording of the report produced by Sir Malcolm Ramsay and G H Stuart-Bunning had been approved by the cabinet, there was some official anxiety lest it should be taken to imply a limitation on the Government's authority. A special committee of the National Council was set up to clarify the constitutional position and the statement quoted above was the result. Since the possibilities of arbitration were limited, and for several years excluded altogether, it followed that when associations considered that the official side was guilty of breaches of faith or of decisions contrary to national justice, as on occasion they did, their only appeal was to Parliament. Appeal to ministers was useless since the official side would not take important policy decisions without prior approval by a minister or the Cabinet.

When boom turned to slump

When the post-war boom turned to a slump and there was clamour for economies from MPs and the Press, particularly in the Civil Service, the associations, with Brown in the lead, found themselves driven to press their case through the House of Commons and won some astonishing victories. Before, that, however, there had been a brief honeymoon until the boom ended.

The Whitley machinery itself gave the associations much of what they wanted, but it did not give them the one thing on which their leaders had placed greatest stress – replacement of the Treasury officials by political or independent representatives on the other side of the negotiating table. It is true that it left the door open. The Official Side was to consist of persons of standing appointed by the Government, and in fact three Government MPs were asked to join the Official Side in 1922, but they contributed little and resigned, at the suggestion of the Tomlin Royal Commission, in 1931. The official side for practical purposes consisted of the Treasury and heads of departments, until the creation of the Civil Service Department nearly half a century later. In any case, the Treasury was bound to have the last word on questions of pay because it held the purse strings.

However, it began promisingly with Malcolm Ramsay as chairman and G H Stuart-Bunning as vice-chairman and these two usually presented the case of the official and staff sides respectively. The Staff Side represented some 200 associations recognised as having adequate representation in some class or grade. Generally, a membership of 40 per cent of the organised staff was considered adequate. The majority were represented through the Civil Service Federation or the Alliance, which later merged into the Civil Service Confederation. Each side had two part-time joint secretaries, one of those for the Staff Side being David Milne, who had previously turned down the post of full-time secretary of the Alliance.

The first step of the National Whitley Council was to set up joint committees to consider some of the major Civil Service problems. The Reorganisation Committee, hurried along by Bill Brown, produced in only four months its first agreed report, which not only established the structure of the Service for the ensuing half century, but also introduced new salary scales for many civil servants, including the clerical class. The new scale was much better than that of the old Assistant Clerks, rising from £80 at 18 to a 'marrying wage' of £150 at 26 (the official side wanted it at 27) and a maximum of £250. The leave of Assistant Clerks on assimilation into the new Clerical Class was to be raised from 14 to 24 days and overtime pay was substantially improved.

All this was accepted, but trouble began when the official side submitted its proposals for the assimilation of Assistant Clerks' pay into the new clerical scale. The Association wanted them to come in at the points appropriate to their age. The Treasury would not accept this but offered an increase on transfer of £25 for Assistant Clerks and £20 for Second Division clerks. These increases would have left them substantially below the proposed Clerical Class scale. Many of his senior colleagues favoured acceptance, but Brown thought the terms quite inadequate and succeeded in getting a majority of one on the Staff Side for rejecting them. The issue was referred to arbitration.

Brown launched one of his most spectacular attacks on these proposals. In June 1920, the whole of the front cover of a special number of *Red Tape* was devoted to the following statement in black type heavily underlined:

TO ASSISTANT CLERKS!

THE RECONSTRUCTION COMMITTEE
HAS

BROKEN DOWN
ON

ASSIMILATION TERMS!

THIS ...
MEANS
WAR!!!

Notice was given in the same issue of a general meeting of the Assistant Clerks Association in the Central Hall on June 15 and members were called upon to cease work in time to attend at 6 p.m.

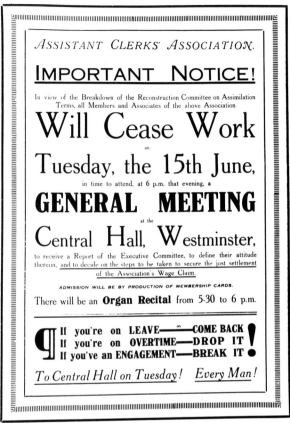

Red Tape also published two short poems attacking the Treasury by Donald Cox, who shortly afterwards became treasurer of the Clerical Officers' Association, one of which went like this:

To the Official Side:

Oh, noble men! Oh, upright, worthy men
With lying lips and facile, easy pen,
Take my best thanks. I did not know till now
How low mankind had sunk in Falsehood's Slough,
Or how bemired they were in Lying Fen.

I've seen you in Whitehall, just after ten,
With sneering lips, I did not know you then
For what you are; I would not know you now,
                    Oh, noble men!

Justice, it seems, is far beyond your ken,
And Honour's but a word. You dream that when
You've fooled us once, with smooth, untroubled brow,
We are for ever beaten. Hearken now –
You'll not be smiling when we meet again,
                    Oh, noble men.

About 3,000 attended a crowded Central Hall meeting of the ACA on June 15 which was stirred to a high pitch of emotion. One resolution instructing the Council to institute a strike fund was carried without dissent (and without visible result). Another asked for a considered report on the advisability of continued participation in Whitley proceedings. A month later 8,000 civil servants were at the Royal Albert Hall for an all-grades meeting on the same lines.

When the Arbitration Board's hearing took place on July 26, the chairman said the two parties should endeavour to arrive at an agreement through the Whitley machinery. On August 7, 1920, a Saturday, the two sides met at the Treasury and discussion and argument continued through the afternoon and evening, according to Brown's account. 'I dug in my toes until I got what I wanted. Again and again I was charged by my colleagues with being unreasonable, and with jeopardising a settlement which by now was beginning to appear a very good one. But I reasoned that the Treasury would be very reluctant to have to go before the Court again, and I was resolved to extract the last possible penny from them. Finally, near midnight, we reached a settlement; the £25 originally offered for the Assistant Clerks became £40.' When they got outside, Brown added, he and one of his colleagues joined in a little dance of triumph in Whitehall. 'I was particularly elated, for I had beaten not only the Treasury, but all the old hands on our own side. That didn't make me popular with them, needless to say, but that worried me then, and ever since, not a jot.'

Brown dances in Whitehall

Another important agreement reached by a National Council Committee was on promotion procedure. This established a formal constitution for promotion boards and appeals by individuals who were passed over and for annual reports, including a provision that adverse annual reports must be communicated to the civil servant reported upon. Promotion remained a contentious subject because of the limited opportunities in the post-war period, but the broad framework stood the test of time.

A cost of living committee was set up to revise the war bonus and establish a long-term relationship between the bonus and prices. Again there were differences between Brown's group and the old hands. At one point Stuart-Bunning, according to Brown, committed an unpardonable offence by disclosing the latest Treasury offer to the staff sides of departmental councils in the hope of provoking such a clamour for acceptance that Brown's resistance would be overcome. But Brown stuck to his guns and eventually got a further improvement.

The war-time bonus increases had fallen far behind the rise in the cost of living and the eventual settlement provided for full compensation for price rises on the first £1 15s (£1.75) a week of salary, half compensation between £1 15s and £3 17s (£3.85) a week and one-third compensation above that. The index was still rising in the first half of 1920, when the talks were going on, and a sliding scale was agreed under which the bonus would rise or fall by one-twenty-sixth with every change of five points in the index. As it turned out, the associations would have done much better to press for immediate consolidation in the basic rates. Prices reached their peak in the last quarter of 1920 and from then on fell steadily until the early 1930s, so that for a decade civil servants found their bonus being reduced by one-twenty-sixth or more nearly every six months. Between 1921 and 1932, the bonus of the lowest-paid civil servants fell from 165 per cent of basic pay to 50 per cent in spite of minor concessions. By this time there had been intense pressure by the Staff Side over many years to revise the agreement with the slogan, 'stop the drop'. Eventually, consolidation was carried out in 1934 on the basis of recommendations by the Tomlin Royal Commission for a 60 per cent increase in consolidated rates over basic rates at £50 a year, going down to 8·3 per cent at the £1,800 level.

In a booklet examining the first year's working of the Whitley system, *Whitleyism on its Trial*, Brown emphasised that, with all the faults and weaknesses he saw in it, the system was a great improvement on anything they had known before. 'The work of the year has shown that in Whitleyism we possess a much better method of dealing with staff grievances than hitherto existed; that the results yielded have been bigger and better than we could have got by earlier methods; that, nevertheless, there are many weaknesses which need correction and that of all our needs the most important is the unification of the staff machinery and the creation of more power to drive it.'

In the next two or three years, however, Brown found himself having to go above the Whitley machinery to do battle with the Government itself. During the economic decline which began in 1921, the Treasury was not free, whether or not it wished to be, to make the sort of concessions which made possible the agreements of 1920. Three issues among the many were outstanding: One was another aspect of assimilation, that of the war-time temporary clerks. The second was the result of a political decision, to withdraw civil servants' right to arbitration. The third was a new attempt to introduce the eight-hour day.

Brown led the fight in these three major battles simultaneously and by and large he won all of them. The struggle over the temporary clerks, which became known as the starting pay case, dragged on for three years. During the war, entrance examinations to the civil service had been suspended and at the same time many thousands of temporary clerks had been recruited so that by the end there were large numbers of vacancies in established grades and an even larger number of temporaries seeking pensionable employment. After a report by a committee of the National Council had been fiercely attacked by the Association of Ex-Service Civil Servants, the Government set up a special committee (the Lytton Committee) which recommended that ex-Service clerks who were successful in an examination should be established on the rate they received on July 1, 1921. This meant that many of them, including middle-aged men with families, with several years' service, would start at the same rate as youngsters from 18–22, in some cases as low as £80 a year. Brown considered this outrageous and so did a lot of other people in the Service.

The National Staff Side, the CSCA and other interested unions protested vigorously. Representations to the Treasury by Brown proved fruitless and when he went to arbitration the claim was rejected, on March 13, 1922, though with a recommendation that departments try to mitigate individual hardships. There was no way to appeal against the Board's decision, but the unions continued to seek the support of the public and MPs, in the hope of getting the Government to appoint a special committee to inquire into the case. The CSCA literally entered new ground in September by organising a demonstration in Trafalgar Square. *Red Tape* estimated the crowd to be about 2,000, and in spite of a downpour of rain several hundred followed a deputation to No 10 Downing Street. There were still some members of the Association, however, who deprecated the use of public demonstration by respectable civil servants.

In November, a general election gave the associations their opportunity. The CSCA, the Association of Officers of Taxes, the Ministry of Labour Staff Association and the AECS agreed to bury their differences for the time being and formed a joint committee to co-operate on the starting pay case. It was not long before the AECS dropped out, but the other three organised a campaign to secure

Fighting on three fronts simultaneously

Brown addressing the demonstration in Trafalgar Square

promises of support from candidates and reported satisfactory results. When the new Government was formed, the associations sent a deputation to see Major Hills, the Financial secretary to the Treasury, whose written reply, according to Brown bore 'all the marks of complete inability to comprehend the circumstances in which the men and women affected are placed.' The next step, he announced in *Red Tape*, was Parliament. A printed statement was being sent to every Member. Provincial MPs were being interviewed by provincial branches and all London MPs were being lobbied. It was proposed to convene a meeting of all Members to explain the case orally. A fund was set up to help Lytton entrants in distress.

In March 1923, Major Hills had to contest a by-election in Liverpool's Edge Hill constituency. The associations threw all they could into support for his Labour opponent, Jack Hayes. Stan Slocombe, CSCA Assistant Secretary, called a meeting of Liverpool civil servants and built up a strong team of workers. Leaflets addressed to ex-Servicemen and female voters were distributed everywhere and Hills was defeated. This and other by-elections in the same period seem to have made politicians realise that Civil Service votes can be made to count. Meanwhile Brown and Houghton, with Edward Thomas of the Employment Exchange clerks, were spending their time canvassing MPs.

On April 10, on a private Member's motion, there was a debate on the subject in the House of Commons, and the incredulous Government ministers found themselves defeated by 145 votes to 138. With the House in a state of great excitement, Neville Chamberlain, the Minister of Health, moved to adjourn. The next day, when the Government attempted to move on to the next business after stating the situation was under consideration, Labour members were provoked to a storm of anger and there was such pandemonium that the Speaker adjourned the sitting. On April 12, Stanley Baldwin gave way and announced the formation of a committee (the Southborough Committee) which would be instructed to report at the earliest possible moment. A jubilant Brown declared it was the first time any

Government had been defeated on a question of Civil Service pay.

The practical gains resulting directly from the victory were limited. The Southborough Committee did not accept the associations' argument that the age of ex-Servicemen should be taken into account in fixing starting pay, but it did award increases of £20 and £10 on the lowest starting salaries of £80, £15 on starting salaries of £90 and £10 on starting salaries of £100. In gratitude, many of those affected contributed to a testimonial fund out of which a piano was presented to Brown and a weekend case to Jean Cormack.

The indirect results of this demonstration of power by the associations were, however, substantial. The second battle with the Government, over arbitration, was reaching its climax at about the same time. The Geddes Committee on National expenditure in 1922 argued, rather curiously, that the Conciliation and Arbitration Board had been rendered unnecessary by the institution of Whitley councils. The Government promptly abolished the Board, although the Whitley agreement had appeared to assume its continuance. There followed a fierce policy struggle between Brown and Stuart-Bunning, chairman of the Staff Side, who thought that the position could be put right by negotiations with the official side. The Staff Side ignored Stuart-Bunning's advice and demanded the restoration of an appeal tribunal. The Confederation, of which he was also chairman, initially supported him but Brown put a new resolution to its council, advocating extensive political action, which was carried by 16 votes to 14. Stuart-Bunning promptly resigned from the chairmanship of both bodies. Brown was delighted.

Stuart-Bunning, said *Red Tape* in May 1922 'who has strenuously opposed any effective action being taken on this most vital matter, has now resigned for (approximately) the fourth time because the Executive Committee of the Confederation has persisted in disagreeing with him. This, we understand, may be regarded as positively his last disappearance . . . The Service may well hear with relief of the passing of a danger (of disintegration) which might have weakened the finest and most representative organisation which it has yet created.' But Stuart-Bunning was re-elected chairman of the Staff Side in July.

The associations set up a joint committee representing the whole service which organised a campaign along now familiar lines, including mass meetings, lobbying of MPs, meetings in the House and a deputation to the Chancellor of the Exchequer, Sir Robert Horne, who discussed possible alternatives, but in the end turned them down. The campaign continued and by February 1925, the associations had promises of support from 415 MPs. The following month, this committee saw Stanley Baldwin, then Prime Minister, who promised to consider the question again but could hold out no encouragement. Two months later, after the Government's defeat on the starting pay case, the committee saw him again and found him in a different mood. He agreed in principle to restore the right of arbitration for civil servants. A joint committee, including both Stuart-Bunning and Brown, was set up and after two years of argument over details, the Civil Service in March 1925 was brought within the scope of the Industrial Court, which meant that hours and leave, as well as pay, became arbitrable. In 1936 this arrangement was replaced by the present Civil Service Arbitrational Tribunal.

Baldwin restores the right to arbitration

Brown believed that the Government agreed to restore arbitration and dropped the demand for an eight-hour day, at least for the time being, because of the defeat on the starting pay case. The case for an eight-hour day for civil servants then working seven hours was put to the National Council by Sir Russell Scott on behalf of the Official Side in October 1922, because of the need for economy, keeping Service conditions in line with outside conditions, and mitigating public criticism of the Service. The proposal provoked an outburst of anger from the associations, partly arising from memories of the war-time struggle and partly because only two years earlier the Reorganisation Report had confirmed the seven-hour day for the 30,000 or so civil servants to whom it applied. The Treasury did not press the eight-hour day.

As a result of these experiences, Brown planned to build up the political power of the Staff Side, particularly after Stuart-Bunning finally retired from the chair and was succeeded by George Middleton. Middleton came from the Union of Post Office Workers but, nevertheless, Brown found that after Middleton's advent there was a tremendous improvement. 'The Staff Side,' he told the 1926 CSCA conference, 'has at last faced the logic of the situation and has decided to go to the Prime Minister with a view to overhauling the Whitley machine and, what is more important, to equip itself with the power without which no conciliation machinery will be effective. There are only three things that will enable conciliation machinery to function. One is industrial power, and that we are not likely ever to possess so far as we can judge. The other is an Arbitration Board that covers all the issues that arise. That for the moment is denied us. The last thing is political power (hear, hear) which will convey to the other side when they say "no" to our just claims that they have not heard the last of those claims and they will have to face the issues in a place where it will be more inconvenient than in the National Whitley Council chamber itself.

'In the last two weeks steps have been taken to set up a Civil Service Committee in the House of Commons consisting of members of all parties (applause) to urge a national programme for the Civil Service in which will be included the minimum wage, and between now and the next general election we have got to educate the Service in that programme and make sure when the election comes that the whole 300,000 of us are politically active upon it.'

This emphasis on the need to develop the associations' political muscle was partly the result of exasperation at the way in which the Treasury was evading its obligations under the 1920 Reorganisation Agreement, particularly by restrictions on the employment of low-paid writing assistants, and by using dubious devices to prevent associations from operating the new arbitration machinery. In October 1925, *Red Tape* published an article by Brown under the headlines *Service Maladministration – Treasury Sharp Practices – The Need for Revolt*, which contained specific attacks on Sir Russell Scott, chairman of the Official Side, and created a sensation. 'Why do Treasury officials do things which are dishonest and unworthy and contemptible?' demanded Brown. 'The Treasury acts as it does because it feels it is safe to do so. And the first thing the Civil Service needs to do to stop these things is to demonstrate that it is not safe.' The Service organisations, he urged, should go in a body to the Prime Minister and demand an independent inquiry into the way the Service had been administered by the Treasury in recent years.

This was a period of constant attacks on the Service and calls for cuts in expenditure in the Press and elsewhere. Some Association leaders, particularly Brown, were also accused of being reds and Brown felt it necessary to issue a statement pointing out that he had been a critic of the British Communist Party and had opposed its affiliation to the Labour Party. In December 1925, there was an all-grades demonstration in the Royal Albert Hall which condemned ill-informed and prejudiced attacks, drew attention to the fact that less than 50 per cent of the Service received full compensation for the rise in the cost of living and pointed out that gross under-payment existed among large sections.

Brown's plans for effective political action were hampered, however, by

Brown plans to build up the political power of the staff associations

He accuses the Treasury of maladministration and sharp practice

major outside events: the 1926 General Strike and its aftermath, the appointment of a new Royal Commission on the Civil Service and the world-wide economic crisis which reached its climax in 1931. The General Strike, called by the TUC in support of the miners who were faced by a lock-out to enforce cuts in pay and longer hours, involved 4 million workers and lasted nine days. The decision to call it was taken at the end of a three-day conference of executives in Memorial Hall, London, in which Brown and members of his Executive took part. Brown himself moved an amendment to the official proposals in a speech in which he criticised the TUC leadership for contemplating a revolutionary act without any intention of creating a revolution and urged that full warning of their intention should be given to the Government, but he got only one vote, his own. He said afterwards he was anxious they should not blunder into war because each side was playing a game of bluff, and that his speech was the most unpopular he had ever made but one in which he felt most satisfaction.

The CSCA and the General Strike

On the last day of the conference, two questions were put one by one to the assembled executives, and Brown was afterwards accused of undertaking to call the CSCA members out on strike if required to do so, which he hotly denied. There has always been argument about the exact implications of the questions, but Brown's interpretation was clear. The unions were divided into two groups, those who might be called out and those who would not. Those in the first group were asked whether they would place their powers in the hands of the TUC General Council and carry out its instructions concerning the necessary action and conduct of the dispute. Those in the second (including the CSCA) were asked whether they would place their powers in the hands of the General Council and carry out instructions regarding the conduct of the dispute and financial assistance, but the word action was not used. Brown answered 'yes', but considered he was committing the CSCA to financial assistance, not action.

Whatever the interpretation of the questions, the CSCA had already told the General Council that it could not undertake to call its members out on strike. The CSCA Executive met for an hour before the executives' conference resumed on May 1 and passed a resolution 'that the question of calling CSCA members out on strike did not, and could not arise and that CSCA help must be limited to financial help.' Brown was instructed to put this in writing to the TUC and did so.

The strike began at midnight on Monday, May 3. Earlier that evening, delegates had assembled at Corton Holiday Camp for the CSCA annual conference and first thing the next morning they went into private session to discuss the industrial position. Brown gave a detailed account of the events leading to the strike and the proceedings at the conference of executives. The CSCA Executive had said 'yes', he told the delegates, because it knew that if the miners went down attacks would be launched on conditions both outside and inside the Service. 'We gave our 'yes', Brown continued, 'for other reasons besides the practical ones. Some of us felt that if this was not an issue on which we could carry our people with us, then our people were not worth leading anywhere; some of us felt that if our people would stand by and see miners condemned to a wage of £1 7s 4d (£1·37) per week, or a little more, then there was something wrong with the education we had given our members or something wrong with our members themselves. Some of us felt that if the trades union movement went down in the struggle, life would not be tolerable for any man who is used to breathing the air of freedom.' He submitted a resolution confirming the action of the executive and continued: 'The conference determines that the policy of the CSCA during the crisis shall be to render all possible assistance, moral and financial, to the General Council in its efforts to resist the attack of the Government and the employers on the standard of life of the people.' The plan was to make a contribution from Association funds and to carry out a voluntary levy of members.

There was general support, but some anxiety about the attitude of the membership. One or two delegates feared it might split the Association in half and there was much emphasis on the need to conduct propaganda in the branches. There were warnings that under the Emergency Act it would be possible for the Government to appropriate its funds, smash the union and take action against leaders. R McC Beamish of the Admiralty, a Conservative who had been the second honorary Secretary of the Assistant Clerks' Association 20 years earlier and had become a sort of father figure in the CSCA, asked the question: 'Is it compatible for us as State employees, owing allegiance to the State, to take sides when the State has taken one side and another body of the community another side?' He then asked himself: 'Is it compatible for me to resist the State on certain occasions?' To that he replied: 'The State has the right to make me do the work for which I contracted, but the State has no right whatever to make me do anything outside those functions. I do not admit that any government, by merely saying it is the Government, has the right to force people, against their will, to do things at which their consciences may revolt.' Nevertheless, he thought it would be wise to omit from the motion the reference to the Government. This was accepted and the amended motion was carried by 258 votes to 2.

The problem of how the delegates were to get home when the conferences was over was resolved by obtaining permits from the TUC for the passage of 11 coaches, which scattered over the country to deliver them.

There were resignations as a result of the Association's policy but far less than some people feared. Membership fell from 20,468 to 19,123 during 1926, largely through a reduction in the number of women members, but more than made up the lost ground in 1927. A ballot of members in October on whether to continue TUC affiliation resulted in a vote of 9,986 in favour and 5,645 against.

The effect on the Staff Side of the National Whitley Council was more damaging. Its General Purposes Committee met on the day the strike began and adopted two resolutions. The first asked for an assurance from the Treasury that civil servants would not be asked to perform any work other than their normal duties and was carried without opposition but with one abstention. The second said that advice should be given to all civil servants not to perform any work other than their normal duties and to report to their Association headquarters any attempt to cause them to do so. This produced a sharp division between the higher grades and the rest, but was adopted by 4 votes to 2, with one abstention and one absent. The resolutions were circulated to departmental staff sides, but the Joint Consultative Committee (JCC), representing the First Division Association, the Society of Civil Servants, the Legal Society and the Inspectors of Taxes, produced their own circular saying that every civil servant in times of emergency should inform his departmental superiors that he was ready to perform whatever work the Government considered necessary and to the national advantage.

After the General Strike was over, a full meeting of the Staff Side ratified the action of the general purposes committee by 16 votes to 6. The Institution of Professional Civil Servants (IPCS) voted with the JCC, taking the view that members should make their own decisions without guidance. The debate went on until in October the JCC associations withdrew from the staff side. But the IPCS, under the influence of its able honorary secretary, Freddy Menzler, retained its membership.

Freddy Menzler, Secretary of the Institution of Professional Civil Servants

Brown expressed the view in *Red Tape* that the resignations would hurt the JCC more than the staff side. Its total membership was less than 10,000, he said, its fighting capacity was nil and it was carried on the backs of the well-organised, low-paid grades. Nevertheless, without the Institution it would have been hard for the staff side to maintain its position as representing the Service as a whole.

Government reaction to the General Strike was to pass the 1927 Trade Disputes and Trades Unions Act which, in Clause 5, prohibited civil servants from belonging to any organisation affiliated to bodies with outside members. The CSCA and other affiliated associations had to leave the TUC and Labour Party and other bodies and were thus officially cut off from the main labour movement until the Act was repealed in 1946. Brown said that what the Government wanted was not civil servants but civil serfs, and there were protest demonstrations supported by the TUC and the Labour Party, but in the atmosphere of the time they can hardly have hoped to achieve anything. When Labour was back in office in 1929, the Government attempted to amend the Act but it was again a minority government and could not get Liberal support for a bill that would satisfy the TUC.

A government act forces the CSCA out of the TUC and Labour Party

The 1927 Act and the withdrawal of the JCC resulted in the rest of the Staff Side becoming more united than before. In 1926, Brown started a campaign for a Civil Service minimum wage. He got the staff side to take it up and in 1928 expanded this into an All-Service Programme of Action, which was adopted unanimously at a conference of executives. The four-point programme included a national minimum wage of £3 10s (£3·50) a week, which would have affected about 180,000 out of the 300,000 Civil Servants; a provision that all service, including temporary service, should count in calculating pensions; equal pay for women, which associations were not allowed to take to arbitration, and restoration of the 'supercut'. This was a reduction in the bonus for those with salaries over £500, introduced in 1921, which the staff side considered a violation of the previous year's bonus agreement.

Brown was still developing his plans for the exercise of political pressure. Nothing could be done on the programme, he said, through Whitley or Industrial Court channels. What was called for was a great campaign culminating at the time of the next general election, due in 1929. The 300,000 civil servants scattered throughout the country, with their wives and dependants, constituted a force which no party would want to flout. It was proposed to create constituency committees throughout the country as permanent machinery and it would be their task to tackle candidates of all parties.

Shortly before the election, Baldwin dragged the carpet from under his feet by announcing his intention to set up a new Royal Commission on the Civil Service. Now candidates were able to get away with expressions of sympathy and assurances that all would be considered after the Commission had reported. Ramsay MacDonald, succeeding Baldwin as Prime Minister, duly set up the Commission with very wide terms of reference and a judge, Lord Tomlin, as chairman. The associations got busy with their evidence and agitation declined, except in regard to the bonus. With the cost of living index still falling, civil servants were increasingly disturbed by the constant cuts in their wages. Hopes were aroused when Philip Snowden, again Chancellor of the Exchequer, stopped one cut, but in view of the country's financial plight he felt it necessary to impose the ensuing ones, to the accompaniment of storms of vain protest.

CHAPTER EIGHT
Triumphs at the Tribunal

We wish it to be understood that our recommendations are subject to the overriding condition that the financial position, of which we cannot be the final judges, admits of their adoption.

In normal circumstances this quotation from the report of the Tomlin royal Commission might have been regarded as a conventional statement. But in July 1931, when the report was published, Britain was in the midst of economic crisis. The following month, the Labour Government resigned and was replaced by a National Government committed to retrenchment, increased taxation and financial reform. In September, a new economy committee, presided over by Sir John May, recommended drastic cuts in expenditure, including abolition of the marriage gratuity for women in the Civil Service. In November, the new government won a sweeping election victory in which W J Brown and other Civil Service MPs lost their seats. Reductions were imposed on the pay of many public servants, including teachers, police and armed forces. A five-point cut in the cost of living bonus in September 1931, was regarded as the Civil Service contribution. Many temporaries were sacked. Many more civil servants on low pay found themselves liable to income tax for the first time. The public was convinced that the nation was in a near desperate situation which made sacrifices inevitable. The Treasury ruled out any settlements involving increases in costs and it was nearly three years before Brown and his colleagues, threaten and plead and agitate though they did, could begin to effect improvements in pay.

Economic crisis and pay cuts

Improvements were not needed in order to recruit staff. An earlier committee dealing with Civil Service pay, the Anderson Committee, had enunciated the old management principle that 'the employer should pay what is necessary to recruit and retain an efficient staff.' Brown, like many another workers' leader before and since, had replied with a statement of the case for a living wage. But seldom had his objective seemed so hard to reach. Competition for Civil Service jobs, and within the Service for pensionable jobs, was intense. The number of unemployed exceeded 2·75 million and was to reach a peak in the winter of 1932–33 of nearly 3 million. It had been growing for a decade. Work and security were at a premium. Evidence to the Commission had shown that in 1928, of 1,160 members of grades like sorting clerks and telegraphists competing for clerical officer posts, only 167 were successful, and of 2,017 school leavers only 631 succeeded. For the humble job of writing assistant, there were five candidates taking the examination for every vacancy.

Even for those who have known the unemployment of the 1970s, it is difficult to recapture the feeling of the workless of those days when there was nothing to fall back upon but the dole and the administration of the Poor Law by local authorities. One of the oldest CSCA jokes described how a temporary clerk notified of selection in an establishment scheme, rushed home with the news that he had been promoted to a permanent job shouting with triumph: 'I'm established! – I'm established! – Of course it's poverty, rank poverty, but thank God it's permanent!' One of the nails in the coffin of the Association of Ex-Service Civil Servants was its 'P' (Permanent) class agreement of 1925 whereby the AECS accepted permanency without the accompaniment of pension rights.

During the four days Brown spent giving evidence to the Royal Commission, Lord Tomlin asked him if he did not think that on the whole there had been a fairly steady improvement in organisation and wage conditions from 1890 to the present time. 'Today we are fighting precisely the same battle that we were fighting 20 years ago,' replied Brown. 'The only thing that has changed is the class in respect of whom we are fighting it. My first task in coming into Civil Service agitation was to abolish the temporary nature of boy clerk employment, and after 20 years I find myself still fighting to abolish temporary employment in the case of temporary clerks. My second task was to rescue the old Assistant Clerk class from a condition of permanent poverty. To an extent we succeeded in that task, only to find the burden of that poverty passed down to classes underneath, like the writing assistants and the 'P' class. We are still fighting for the same things that we were fighting for 20 years ago, namely establishment where the work is permanent, and a rate of pay for the subordinate grades that gives them something like a reasonable standard of life.'

By and large, there could hardly have been a worse time than 1931 to sit down with the Treasury to discuss the Commission's recommendations on every aspect of Service pay and conditions, knowing that the Treasury would inevitably make the most of the 'overriding' financial position. The recommendations were not, indeed, in any way radical or likely to prove excessively costly. It was largely an as-you-were report, chiefly remembered for the formula for fixing Civil Service pay which remained a guideline until the report of the Priestley Commission 25 years later: 'Civil Service remuneration should reflect what may be described as the long-term trend, both in wage levels and in the economic condition of the country.' The Commission turned down the CSCA's revived plan for abolishing the Executive Class, found arguments for retaining the departmental clerical grades and, on equal pay for women, since the members of the Commission were equally divided, had nothing useful to say, though it accepted the principle of 'a fair field and no favour' for the employment of women.

The report of the Tomlin Royal Commission on the Civil Service is found 'terribly disappointing'

Brown thought the document terribly disappointing and observed: 'If Royal Commissions are to be used merely as convenient media for turning down every claim of importance put to them and for dodging every main issue, then we hope the Service will not see another Royal Commission for the rest of its days.' Yet there were things in the report on which the associations could work.

Its most welcome proposal concerned temporary civil servants who, as things were, could remain temporary for an indefinite period of years with little pay and no pension to look forward to and without the advantages in leave and other conditions that went with establishment. The Commission thought that five years should normally be the limit for temporary work. It recommended the creation of an 'obsolescent' class of permanent and pensionable male civil servants, which became known as the 'S' (Special) Class, into which the 'P' class would be absorbed as well as male temporaries with five years' service. Temporary female clerks were to go into the writing assistants' class and temporary typists and shorthand typists into the established typists' class. The Treasury made six years the normal limit for temporary work instead of five, but nevertheless, in October 1932, some 15,000 temporary clerks, typists and shorthand typists were established. The CSCA had admitted female temporaries into membership in the autumn of 1931 – they had not been admitted with male temporaries two years earlier because of an agreement with the Association of Women Civil Servants which the AWCS had now terminated. The CSCA was actively recruiting among women as well as men and did not hesitate to claim much of the credit for the permanent establishment of

A section of the great Civil Service demonstration against the cost of living pay cuts as it passes through Piccadilly Circus

typists. On pay questions no such early benefits were possible. A series of committees was set up during 1932 by the National Whitley Council to deal with various aspects of the report but none could make any progress.

The future of the cost of living bonus was the most urgent question. The Tomlin Commission had recommended by a majority that the bonus should be consolidated into basic pay immediately. The cost of living index was going down more rapidly than ever and the consequent cuts in pay were arousing ever-growing resentment. Protest demonstrations had continued while the Commission was sitting and were embarked upon with renewed vigour as soon as it reported. In October 1931 there was a great march through London from the Embankment to Hyde Park, where it was claimed that 100,000 people gathered. '23 Cuts Since 1920. We are still Civil but would you be?' demanded one of the scores of banners. 'Served in 1914, Serfs in 1931', proclaimed another. Ten days later there was a crowded Staff Side demonstration in the Royal Albert Hall and other demonstrations followed in every great city.

By the summer of 1932 the index, which had been 165 in 1921, had fallen to 44 and was still dropping. A joint committee failed to agree on a basis for consolidation and decided, as a temporary measure, to stabilise it at 50 for 19 months until April 1, 1934. Agreement could still not be reached, however, and the Government effected consolidation by administrative action on the lines recommended by the Commission. The other committees were deadlocked.

'In no area of the Service is there any possibility of securing improved

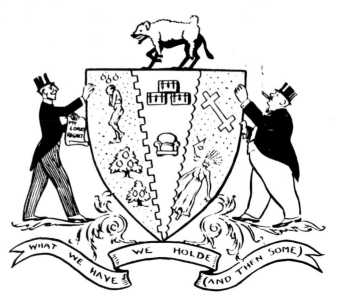

'Red Tape' suggests a coat of arms for the Treasury

conditions of remuneration unless the present correlation of forces as between staff and Government can be altered,' Brown wrote in March 1933. 'To do this,' he argued, 'a campaign involving the whole Civil Service is not enough. What is needed is a widespread agitation by public servants generally, including teachers and municipal staff and other sections of State employees. The basis of the campaign should be a few simple points expressing the will of that section of the community for a higher standard of life.'

The idea did not get very far, though the General Secretary of the National Union of Teachers did speak at an Albert Hall demonstration organised by the Civil Service Confederation a couple of months later. The only other speaker from outside the Service was Lord Beaverbrook, proprietor of the Express group of newspapers and a friend of Brown, whose papers were advocating reductions in income tax and a restoration of the 1931 cuts.

Brown turned with some hesitation to the possibilities of arbitration. He argued that if the economic situation improved, it would be advisable to wait for a while, but if it was going to get worse their only chance was to go to the Court straight away. He thought it would probably get worse, but wondered how far the Industrial Court would be swayed by the Treasury. Having obtained the endorsement of the 1933 annual conference, against some opposition, he wrote to the Treasury presenting seven pay claims covering all the general classes the Association represented. About the same time a manifesto was issued by a joint committee representing the Post Office and Confederation organisations declaring their intention to wage an unceasing Parliamentary, press and public campaign until the general level of remuneration was improved. Widespread publicity in many parts of the country was obtained by local action.

It was some time before the claims reached the stage of arbitration as the Treasury insisted the cases should be presented in detail, while Brown held this was unnecessary since the Treasury had said it could not even discuss any recommendations which involved increases in expenditure. However, by March 1934 terms of reference to the Court were agreed.

In the meantime, the Association had been encouraged by an award on provincial differentiation which they considered a substantial victory. The 10 per cent difference between the pay of many staff in the country and those in London was reduced to 5 per cent. 'The award is very important as marking the rejection by the Court of the plea that the national financial situation (a point strongly stressed in the Treasury statement of case) precludes anything being done on any Civil Service case,' Brown said. There were also gains in other small cases.

This was the beginning of two years during which Brown achieved the most intense and successful use of arbitration the Civil Service has known. The Court never gave reasons for its decisions, but Brown must have been helped by the fact that there were at last signs of an upturn in the economy. Unemployment was beginning to fall. Wage rates were beginning to rise. The budget was balanced and by the end of the period prices had begun to increase.

During the two years to March 1936, the CSCA, usually alone but sometimes with other associations, practically monopolised the Industrial Court in 20 successive cases covering both men and women, including large grades such as writing assistants, typists and the 'S' class. One or two of the awards were disappointing, but something was won every time and in many cases the gains were substantial.

One remarkable case affected only 35 Land Registry Mapping Assistants, whose tiny association had merged with the CSCA in 1934, but it lasted a week and was full of high drama. Brown succeeded in working into his presentation of the pay claim accusations that, for years past, the Land Registry had been maladministered and that the top management was anti-trade union. Among the witnesses he called was George Green, who 20 years later became the CSCA general secretary. When Sir John Stewart-Wallace, the head of land registry, came to cross-examine on the second day, he found himself thrown on the defensive and apparently more concerned to clear himself of the charges than with the merits of the claim.

On the morning of the third day, Sir Claud Schuster, KC, secretary to the Lord Chancellor's Department, displaced Stewart-Wallace and took over the case himself. Schuster was sometimes regarded as the Bill Brown of the official side, 'willing to take on anybody at any time', and Brown was delighted at the opportunity to cross swords with him, particularly as Schuster was in general charge not only of the Land Registry but also of several other quasi-legal departments such as the Public Trustee Office and the Treasury Solicitor's Department, and there had been a lot of trouble in most of them.

Schuster started by accusing Brown of enveloping the case in a cloud of reckless misrepresentation and indiscriminate slander. Brown listened and waited until a little later Schuster said that Brown had deliberately tried to mislead the Court by making charges of fraud in connection with an agreement reached in 1930. Brown was on his feet in an instant, demanding Schuster produce evidence in support of the charge or withdraw it. Otherwise, Brown would invoke the protection of the Court.

After a tense three-quarters of an hour, the President of the Court said he thought Schuster's position was untenable and Schuster reluctantly withdrew. Before the six days were over, Schuster had made more than one concession, and the eventual award was highly satisfactory to the Association. The battle between Brown and Schuster became a Civil Service legend and it was firmly believed that changes in top Land Registry personnel were one result. George Green became a CSCA Assistant Secretary just over a year later.

Sir Claud Schuster, described as 'the Bill Brown of the Official Side'

There was still to come the departmental classes case – the greatest *tour de force* of Brown's career and probably the most notable arbitration case in Civil Service history. It began during the negotiation of an important Writing Assistant/Clerical

Class settlement which turned writing assistants into clerical assistants by giving them minor clerical duties and substantially increased their maximum as well as that of the Clerical Officers. In return, the Clerical Officer scale was reduced at the lower end and other concessions were made. Parts of the complex agreement were criticised by other associations but it seems to have worked out favourably.

During the concluding stages of talks, the Treasury, under pressure from Brown, agreed to central negotiations over the whole departmental clerical classes field. These classes were formed when the Ministry of Labour introduced an inferior scheme for Employment Exchange clerks to that being negotiated by Brown for the general Clerical Class in 1920 and was followed by other departments until about 40 per cent of clerical staff were covered. Since then, Brown had been trying to bring the exchange clerks up to the general class level, but the Treasury always insisted it was a matter for each department.

With the Treasury apparently ready to negotiate collectively, the CSCA presented its cases in detail. Replying on June 19, 1936, the Treasury said it had consulted the departments and come to the conclusion that central discussions were not appropriate. The Association negotiators, according to Brown, could hardly believe their ears. Brown startled his hearers, on both sides of the table, by warning the Official Side that if that was the way it was going to behave it might consider the effects of a possible sit-in strike in the defence ministries. Craig, the Official Side spokesman, asked if this was a threat and Brown replied that he could take it as he liked. After a few further icy exchanges, Craig adjourned the meeting.

Brown's colleagues were convinced that his threat was unpremeditated, the result of his reading reports of sit-in strikes in France in that morning's papers. But he immediately realised what could be made of it, and made sure that the Press were promptly told what happened. The threat of a Civil Service sit-in strike was front page news and the case of the departmental classes, which had until then aroused little interest, suddenly became a national issue. There were questions in Parliament and angry protests and Brown wrote a letter to *The Times*.

If the Government was worried, so was the Association. The Executive, which, of course, had not been consulted, was disturbed, and anxious questions came in from the branches. There had been no preparation and the possibility of effective action was remote. Emissaries were hurriedly sent round the country assuring the branches that everything would be all right and urging them to keep calm and look warlike. Face was saved by the arrival of an offer of mediation from a distinguished former public servant, Sir Guy Fleetwood Wilson, who hated the idea of a strike in the Service. Brown immediately gave Wilson's letter to the Press, with a statement that the Association would be glad to accept the offer.

In the House of Commons, Neville Chamberlain, Chancellor of the Exchequer, rejected the offer of mediation and condemned the idea of a Civil Service strike. Brown retorted by getting an opinion from Sir William Jowitt, former Attorney-General, that nothing in any Act of Parliament precluded civil servants from using the strike weapon. Chamberlain told the Commons that the question was not one of law. If a civil servant indulged in a strike he rendered himself liable to instant dismissal.

Meanwhile, there had been letters from the Treasury. Three days after Brown's threat, Sir James Rae, Chief Establishments Officer, asked Ross Wyld, the Association President, to see him. Wyld was on leave and the letter came to Brown. When it was passed on, according to Brown's account, Wyld told him he intended to go. Brown got the negotiating team to veto that and Wyld replied to Sir Rae that instead of seeing him alone it would be preferable for him to see the

Brown threatens a sit-in strike in the defence ministries

The CSCA team at the departmental classes arbitration case: (from left) Stanley Mayne, Bill Brown, Min Jackson, George Green and Len White

whole team, which included the two Vice-Presidents, the Assistant General Secretary and the Woman Officer, Leslie Sweet, as well as Wyld and Brown.

Rae then wrote to Miss Min Jackson, the senior Vice-president, saying that certain statements by Brown were 'purely inconsistent with discussions under the Whitley scheme', and that if those statements represented the considered policy of the Association, the Government would have to consider whether it was willing to continue to authorise departments to negotiate with the Association. With Brown's aid, Miss Jackson replied that, with regard to the threat to sever relations with the Association, Rae appeared not to appreciate that what was at issue was whether any relations with the Treasury could be regarded as possessing any value in the light of recent events. She added, in what was as near to a withdrawal as anything in Brown's career: 'The Treasury must be well aware that what Brown said was not a declaration of considered Association policy, but a very natural reaction to what everyone of us who was present regarded, and regard, as a complete breach of faith.' Giving the letter to the Press, Brown observed: 'Treasury officials are never heroes when dealing with free men, but they can be surprisingly brave when dealing with women civil servants over whom they think they have an economic free hand. The letter to Miss Jackson is the measure of the moral and intellectual stature of the epigones who unhappily are in charge of the finest Civil Service in the world.' It was typical of Brown to use a word such as 'epigones', which must have made correspondents rush to their dictionaries, to suggest the moronic nature of the Civil Service leaders.

However, the Treasury noted Min Jackson's statement that Brown's threat was not considered Association policy, and there was further prolonged correspondence between Brown and the Chancellor as well as with the Treasury, all published in the next issue of *Red Tape*, and finally a compromise was reached. The cases were to be heard separately, but consecutively, with identical terms of reference, and all the cases would be heard before an award was given.

This gave Brown what he wanted: to bring in the Treasury and to obtain decisions covering the whole field. The hearings began on August 25 and the Court met continuously, except for weekends and one Monday, until September 17, a total of 17 days. Brown led the Association's case throughout, in spite of a bad attack of shingles, while the Official Side had a different team for each of six departments, which enabled him to use the evidence of one against another. By common consent his handling of the whole exhausting task was masterly.

The final awards gave the Association not quite but nearly all it asked for in five of the six cases, covering some 2,400 civil servants. In the sixth case, 49 Home Office factory inspectors' clerks got only a small increase. Since their work was similar to that of the others, no one ever understood why. Apart from the

Leslie Sweet, who led the 1935–36 equal pay campaign

immediate gains, an increase of £67 5s (£67·25) on the men's maximum and £27 7s (£27·35) on the women's maximum in the main cases, the awards put the Association in a strong position to claim substantial increases for thousands of civil servants in other grades, which it usually did with success.

The one important issue on which the Association could not hope to make progress either by negotiation or arbitration, because of a ruling that it was a matter of high government policy, was equal pay for women. The general election of 1935 provided the opportunity for a joint association committee, of which Leslie Sweet was Secretary, to seek promises from candidates for election, which it did with some success. At the same time it ran an energetic public campaign and when the new Parliament assembled it sent every MP six folders, each explaining one aspect of the issue, and arranged a meeting of Members to hear its case.

Ellen Wilkinson, a Labour member, was successful in the ballot for private Members' motions, and on April 1, 1936, she moved an amendment to the formal motion, 'that the Speaker leave the chair', which referred to the 1920 Commons resolution and requested the Government to place women in common classes on the same wage scales as men. The Government opposed the amendment and, for the second time, a Government was defeated on a motion concerning Civil Service pay, by 156 votes to 148. When the Speaker put the amendment as a substantive motion it in turn was defeated by 149 votes to 136. With the House in confusion, Baldwin, the Prime Minister, moved the adjournment, remarking that Members might go away less dissatisfied if they remembered that the date was April 1. Five days later there was another debate on equal pay as part of a general motion, with the Whips on, and this time the Government won by 361 to 145.

Nothing came of that, but the Whitley council set up a joint committee on unequal pay which eventually reached an agreement that in common grades the women's maximum should not be less than 80 per cent of the men's maximum, which meant many gains.

CHAPTER NINE
Getting Rid of a President

W J Brown speaking to Len White, newly-appointed Assistant
Secretary:

Brown: *And we must be solidly united against the common enemy.*
White: *Yes, I hate the Treasury as much as you do.*
Brown: *Who said anything about the Treasury? I'm talking about the
National Executive.*

Len White was fond of recounting this little piece of dialogue. When Brown heard
it, he declared it was of doubtful authenticity but conceded that there was sufficient
basis for the story to give it the appearance of truth. He never had any doubt as to
what to do with the Treasury or the departments, he said, but rival factions and
groups on the Executive took more out of him than all the other work he did. On
policy he usually got his own way, he added, 'But Lord, the expense of spirit in a
waste of shame.'

The long, and at times ruthless, struggle within the Association had its origin
in a clash between Brown and Ross Wyld in 1922 and built up in the 1930s until
in 1937 Brown forced a special conference to choose between them. At this
conference both men went back over the years to tell the story of their antagonism.
Their accounts conflicted on many points, but the main course of events is clear.
Behind the personal rivalry was a growing resistance to the domination by the
leaders of the Post Office Section, many of whom had come into the Association
through the amalgamation with the Clerical Assistants, allied with those of the
Admiralty, who had come in with the Civil Service Union. Both had been accorded
places on the National Executive as part of the merger terms.

Wyld was the chairman of the Post Office Section. He was a small, very able
man, less flamboyant than Brown but a powerful Labour Party supporter and one
of the most impressive speakers at the mass demonstrations of 1919 and 1920. By
1921 he had become a vice-president and was appointed an assistant secretary of the
CSCA for a year. At the end of the year he was induced to resign. Brown claimed,
with the support of some of the Executive, he was inefficient in the job, though not
in his capacity as a civil servant. Wyld showed in his speech at the special conference
that the episode had continued to rankle, not so much because of what was done,
but because of the way in which Brown handled it.

The President at this time was William Thomas, a PO clerical assistant who
had been given the job in the 1920 amalgamation. Sometimes known as Big Bill
(with Brown as Little Bill) he was a massive, bluff, sometimes irascible and
sometimes fatherly man, fair, honest and decisive. Brown respected his judgement
but had no cause to fear him as a rival influence in the Association. Thomas had
worked with Brown on the Reorganisation Committee and regarded him with
something akin to parental pride. There was no limit then on the number of years
a president might hold office, but in 1925 Thomas had to resign, while not yet 40,
because of ill health. At the conference that followed Wyld was elected his successor
without opposition and remained President for 11 years.

At this conference, the first at Corton Holiday Camp, it was decided that the
two vice-presidents should be chosen by the conference instead of by the Executive

*'Big Bill' Thomas, first
President of the CSCA*

and Bert Broadhead of the Post Office and Ted Rundle, chairman of the Admiralty Section, were elected.

In the following five years these two Sections entrenched themselves in a dominating position, at first apparently co-ordinating their votes in an informal way and later, there seems little doubt, holding regular meetings of what became known as The Caucus. Probably many conference delegates, and certainly most Association members, knew little of what was happening. Those who did were unwilling to advertise dissension within the ranks. But signs of restlessness within the other departments grew. By 1929, The Caucus held 18 of the 27 places on the Executive and from then on motions to limit the number of Executive members from one department, and to limit the period of office of the president or Executive members, appeared regularly on the agenda but were always easily lost.

During a 1928 debate on an unsuccessful motion to abolish the card vote in elections, delegates for the first time openly complained of the existence of a caucus and of rival block voting. Generally, over these years, the Post Office–Admiralty leaders, assured of their domination, had confined themselves to pin-pricking counter-attacks on such things as the salaries of officers. By 1930 Brown was an MP and openly critical of the Labour Government. He had been critical of the first Labour Government in 1923–24 from outside, with the unwelcome result, as was pointed out, that some delegates were encouraged to ask for a referendum as to whether Labour Party affiliation should be continued. Brown had to work hard to kill the idea.

Brown was now attacking the second Labour Government from inside the House of Commons and some delegates did not like it. The Post Office and Admiralty leaders tended to be loyal supporters of the party on traditional lines and were disturbed by some of his criticisms of it, just as they had been disturbed by his unconventional assaults on some other Civil Service associations. An Admiralty delegate asked whether it was possible for the general secretary to be a fully-fledged politician and at the same time hold down the general secretaryship of the Association. 'Ask yourselves whether you are prepared to continue for another 12 months on similar lines to the last 12 months,' he urged the delegates. Brown claimed he had done a good year's work in both jobs. 'If ever the time comes that I find it impossible to combine these two functions, it is the Parliamentary and not the trade union function that I propose to relinquish.'

The issue was not carried to a vote then, but by the time of the 1931 conference Brown had resigned from the Labour Party, and the pent-up antagonisms exploded. The attack on Brown took place at Corton during the conference, but technically, because of the Trade Disputes and Trade Unions Act, it was at a meeting of 'representative subscribers to the W J Brown Parliamentary Candidature Fund'. *Red Tape* devoted only half a cautious diary note to the occasion but Brown himself later gave a colourful description of it in his autobiography.

The strain of his two jobs, in neither of which had he spared himself, had proved too much, and on doctor's orders he spent from March to April 1931 on a Mediterranean cruise, returning refreshed for the coming battle in May. The issue, as Brown put it, was on the Executive's recommendation by 17 votes to 2 that they should have power to terminate his Parliamentary candidacy. They had, he wrote, left nothing to chance. Each of a long team of speakers had his brief. Whereas, on his side, there was no organisation whatever. 'In all my Association life,' he added in his self-righteous way, 'I had regarded it as my business not to organise caucuses, manipulate votes, pre-arrange debates and the like. Perhaps out of pride, perhaps out of an instinctive recognition that those who organise caucuses become the

A Post Office and Admiralty caucus of members dominates the CSCA Executive

prisoners of their own creation, I had steadfastly kept clear of them, had never lifted a finger to influence an election, and had relied for influencing policy solely upon fair diagnosis, and the best advice I could give.'

He expected support from one Executive member, Stanley Mayne, and from Len White, then an assistant secretary of the Association, but beyond this he knew nothing of the support he would get.

For several hours, speaker after speaker was against him. His chief opponent, Ross Wyld, left the chair to support the resolution and then resumed it. Brown made no complaint. 'I myself would rest on nothing but the record of work I had put in and my right as a free man to take whatever political line my conscience dictated or approved . . . I would say nothing about the intrigues which had been going on behind my back. I would win gloriously or not at all. I would be defeated or I would so win that the principle of the political freedom of officers of the Association should be established beyond possibility of subsequent dispute, then and thereafter, for so long as there should be an association at all.'

The arguments against him, as he remembered them, were that as an isolated MP, he would be useless to the Association, that he should have stayed in the Labour Party and tried to reform it from within, that his break with the Party would prejudice the Association's relations with it and indirectly with the TUC, that since the Association had 'made him', it had a right to control his political activities. Then came Brown's turn. He made a long speech and even *Red Tape* found space to describe it as magnificent. It was certainly among the most effective of his career.

'It was dusk when I rose to speak,' Brown recalled. 'It was dark ere I had finished. Half-way through someone brought in oil lamps [the hall, being used only in summer, was not wired for electricity], and these cast a subdued light over part of the hall, leaving the rest in near darkness, and heightened the tenseness of the atmosphere in the crowded place.'

Brown's eloquence overwhelms his critics

Brown avowed his faith, since he became capable of conscious thought, in socialism and the trade union movement, and explained why he believed the leaders of the Labour Party and the TUC had failed. Then he looked realistically at the reasons which had prompted Civil Service unions to sponsor Parliamentary candidates. The idea of being associated with the political expression of working class organisation was only part of it. Another factor was the belief that Civil Service interests demanded someone in the House of Commons to speak for the Service, and that weighed very heavily. In 1927, when an appeal had been made for a voluntary fund, he recalled, it had spoken of the need for somebody in the House with a special knowledge of Service conditions to further the interests of the Service. The appeal had continued: 'We look for this response not only from those who happen to share Mr Brown's political views, but equally from those who hold other political views.' Yet now it was suggested that, because he was no longer a Labour Party man, he was not giving a fair deal to the subscribers. As soon as the candidacy was made dependent upon any particular Party label, it would do the organisation more harm than the candidacy could ever do good. There was only one basis for keeping the membership solid, and that was to regard the candidacy from the point of Civil Service economic interests. Was there to be a political test for members of the Executive?

Earnest and intense in the circle of light among the shadows, Brown moved to his peroration: 'I will give you no pledges about my future, none whatever, except the pledge I gave you a year ago in this place when I was being criticised for the line I was taking. I told you there were two sets of vows that a man made – his public vows and the vows he made to himself – and that the private vows were the more important. I told you that I had made a vow to the CSCA that I would play the game with them (and there is not a man or woman here who will say that I have not done my best for the Civil Service), so also I had made the same vow that I would serve in my political life faithfully and honestly the interests of the men and women who sent me to Parliament, regardless of where that vow took me. I ask you as Liberals, Labours, Tories or Communists to trust me in my Civil Service work, and to give me freedom in my general political work . . .

'When I was ill, and the Executive was good enough to give me some money to go away with, I went, amongst other places, to Palestine, and I saw Jerusalem and Nazareth. You cannot go through that experience without learning something from it. I saw the same difference between Nazareth and Jerusalem as I see between Wolverhampton and the House of Commons, the same difference between circumference and centre as I see here. I saw the simplicity and beauty of Nazareth; I saw Jerusalem with its shameless prostitution of beautiful things. There is a Jerusalem as well as a Nazareth in every country. I sat on the hill above Nazareth and looked down upon it. There I made to myself again the vow that I would not go the easy way – the way that brings you popularity, friends, power and money – for I have looked at all these things and I despise them.

'I do not know what is going to happen to me on the road I have chosen. It does not matter very much. The biggest and the smallest of us alike are infinitesimal atoms seen against the background of an eternal past and an everlasting future. I do not ask you to come with me on my road. I do ask you to let me go on. And if the CSCA is what I believe it to be, if it possesses that love of liberty which has been its hall-mark for 20 years, it will not, I know, deny me the liberty for which I ask.'

When Brown sat down, he said in his account, there occurred a scene without parallel in his life. The audience rose and cheered as if they would never stop. When the vote was taken, 299 of the 300 delegates supported his request for complete freedom. One solitary vote was recorded in favour of the Executive Committee's resolution and Brown sat and wept for sheer relief.

The Executive had a second string to its bow, a motion submitted to the conference that the general secretary should be allowed to continue as an MP and Parliamentary candidate 'if he can secure the necessary financial support.' This was understood to give the Executive authority to decide what was the necessary financial support and the conference carried an amendment deleting the clause.

In the election that year, Stanley Mayne of the Ministry of Health displaced Ted Rundle, as junior Vice-President. It was the first breach in the Post Office–Admiralty monopoly of the senior offices. Since 1926, Ross Wyld, chairman of the Post Office Section Committee, had been President of the CSCA; Bert Broadhead, Assistant Secretary and Treasurer of the Section Committee, had been senior Vice-President, and Rundle, Chairman of the Admiralty Section, had been junior Vice-President.

Mayne, who for many years was to be a notable left-wing figure in the world of Civil Service associations, made his name in the CSCA in 1929 by his able support of a motion providing for the general recruitment of male temporary clerks. The motion was carried with one dissentient despite Executive opposition. The following year he was elected to the Executive, so he had spent only one year there when he was made a vice-president. A *Red Tape* commentator on the 1929 conference, picking outstanding delegates, described him as 'that tall, fair, forcible and sincere speaker from the Ministry of Health.' Mayne had known Brown from the early post-war days, when both were Independent Labour Party (ILP) speakers.

Stanley Mayne,
Vice-President

He had continued ILP activities in the 1920s until an MP protested and he was warned by the Ministry of Health establishments officer that he must decide whether he wanted a political or a Civil Service career. After consulting Brown and Len White, he decided to concentrate on Association work, which accounted for his meteoric appearance in the CSCA in 1929 at the age of 29.

After the 1931 conference, opponents of the Post Office–Admiralty caucus associated more closely, and in November formed a rival caucus which became known as The Group, led by men from the younger ministries, such as Health, Labour and Air.

The inaugural meeting, held at the Department of Overseas Trade, passed a resolution expressing deep concern at the action of the National Executive 'in allowing outside interests to affect their judgement and actions.' The aim of The Group, it was agreed, would be to give mutual assistance in reaching decisions on nominations which would provide that, so far as possible, only the most efficient candidates, who could be relied upon to carry out the wishes of conference, would be elected to the Executive Committee. Frank Dean of the Air Ministry, a big, shrewd, formidable man was elected chairman of the group, and Joe Pepper of the Ministry of Health as secretary.

Leaders of The Group: Frank Dean (left) and Joe Pepper

It was a year of constant bickering inside and outside the Executive, and the 1932 conference began with even the weather more depressing than it had ever been at the Corton meetings. 'We ran through the rain from our huts to fetch our morning shaving water, hurried through the rain to the Pavilion, strained our ears to listen to speeches delivered to an obligato of hail on the roof, and paddled back to camp through pools of water,' wrote a *Red Tape* commentator.

The conference began with a full-scale debate on a paragraph in the annual report which referred to The Group, and representatives of both factions let themselves go with little restraint until 9 p.m. Post Office leaders and their allies, in speech after speech, defended themselves and attacked The Group and a document The Group had issued on the eve of the conference, and their opponents replied in kind, with Brown for once in the sidelines. Broadhead of the Post Office said that in every question the Executive had had to consider, definite steps were taken to destroy them, discredit them and blackguard them. Mayne accused the Executive of developing an atmosphere of hostility and distrust. He had not been alone, he added. He and five other colleagues had stood as solidly together throughout as the remainder of the Executive had stood against them. The offending paragraph was approved by 616 votes to 527 and the day's proceedings concluded with Wyld resigning the presidency because of aspersions on his good faith and The Group leaders persuading him to withdraw his resignation.

The next day the delegates turned their attention to union business – until the evening when the election results were announced and showed that The Group had almost swept the board. There was fury among the Post Office and Admiralty leaders and The Group itself was embarrassed by the scale of its success. Ross Wyld's position had not been challenged, but old stalwarts of the Association like Broadhead and Bill Boddy of the Post Office and Arthur Beard of the Admiralty had been removed from the Executive. Mayne retained his position as a vice-president and The Group was in control.

Leaders of the Caucus: (from left) Bert Broadhead, Bill Boddy and Ted Rundle

The next morning, Wyld opened the proceedings with a grim warning: 'The result of the elections shows that conference as conference is not master in its own house. Action has been taken by a section outside of conference in order to decide conference matters. I therefore, as president, do not feel in a position to accept such a state of affairs in the interests of the good government of the Association.' He suggested that the only way out of the difficulty was to reconsider the constitution of the Executive Committee so it would provide for the sectional, grade and sex interests, for which purpose a special conference should be held in three months.

Brown now entered the fray. For years, he said, he had served an Executive Committee the election of which had been determined outside the conference. For years past the Association had been ridden with caucuses. Every caucus ultimately produced its counter-caucus and in the clash of caucus and counter-caucus the very organisation itself might be destroyed. There had been a Post Office caucus years ago, and there still was. The Post Office had been heavily over-represented on the Committee and, consequently, others had been under-represented, so there were all the elements of trouble. Instead of a special conference in three months, the new Executive should look at the constitution from top to bottom and bring considered proposals to the next annual conference to be discussed in a calm atmosphere. Brown's speech provoked further retorts, but eventually it was agreed that the chief officials and leaders of the Post Office and Admiralty and The Group should meet to discuss peace proposals.

The 350 delegates waited. Someone from among The Group delegates, according to the *Red Tape* commentator, started to sing *Abide With Me* and the whole of that section took it up. The Post Office section tried to outdo The Group with its version of the hymn. The Group struck up another tune and before long the whole conference was engaged in community singing, finishing, as the principals came back with a peace treaty, with *The More We Are Together*. Settlement was agreed on the basis that a revised constitution would be submitted and that in the meantime the Post Office Section Committee would not be interfered with.

However, the truce was not followed by peace. In the following months there were fruitless talks. The Group did not disband itself. Documents were issued by the rival parties on the eve of the 1933 conference. The Post Office–Admiralty

Bill Bird, the diffident peace-maker

caucus decided not to make nominations for the Executive. The Executive had set up a Constitution Committee to prepare revisions but the Committee's chairman was Frank Dean and as soon as the delegates met it was moved that its report should not be received. At the Post Office Section meeting before the main conference there were motions advocating secession from the Association, but it was agreed to defer a decision on them until the conference had met. It looked as if there was to be another bitter and prolonged battle which might end in the splitting of the Association when a *Deus ex machina* appeared in the shape of a tall, thin man with a diffident manner but a sense of humour named Billy Bird. He was editor of *Red Tape*, and had never before addressed a conference except on the subject of *Red Tape*. He proposed an amendment that the conference should appoint a committee of five people who had had 'no hand, act or part in any of the controversy' to find an agreed settlement. He had already chosen the five, including himself. Post Office and Admiralty speakers supported the amendment. Joe Pepper opposed it, but it was evident the delegates wanted anything that might lead to a peaceful settlement and they liked Bird's choices for the committee. Only about ten voted against it.

In 48 hours the committee, after talks with all the power groups, produced its report, which was adopted unanimously. The Group met and decided to disband forthwith. The Post Office and Admiralty accepted with gratitude. Both sides agreed to withdraw the wounding documents they had produced. The President and General Secretary agreed.

The basis of the settlement was that no section or branch should be in a position to secure an unfairly large share of representation on the Executive. This was brought about by introducing a rule that of the total number of seats on the Executive, excluding the president, no greater number should be filled by the nominees of one department than was warranted by the ratio which the membership in that department bore to the total membership. This rule, which in modified form has been retained ever since, would come into operation the following year. In the meantime the Post Office would be asked to nominate six of the 27 Executive members and the Admiralty two.

For three years after this there was outward peace, but antagonisms continued to bubble and rumble beneath the surface. In September 1936, on the day before the departmental classes case went to the Arbitration Court, the volcano erupted. Brown resigned as General Secretary. 'I did so deliberately,' Brown wrote afterwards, 'to force a showdown between myself and the President. Either he would go, or I would.' The immediate reason, or pretext, was the behaviour of Ross Wyld during the struggle with the Treasury which preceded the arbitration hearings. As Brown saw it, the timing of his resignation was forced on him. If he did not win the case, Wyld would make the most of Brown's failure. If he did win and then resigned, he would be accused of cashing in on the victory.

Brown says either he or Ross Wyld must go

The other officials and the Executive made desperate attempts to get Brown to withdraw his resignation, or to get Ross Wyld to bow out on the understanding that he would remain assured of retaining the position of secretary of the National Staff Side, to which he had been appointed a year or two earlier. But neither man would give way. Brown made it clear that the only thing which would induce him to withdraw his resignation was the removal of Wyld. Wyld refused to resign voluntarily. Eventually the Executive called a special conference which was held in London's Caxton Hall on January 7, 1937.

It was a fight to the end between the two most powerful men in the Association, leading closely matched forces. Wyld had been President for 11 years. He was an able negotiator and committee man, a forceful speaker and a skilled and good-humoured conference chairman. His qualities had been recognised by the wider Civil Service. He was Vice-President of the Confederation and Staff Side secretary. He had behind him the Post Office Section, representing a fifth of the Association's membership, and his personal following was hardly less loyal and determined than that of Brown.

Brown had tremendous magnetism, carried the aura of success in his battles with the Government and with other unions and was accepted as the man who had built up the Association and raised the standard of living of its members. The majority of the Executive and the full-time officers were with him. Above all, perhaps, he had the oratorical power to arouse an enthusiastic emotional response from an audience.

On the eve of the conference, the Post Office leaders had a meeting in the Grafton Hotel and Charlie Inskip, a popular character who did the conference report single-handed for many years, moved that if Wyld was defeated the Post Office group should go over to the Union of Post Office Workers. There were impassioned speeches in support but the motion was lost because Ross Wyld himself opposed it.

When the special conference assembled, there were 419 delegates representing

46,079 members and holding 1,927 card votes. Brown was called on to explain the circumstances which led to his resignation and made a speech which was, as he described it an *apologia pro vita mea*, a speech no less emotionally effective than that of 1931.

He had taken up a trade union career, he said, 'because whatever Gods there are gave me, as part of my equipment, a profound and abiding hatred of injustice, and a passionate need to strike at it wherever I go.' He then summarised his achievements for the Association. But as success bred confidence in the Association, 'The politicians made their appearance. The parasitic growths appeared. The spirit of institutionalism grafted itself on to our crusade. In the beginning we knew little of vote bargaining and manipulation. A man got office on his merits, and not as the result of "you scratch my back – I scratch yours" bargain. Now these things crept in. And at their centre was always Wyld.'

By 1928, Brown continued, the Post Office–Admiralty caucus had conquered complete power on the Executive Committee. Executive decisions were being settled by prior understandings. The full-time officers became the whipping boys of the caucus. They were contrasted with serving civil servants as if they were somehow of a lower and a different order. They were spoken of as paid servants.

Brown accused Wyld of undermining the Association's policy in a number of respects and particularly in the situation which followed Brown's threat of a sit-in strike. Wyld, he said, had never believed in the possibility of success in the departmental classes case, which he had described in conversation as 'one of Brown's stunts'. Brown continued: 'When the President's conduct reached a point where it might easily have completely ruined a case affecting thousands of our members, upon which I had worked for 16 years, I could bear it no longer. I resolved that never again would I go into action on a Civil Service case with Wyld at my side.'

Brown defended himself against the accusation of being a dictator. Democracy he defined as 'that form of government which, whatever its label, best realised in the world of actual things the hopes and the aspirations that men carried in their hearts', and claimed by that definition to be a superb democrat. He contrasted this with the moral weakness of democracy on the national and international scene. Finally, he came to his peroration: 'I have given to the democracy of the CSCA the kind of leadership which alone could have made it the force that it has become. Now I lay down the leadership, for I can no longer endure a situation in which my biggest obstacle is not the enemy with which I contend without, but the foes of my own household. What the future holds for me I do not know. I have made no plans and accepted no posts, but I believe the law which I have sought to serve in my work for you, and through which alone I have achieved whatever successes I have achieved, will not fail me now.'

Brown denies the accusation that he is a dictator

He finished with a few words of thanks to colleagues, particularly Miss Cormack, who had stood by him through the years, and a quotation from John Bunyan concerning the summoning of Mr Valiant-for-Truth: 'Then said he, I am going to my Father; and though with great difficulty I am got hither, yet now I do not repent me of all the trouble I have been at to arrive where I am. My sword I give to him that shall succeed me in my pilgrimage, and my courage and skill to him that can get it. My marks and scars I carry with me, to be a witness for me that I have fought His battles who now will be my rewarder.' Brown received loud and prolonged cheers and applause, noted the conference report.

Loud and prolonged cheers and applause also greeted the calm, diminutive figure of Ross Wyld when he rose to put his case. His speech was quieter in tone, less emotional in content, but clear, factual and hard-hitting. He opened with an expression of sympathy for the delegates who had to choose between a restriction of their own freedom (to choose whom they wished as President) and the retention of the General Secretary whose capacity had been amazingly high and had at times fallen little short of genius. The simple fact was that the General Secretary said, 'I won't work with Wyld', and half the Executive said that in those circumstances Wyld must go. No one else, of the many with whom Wyld had worked, had found it impossible to work with him, but Brown suffered from an inability to work with anybody. He could not subordinate himself as a member of a team. 'As a leader he shines, he knows he shines, and enjoys shining. The absence of limelight irks him, and if it shines on any other person he resents it. Brown's idea is that there shall be "no other God but me". Brown's God is himself. Chronos, of old mythology, who is said to have swallowed his children, lest a power arise near his throne, must be regarded as the patron God of general secretaries from Brown's point of view.'

Wyld says Brown's God is himself

Wyld denied, as had been suggested, that he had ever wanted to take over Brown's Parliamentary candidacy. He had declined a nomination for East Woolwich, and thus thrown away a Parliamentary career, because he knew that if he accepted, just as Brown was leaving the Labour Party, Brown would regard it as a personal affront to him and create difficulties inside the Association.

Wyld went on to describe in detail how, as he saw it, he had sought to work amicably with Brown in spite of provocation. He gave his reasons for thinking that Brown actively co-operated with The Group. His central theme was in a document he had prepared: 'For the General Secretary or the Executive to indicate to Conference that in their opinion a specified individual should not be elected to a particular office strikes at the root of conference's right freely to elect whomsoever it pleases, and is directly opposed to the many declarations of recent years that conference should be master in its own house.' If he had taken the easy course and resigned, said Wyld, then members accepting nomination for the presidency in the future would have had to say: 'I gladly accept and I have obtained Mr Brown's approval.' He concluded: 'There are some things that every man will fight for if driven to it. The two things for which I have striven are honesty of Association life, coupled with rank and file control. If ever the CSCA allows itself to become dependent upon one individual and is prepared to pay any price for his retention, then the CSCA is already doomed and will have to give way to a real trade union. We men and women come together as members of an organisation for the development of our own interests and not for the aggrandisement of any individual personage.'

During the vigorous discussions that followed, it was clear that many delegates wanted to keep both President and Secretary but became convinced it was impossible. C Holock, the finance officer, read a statement by the full-time officers paying tribute to Brown's work, testifying to their good relations with him and to the smooth working of headquarters' machinery and expressing the view that his resignation would be a disaster to the Association.

Min Jackson, who as senior Vice-President was in the chair during the conference, was invited to make a statement. She had in a sense had a foot in both camps. She was in the Post Office, where she was a member of the branch of which Wyld was chairman and greatly admired him. But since she became a vice-president she had seen Brown at work at close quarters and sat alongside him at the departmental classes arbitration. To the dismay of the Post Office contingent she came down firmly on Brown's side. A resolution expressing regret at Brown's

*Min Jackson, first female
President of the Association*

resignation but refusing to agree to his demand that Wyld should be removed from office was defeated by 975 votes to 734. The conference then carried by 963 votes to 774 an Executive resolution noting it was clearly impossible to keep the services of both men and declaring it was imperative that the services of the General Secretary should be retained. A motion asking Wyld to continue in his Staff Side job was carried unanimously. There was no less unanimous support for another expressing deep appreciation of the services to the Association of both men.

A fortnight later Wyld sent in his resignation and Brown returned to the General Secretary's desk. Wyld continued as Staff Side Secretary, but the following year he was promoted to the Executive Class and said good-bye to the Post Office Section, of which he had been chairman for 14 years. He had been mayor of Walthamstow in 1935 and continued his local government activities there.

At the 1937 annual conference, Min (Mary Anne) Jackson became the first female President of the Association, but it was a long time before her Post Office colleagues forgave her for supporting Brown. A girl from Northern Ireland, she was a dominating character and eventually became Controller of Typists for Great Britain and Northern Ireland. Neither Boddy, the Post Office Section Secretary, nor Broadhead stood for the Executive at the annual conference. A Ministry of Labour man, Reuben Berg, joined Mayne as Vice-President.

Ross Wyld

Finally, the conference passed resolutions that neither presidents nor vice-presidents should be eligible for election for more than two consecutive years.

CHAPTER TEN
Into Another War

W J Brown at Cardiff:

There's a breathless hush in the hall tonight, in a well-known South Wales town. Is it Tommy Farr* that they wait to see? No! – William 'Knock-out' Brown. The Sec of the YAC has made his speech, the Chairman's shed his frown. Even the Youth Committee now is silent for Mr Brown.

He rises, and speaks of achievements past, of deeds of great renown that were done by the pioneers of old, with the help of Mr Brown. Then he tells that the cost of living figure is going up, not down. 'Now is our chance, we'll fight and win this battle, too,' says Brown. 'Air raid precautions!' – these he calls an adjectival noun! 'This Government's ineffective plans won't do,' says Mr Brown.

Then onto higher, nobler things than that extra half-a-crown. (We too want peace and brotherhood; we're with you Mr Brown.) The voice of youth is needed now, the drums of war to drown, and 44 is not too old, if you're young at heart, like Brown. The HCO forgets his pipe, and the young CA her gown; there's a breathless hush in the hall tonight – then applause for Mr Brown.

A recruiting poster used during the 1937 campaign

In the autumn of 1937, when that effusion was inspired by his visit to South Wales, Brown was at the peak of his Civil Service reputation. The departmental classes victory, the 1937 special conference and the end of the battle with the Ministry of Labour Staff Association had all come within a year. The associations of Women Civil Servants and Ex-Service Civil Servants had been reduced to impotence. Arbitration was producing more gains. A keen struggle to represent the staff of the new Unemployment Assistance Board resulted, in the same year, in the CSCA obtaining sole recognition. Only one or two small associations, such as the Post Office Sorting Assistants, had merged with it in the 1930s, but it was growing fast. A campaign to reach a membership of 50,000 during 1937 actually brought the figure up to 57,000, an increase of about 10,000, and another 8,000 were recruited the following year. Among the most enthusiastic workers in these recruiting campaigns were members of the Youth Advisory Committee (the YAC mentioned in the verse quoted above) which had been formed in 1936 and was spreading rapidly throughout the Association, attracting young people into CSCA activities.

In these euphoric days Brown endorsed a scheme, dreamed up by George Green, then an assistant secretary, for a magnificent new building which would combine headquarters offices, club and housing accommodation. There were to be club rooms, squash courts, billiard tables, tennis courts, a gymnasium, a swimming bath, a rifle range, a theatre to hold 1,000 people, lecture and committee rooms, reading rooms and library, restaurant and cafeteria, shops and garages, furnished flats from 9s 6d (47½p) to 17s 6d (87½p) a week and male and female hairdressing salons. It was to be financed by 30,000 members providing share capital of £20 a head spread over three years. Capital cost was estimated at more than half a million

* Welsh heavyweight boxer.

pounds, annual income and expenditure at £43,000. The annual conference approved it by 1,061 votes to 477, but the size of the opposition seems to have killed the scheme.

The following year, the conference gave the officials authority to find new headquarters in place of their premises in 2 Upper Belgrave Street, which had been outgrown. From the first office in a Penge attic, the Association had moved to 12 Buckingham Street, off the Strand, in 1920 21, to 38a St George's Road, Victoria, in 1921 before going to Upper Belgrave Street in 1930. Premises were found in Park Street but were demolished by bombs in 1940 and the Association remained in Belgravia until 1961, when it moved to its present offices in Balham, with additional space in Nightingale Lane not far away.

A drawing of the CSCA headquarters in Belgravia and the women at work inside

Brown, now 43 and with no major battles in hand, celebrated 1938 as the silver jubilee of his Association career, reminiscing on his victories since he had given evidence to the MacDonnell Commission in 1913. The Executive obligingly established a Jubilee Fund for him. The welfare and educational activities of the Association were developed. Attention was paid to the membership in foreign stations. Brown and Min Jackson visited Malta and improvements were secured for local civil servants in Gibraltar, Hong Kong and elsewhere. Help was given to the struggling guilds of bank and insurance employees, and Brown and Len White together forced through a Whitley scheme on behalf of prison officers.

Brown's position had become impregnable. In the winter of 1938–39, he visited Australia and at the 1939 annual conference a delegate moved a motion questioning the propriety of contributing from Association funds to the costs of his visit. Brown dismissed such criticisms as 'niggardly, parochial, pettifogging, piffling, parsimonious and petty' and the motion was defeated by 400 votes to 30.

At this conference, Min Jackson was involved in a clash over the powers of the President which was to have important results in later years. It arose over the formation of the Civil Service Alliance. The executive had promised to stop recruiting Employment Exchange staff, but the Ministry of Labour branch claimed there was nothing in the rules to prevent it taking such staff into membership and when the Executive challenged this, Miss Jackson ruled in the branch's favour. The Executive said it was for it to decide. Sir William Jowitt, KC, was consulted and gave a legal opinion that under the constitution neither the President nor the Executive had any power to rule on disputed points, which could only be done by the courts. The branch proposed an amendment to the rules vesting the President with the power to interpret them when conference was not sitting. In spite of opposition from Brown, White and Mayne, the amendment was carried by 254 votes to 86.

Min Jackson had now completed her two years as President and Stanley

Mayne was the unopposed nominee to succeed her. Shortly before the conference, Mayne was promoted direct from the Clerical Class to the Administrative Class, a rare occurrence. He was soon active in the First Division Association, which organises top civil servants, and became a member of its executive. In 1948 he left the Civil Service to become General Secretary of the Institution of Professional Civil Servants.

When Mayne withdrew, the Association called for new nominations for the presidency and elected Broadhead, one of Mayne's stongest opponents in past battles, though he was not a delegate and had not been a member of the Executive for two years. The choice reflected a decline in old hostilities and probably a desire to have a strong man with long experience to lead the CSCA into the Second World War, which most people thought inevitable, and was, in fact, only a few months away.

Bert Broadhead (right) is congratulated on his election to the presidency

Behind the comparative peace and vigorous progress of the Association from 1937 to 1939, shadows of the coming war had been deepening. The Nazi and Fascist threats were ever more menacing and impatience grew with what many regarded as the weak policies of the British and French democracies. Those were the days of the United Front, when young men from many countries enlisted in the International Brigade to join the fight for democracy in the Spanish Civil War. The Left Book Club, organised by publisher Victor Gollancz, of which the CSCA formed sections, made the left better informed than in most periods. There were some protests when the Association contributed to Spanish relief funds. One member brought an action to try to stop it but lost his case. They were stirring days for radical youth and it was not surprising that the Youth Advisory Committee found enthusiastic support.

The impact of war was more gradual than that of the First World War. In the summer of 1937, the CSCA was already criticising the Government's air raid precautions. There were criticisms of the gas masks issued. It was demanding bomb-proof underground shelters and the evacuation of civilians. The 1939 conference conditionally accepted the introduction of conscription, on the grounds that it was an inevitable companion to the building up of a peace front of powers opposed to Fascism and Nazism, but at the same time criticising Government foreign policy, demanding guarantees against the use of conscription to make industrial conditions worse and the simultaneous conscription of wealth. There was some criticism from right and left but no one voted against the motion.

The first war-time issue of *Red Tape* was in striking contrast to that of 1914. There was none of the fervour, one might almost say exhilaration, of the First War. Instead, the Association concentrated on the host of practical problems which war had brought: the evacuation and billeting of thousands of members, including parts of the Association staff to East Grinstead, organisation in the new and expanded Government departments, the suspension of the marriage bar, civil pay for enlisted men and organisation of a new flood of temporary clerks. The expansion of the Service created opportunities for patronage and nepotism, examples of which Len White regularly exposed. There was need for constant defence against Press criticisms of the Service. During the first year of the war, the cost of living rose rapidly and the Association campaigned for pay increases. A new bonus was introduced which went part of the way to meet complaints and was raised several times. From the autumn of 1940, Government action kept prices relatively stable by subsidies and other devices.

The 1940 annual conference was cancelled at the last minute when the 'phoney war' turned to *Blitzkrieg*. The Staff Side wrote to Winston Churchill, the new Prime Minister, offering the loyalty and support of civil servants. It offered to forgo overtime pay until 44 hours had been worked in a week and to work whatever additional hours were necessary. It was agreed that a 54-hour week should be aimed for in the immediate future and 48 hours should be the absolute minimum. The CSCA started a long campaign for the more efficient use of Civil Service manpower. Attention turned to such things as fire-watching arrangements and grants for bomb damage.

The Staff Side offers Churchill its loyalty and support and agrees to work longer hours during the war emergency

When Germany invaded Russia in the summer of 1941, Brown wrote a *Red Tape* article rejoicing that the Russians were now fighting with Britain against Hitler and taking pleasure in the fact that the Communist Party ('which for the last two years has demanded the end of "this Imperialist War" and has for practical purposes acted as an ally of Hitler') had now changed its position and was supporting the war. He said that Stalin's action in signing the non-aggression pact with Hitler did more to precipitate the war than any other single thing. If she had not been attacked, Russia would presumably have continued to observe the non-aggression pact and to supply the German war machine, and the British Communist Party would have pursued its line of revolutionary defeatism.

Stanley Mayne, still taking an interest in the Association, wrote a more-in-sorrow-than-in-anger reply: 'Why did you do it, Bill? . . . You seem more keen to vent your spleen on the Communist Party than to drive ahead in the war . . . I am sorry you did it, Bill. God knows there are differences enough between us, but are they not better left while we concentrate on the urgent job immediately before us?' *Red Tape* published a number of letters also criticising Brown's article, at least one from a member of the Executive and some more-in-anger-than-in-sorrow.

It was not the first article by Brown to criticise the Communists and provoke indignant rejoinders.

Shortly afterwards, the Executive passed a resolution which it distributed widely listing nine points which it regarded as essential to victory. They included the recomposition of the Government on the basis of character and ability instead of on Party lines, the purging of Munich elements from the public services, the elimination from the High Command of those whose outlook was bounded by the last war, the removal of a ban which had been imposed on the Communist *Daily Worker*, the taking over of war factories by the State so as to cut out the private motive and the establishment of a Western land front. This too provoked controversy, some readers claiming that the Executive had no right to commit the Association on political, or strategic, questions.

The CSCA executive lists nine points essential to victory

It was evident that new power blocs, quite different from those of the 1930s, were building up within the Association.

PART THREE
A NEW APPROACH
1942-1968

CHAPTER ELEVEN
Whitleyism in Flower

There was general agreement that, apart from the officers, the individual who contributed most to the growth of Staff Side unity was Len White, who succeeded W J Brown as General Secretary of the Civil Service Clerical Association. He was instrumental in 'converting the National Staff Side from a battleground of conflicting organisations to a co-operative effort for each and all, and the contrast for anyone who has lived through both types of organisation is amazing.'
Henry Parris in his book: *Staff Relations in the Civil Service: Fifty Years of Whitleyism.*

It was not only to the Staff Side that White brought more co-operative relationships. He had played an important part in the formation of the Civil Service Alliance just before the war and from the moment he formally took over the general secretaryship from Brown he set to work to make peace with all those with whom Brown had quarrelled over the years: the TUC, the Labour Party, the Official Side and the Press. Within a year it was announced that talks with the TUC had led to an understanding which, given patience and goodwill on both sides, would pave the way to a more cordial and friendly relationship. Greg Challis, a vice-president and later full-time officer in White's time, describes him in that period as 'an immensely diplomatic and likeable man who looked more like a musician than a union leader. A splendid head, the bald dome surrounded by black curls like a crown, the quick, dark eyes, the clever, good-humoured mouth, the short, portly figure – in all a most genial personality who drew affection from every side. He was a man with a tolerant disposition and singularly without malice. His left-wing tendencies were of an individual kind which seemed to contain no class hatred. He was fascinated by people and they by him. He was too sceptical of pretentiousness to be an uncritical adherent of any party. Brown's wit was of a grim type that made his victims writhe, whereas Len White's was of the kind that made its victims treasure it to tell to later generations.'

Len White becomes General Secretary: 'an immensely diplomatic and likeable man'

It was often assumed that White was a Communist because in 1945 he became a member of the Communist *Daily Worker* editorial board and in the Association worked with an Executive dominated by Communists and their allies, but he always insisted that he was a member of the Labour Party and when the internal struggle was at its height wrote in a private letter that he was not, and never had been, a member of the Communist Party. He did not hesitate to criticise and oppose the left on some issues. During the national crisis of 1940, when the Communists were still opposing the war, the Staff Side had agreed to the working of considerable overtime and the shelving of some non-urgent issues.

'The Staff Side's gesture,' White wrote in *Red Tape*, 'caused some rumblings among what is sometimes miscalled the left wing of our organisation. I say miscalled because the term left wing suggests some stability of position. We were accused of selling the pass. We have explained to our critics, who are overwhelmingly more noisy than numerous, that in the situation with which we were confronted it was the duty of leaders to estimate the wish of the Service, and to take responsibility for expressing their conviction to the Government. Crises cannot be

Len White

put in suspense to satisfy every detailed theory of democracy.

'The time has arrived for some blunt speaking to this small minority, most of whom are merely muddle-headed, a few of whom may be motivated by other considerations. The Staff Side's actions spring from the conviction that the very existence of everything fundamental to the trade union movement and indeed the very existence of the trade union movement itself, are bound up with the winning of the war . . . The pressures under which Government departments are now working have made it difficult for many of our effective workers to give the time and attention to the activities of the Association which, in the past, we have had from them. In this situation there is considerable scope for those who are prone to use the Association as a platform for expounding their own particular political theories.'

It may be that White moved further to the left in later years but he never relinquished his independence of mind. Douglas Houghton, an outspoken moderate, said White had a genius for ending feuds and restoring confidence. 'A wonderful gift for saying the hardest things in the most disarming way,' said one Treasury spokesman. 'An immensely decent fellow with whom you could work and whom you could trust,' said another.

Len White established a position in the Association and in the wider Civil Service movement which went deeper than the day-to-day battles. Many veterans will still remember him in his favourite corner of the Horse and Groom, just round the corner from the Belgravia headquarters, to which members would adjourn after executive meetings. There he would lavishly dispense his unassuming wit and wisdom. It was an old-fashioned pub, run by two elderly Irishwomen, Bridie and May. Though they were devout Catholics, they were very fond of White and once threw a man out for accusing him of being a Communist. The

CSCA negotiated to buy the place early in the war and Brown, during his visit to America, sent White a telegram: 'Are we publicans or still merely sinners?' According to White, this disturbed the authorities, who thought it must be some sort of code.

White's contribution to the development of Civil Service trade unionism

It was in the development of Whitleyism that White made probably his greatest contribution to the future of the Association and of Civil Service trade union organisation as a whole. After the first promising period from 1919 to 1921, the Whitley system had fallen into some disrepute, partly because of Government pressures for economy during the long years of depression, partly because many senior officials resented the new rights accorded to Association leaders, and partly because of divisions and rivalries on the Staff Side. The National Council met regularly, taking up the time of many leading civil servants, but its proceedings were apt to be purely formal except when stirred to life by one of Brown's eloquent and provocative speeches, which impressed his hearers but seldom achieved practical results. Some of the 70 departmental councils worked well most of the time, but others did not. Most of Brown's victories were gained by political pressure or by arbitration, not by consultation or negotiation.

The rows on the Staff Side, which emerged as personal quarrels between Brown and many of the others, in reality went deeper than that. There was a difference in approach and background between the Post Office and clerical unions, and in a different way between the associations of higher and lower civil servants, because they believed that their interests were different, which in the short term they often were.

There was also a fundamental difference of policy between Brown and many of the older union leaders who believed the Whitley ideals of co-operation were not assisted by Brown's constant lambasting of the Treasury, and that the Staff Side was weakened by the inter-union battles in which the CSCA was often involved. Brown's justification was his success in fighting specific issues and in forcing the Official Side to treat the associations with respect.

The system was transformed by the Second World War in which the Government and the two sides on the Council shared an urgent and overriding objective. Some ministers appeared from both sides of industry who were unaccustomed to Civil Service formalities. Before hostilities began, the Staff Side promised that if the Official Side would arrange to consult it on any matters of importance, the Staff Side would make it as easy as possible to get things done. A smooth change to the new approach owed much to the 1939 appointment of Albert Day of the Society of Civil Servants as chairman of the Staff Side. He was a man always formal and correct in dress, deliberate and quiet in manner, who had an advocate's skill in dealing with the Official Side, the exceptional patience needed to keep the Staff Side together, and an integrity which assured him of the trust of both. From the beginning of 1947, Day became the first full-time chairman of the National Staff Side.

At the beginning of the war, two small sub-committees were set up. One (Committee A) was concerned with urgent matters and met every few days in the early part of the war, while the other (Committee B) handled less pressing issues. The two sides also developed an effective informal relationship, with many things discussed by officials or small groups before being reported to the Staff Side. The full National Council met only once during the war, in May 1941, to deal with longer hours and shorter leave. In April 1945, a Parliamentary question elicited the information that the Official Side of the National Council no longer existed. White observed that this had not been a cause of inconvenience because all the work had

Albert Day, Chairman of the National Whitley Council Staff Side; a man with 'skill, patience and integrity'

been done by sub-committees, but he was not entirely happy about it because some departments had become completely detached from the Council. However, the Official Side was reconstituted shortly afterwards with 27 members, of whom 20 were knights. The full National Council still did not meet, however, except for a glass of sherry at Christmas. There were only two meetings between the end of the war and the 1970s, both over the 1949 Masterman report on the civil rights of civil servants. But the committee and unofficial meetings continued.

Before the war, Len White wrote in 1945, official sides seldom took any initiative, avoided consultation wherever possible and did little more than acquaint staff sides with decisions which usually remained unaffected by any subsequent joint discussion.

'Today,' White continued, 'we have achieved a position in which, on almost every issue of importance affecting staff interests, we can expect to be consulted while the Official Side is engaged in formulating policy and at a time when it is possible, if the arguments are sufficiently cogent, to influence the decisions reached. Moreover, we can generally rely upon being given facts and considerations which would not previously have been available to us.'

This sought-for situation presented problems. If they were given the facts, associations had to face them even when they were unfavourable to their point of view. For instance, they admitted that the Official Side had made a good case for the dispersal of some government departments to the provinces even though their members were protesting against it. The question, said White, was whether the Service really wanted Whitleyism as originally intended, or were the representations to be limited to statements of what members wanted.

This approach, contrasting so strangely with that of Bill Brown, was argued out at the 1945 conference. There was a motion to censure Staff Side representatives for agreeing to a report on the staffing of the Service during the reconstruction period and another expressing alarm at the 'increasing tendency towards fraternisation'. The proposer of the latter said it was time the Staff Side got round to the proper side of the table. Both motions were lost.

White told delegates there were still some members who apparently believed that, even when the Official Side was disposed to give them what they asked for, it was an act almost of treachery to accept it. He rejected completely 'the fallacy that the Staff Side consisted exclusively of the virtuous and the Official Side exclusively of the vicious.' He had had experience of Staff Side claims that were as immoral and unjustifiable as were Official Side rejections. Although the Staff Side had not spent its time calling Treasury officials rude names, it had nevertheless negotiated with firmness and with an adherence to Staff Side principles as rigid and as effective as at any time in the Association's history.

The result of the new system was that more negotiations were carried through by staff sides and fewer by individual associations. For instance, the CSCA held a conference on post-war reconstruction and arranged a special conference for members returning from the forces, but negotiations took place through the Staff Side. The Government asked the joint body to prepare a report on post-war recruitment which the Government accepted and published as a White Paper. Since entrance examinations had been suspended since 1939, there were thousands of openings for permanent staff, particularly as the size of the Service did not decline nearly so quickly or so much as after the First World War, but the competition for established jobs from those returning from the forces, temporaries and young people wishing to enter the Service was intense.

With those in the Services demanding early demobilisation, evacuated civil servants clamouring to return to London, large sections of departments being dispersed about the country, swollen war-time departments being reduced in size, others returning to peace-time dimensions and new social departments of the welfare state being created, the end of the war found the Service involved in a gigantic game of musical chairs in which hundreds of thousands played. The preparatory work of the Whitley Council and the systematic preparations made by Ernest Bevin contributed to the country's success in sorting it all out with comparatively little friction.

The 'gigantic game of musical chairs' when the war ended

The return of the first majority Labour Government in 1945 so raised expectations that Len White felt it necessary to warn members that the Government would itself be facing serious economic difficulties and unable to do all that it would like to do, at least without pressure from the Association. Nevertheless, a statement by Ernest Bevin that he would like to see the Government become a model employer rather than follow behind on the Tomlin formula and the repeal of the 1927 Trade Disputes Act seemed to promise well for the future.

During the war, the associations had concentrated on trying to get the Act amended to eliminate Clause 5, which prevented them from affiliating to the TUC or Labour Party. The TUC leaders as a whole resented the refusal of the war-time coalition to do anything about an Act, which they regarded as a piece of political spite, at a time when they were doing their utmost to help the Government in the prosecution of the war. In 1943, the Union of Post Office Workers (UPW) applied for affiliation with the Trades Union Congress and was strongly supported by the CSCA. Under strong pressure from the Government, the UPW withdrew the application, but a number of association branches, including many from the CSCA, affiliated to local trades councils, including the formidably left-wing London Trades Council. As late as March 1945, Churchill told Sir Walter Citrine, TUC General Secretary, there was no possibility of amending the Act because of the opposition of the majority of Conservative MPs, but the Labour Government immediately repealed not only Clause 5 but the whole Act. The CSCA and four other associations at once reaffiliated.

A number of other long-standing complaints were altogether or partially removed either by legislation, with Brown playing an active part, Whitley Council agreement or a combination of both. Among these were two Acts raising Civil Service pensions and, in 1949, an unexpected success, attributed by the Staff Side largely to a campaign by Brown in the House of Commons. This secured that temporary service between the years 1919 and 1935, which had been deemed quite lost for pension purposes, would be taken into account for half its length. Legislation based on the agreement also covered the position of 'age-barred' officers – that is to say, officers who were older than 50 at the time of establishment and therefore could not complete the ten years' service then required to qualify for any pension. It was to be a quarter of a century before, in the 1972 Act, the associations made further substantial gains on superannuation, with the CSCA again playing an important part, but the 1949 Act was a major step.

The establishment of war-time temporaries was carried through at a pace which surpassed expectations. By 1943, about 400,000 of the total Civil Service of 700,000 were temporaries, without pension rights. Many of them, of course, wanted to return to their peace-time occupations but there remained a major problem which was dealt with by a series of reconstruction schemes which in five years conferred permanency upon 100,000 in clerical and allied grades. Thousands who had poured into the Service during the war now stayed, including men and women with a wide variety of experience.

Thousands of temporary Civil Servants are established

The problems of promotion were hardly less complex. A war-time agreement set up the 1942 Treasury Promotion Pool, which reduced the worst inequalities between one department and another in respect of promotion opportunities. When the scheme was criticised at a meeting of representatives of London branches, White defended it with some skill, concluding with the characteristic exhortation: 'If it should prove, over a period of years, that the process of imports and exports does not produce complete equity – if it should prove that you have provided your colleagues in other departments with more opportunities than you have received in return, just think what a fine Christian thing you will be doing.' His appeal to generous impulses was received with laughter and acceptance. The pool was placed on a permanent footing for Clerical Officers in 1949. Since then it has been repeatedly amended and has disappointed those who thought of it as the forerunner of a single promotion system for the whole Service, but it has helped thousands who would have had little hope of promotion without it. In 1976–77, for example, 220 clerical officers were exported to other departments with promotion to Executive Officer.

There were occasions on which the Government, without consultation, took important decisions directly affecting civil servants, to the indignation of the associations. Perhaps the two most important occasions were the Prime Minister's 1948 statement on Communists in the Service and national security, and the Government's acceptance of the Masterman report on civil rights the following year which, contrary to established Labour Party policy, tightened restrictions on civil servants' political activity except for manipulative grades. A full meeting of the National Whitley Council was called, as has been said, at the request of the Staff Side, and every candidate in the February 1950 election was lobbied through a combination of 12 associations. Negotiations dragged on through the Whitley machinery until the Conservative Government in 1953 accepted a joint report which modified the Masterman proposals but left Len White and some of the other general secretaries angry and dissatisfied.

Another example of Government failure to consult in advance, affecting not only civil servants but the whole trade union movement, was 'the Cripps freeze',

Bill Ellerby, Deputy General Secretary

Len White as seen by 'Joss' of 'The Star'

the White Paper on Personal Incomes, Costs and Prices produced in February 1948, and outlining a policy of wage restraint. The CSCA was against it, even in a modified TUC version, and Len White produced arguments against Government income policies which were to be developed and elaborated by the Association's leaders over the next 30 years.

The CSCA had already felt the impact of Government economic difficulties the previous year, when there was so much exasperation at delay in replying to 1946 pay claims that there was a return to the policy of mass meetings, including the Association's second in Trafalgar Square. But Len White later criticised the membership because, he said, only 2,000 were there out of a possible 100,000, so 98,000 had demonstrated they did not care.

In those days, Association leaders showed an understanding of the Treasury problems which was never evident in Brown's day. In July 1947, Bill Ellerby, the Deputy General Secretary, wrote: 'Many members tend to look upon the Treasury as an organisation of sadists whose main purpose in life is first to delay making any decision as long as possible, and then to delight in rejecting claims on any pretext and when compelled to make a concession to take back with one hand what is given with another. The truth is that with few exceptions Treasury officials are among the hardest worked and the most conscientious of civil servants, who are endeavouring to do an exceptionally difficult job under the most trying conditions.' He laid the blame on the Government.

Len White was no less understanding at a Central Hall demonstration in December 1950, when resistance to the wage restraint policy was at its height. 'The Treasury were powerless in the face of the restrictions imposed by the Chancellor's document,' he said. 'Our dispute tonight is with the Government and not with the Treasury.'

White argued that for practical purposes the White Paper meant the end of negotiations with the Civil Service associations and the virtual closing down of arbitration. The Treasury, the Staff Side was informed, had been instructed not even to discuss wage claims which had not been settled before the White Paper became effective. White objected that there was nothing in the White Paper which ruled out negotiations. 'So perhaps you would like to settle with us what it is you owe us before you tell us we cannot have it,' he added. The Staff Side sent a deputation to see the Prime Minister, who assured it that the established joint machinery remained available for the exchange of views and the staff were free to take their claims to the Arbitration Tribunal. At the beginning of 1951, the CSCA succeeded in getting a substantial increase for Clerical Officers, the first Civil Service success since the freeze began, followed by increases for other grades.

For some years, Len White had been arguing that claims based on substantial increases in the general wage index should be undertaken by the National Staff Side for the Civil Service as a whole, instead of relying on a host of different claims for different grades. Following the CSCA's 1951 success, the Staff Side adopted this policy with fruitful results and for the following few years regular increases were obtained, by central negotiations when the Government could be persuaded to agree to them.

The CSCA of the post-war decade differed in many ways from the pre-war organisation. It was more than twice the size, reaching a membership of 153,000 in 1948. Instead of concentrated in London, the members were spread over the country as a result of the Government's dispersal policy and the growth of welfare departments. The proportion of women was larger because of the influx of female temporaries during the war and the abolition of the marriage bar after it.

During the war, the Association lost many of its active members to the Forces and not all returned. Many of these who remained were given acting promotion, often at an early age, because of the need for experienced men and women to supervise the mass of newcomers, and these promotions were confirmed when the war was over. The CSCA showed great energy in recruiting these temporary workers, but its soaring membership required more and more branch officers, to replace those who had gone, and to run new branches. To meet this urgent need, the CSCA started educational programmes designed to help actual and potential branch officers, new to trade union activities, achieve an understanding of the trade union movement, the CSCA and Civil Service Whitley machinery, local negotiations and the organisation and management of a branch. The organisation of these programmes was entrusted to Muriel Coult, a woman who had shown exceptional energy on the Youth Advisory Committee and was now a member of the Finance and Organisation Committee. In spite of enemy action, transport difficulties and the complications caused by evacuation and other war-time problems, she made a great success of organizing weekend schools in many parts of the country. Other unions were impressed and followed the CSCA example. The programmes were continued and expanded after the war.

Muriel Coult, who organised war-time educational programmes

The resulting complement of voluntary officers was invaluable, especially after a Whitley agreement, made in 1947, encouraging departments to abolish the Higher Clerical Officer (HCO) grade, the supervisory grade organised by the CSCA, and replace it by Executive Officers, organised by the Society of Civil Servants, for supervisory work as well as other work calling for 'judgement, initiative and resource'. The bargain was attractive to the CSCA because it provided immediate promotion opportunities for Clerical Officers, and consequently for Clerical Assistants. Gradually, in department after department, over the next 25 years, the HCOs disappeared. Critics of the agreement complained that the CSCA had blown its own brains out. Experienced HCOs had played, and for a time continued to play, a major part in Association work from branch to national level. Of the 12 presidents from 1939 to 1968 (including one acting president) nine were Higher Clerical Officers.

Another important factor affecting the CSCA leadership was the decision of the 1950 annual conference to abolish grade and provincial reservations in elections to the National Executive Committee. Ever since the amalgamations which formed the CSCA, candidates for the NEC had been divided into a number of groups, some originally representing merged unions, so that men and women, members from the provinces, permanent and temporary staff and so on were assured of representation. This was changed so that the Executive was elected by the whole conference (subject to the departmental limitations rule) which resulted in clerical officers coming almost to monopolise the Executive.

The Government dispersal of the Civil Service, and consequently of Association members, many of them recruited in the area in which they work, has meant that local attitudes and traditions have increasingly had to be taken into consideration in framing national policy, with which they may on occasion conflict. The first dispersal agreement, the purpose of which was to check the disproportionate expansion of employment opportunities in London at the expense of other parts of the country, was reached by the National Whitley Council in August 1948. By 1963, 25,000 posts had been moved out of London. By 1972 50,000 had been moved and there were plans to more than double that figure. While in 1931 the proportion of civil servants in London was 72 per cent, it had fallen to 26 per cent in 1977.

*Alex McMaster, a firebrand
from Glasgow*

Some of the Association's biggest branches are now to be found in the provinces: there are 9,000 members in the Department of Health and Social Security branch in Newcastle, 5,000 in the Savings Bank in Glasgow and 4,400 in the Driver and Vehicle Licensing Section in Swansea.

Most of the moves were not rushed. There was ample consultation and preparation and they went surprisingly smoothly. An exception was the transfer of the Post Office Savings Bank to Glasgow, which produced a minor Association crisis. The Government announced its intention to move the Bank in 1963 and originally suggested Merseyside, Teesside or Glasgow, of which the members chose Teesside. The following year the Government announced, it was presumed for political reasons, that the Bank was to go to Glasgow. The Branch accused the Government of making a mockery of consultation and urged the NEC to help it get the matter reconsidered.

This aroused the Scottish members, who were naturally anxious to get such an addition to Glasgow's employment opportunities and local newspapers interviewed Alex McMaster, chairman of the Area Co-ordinating Committee in Glasgow, though area committees were not supposed to interfere in policy matters. Among comments attributed to McMaster were: 'Our union leaders are using dirty tactics.' 'What they really fear is that with the move of the Savings Bank, a lot of influence in the CSCA will shift to Glasgow.' 'An unfair picture of Glasgow has been presented by our union people,' and 'People in London are fostering an anti-Scots feeling.' He was even said to have accused the London leaders of race hatred.

Called before a small Committee of Inquiry, McMaster said he had been badgered and misreported by the Press. McMaster was severely reprimanded but the NEC hesitated to go further in view of the feeling in Scotland. 'We believe the NEC must act in such a fashion that charges of victimisation cannot be alleged,' said the Committee of Inquiry's report. 'We fully understand that any conciliatory gesture may be interpreted as a sign of weakness. We would rather be subject to this type of criticism than recommend action which would further exacerbate the intense feeling in Glasgow or produce an actual split in the Association which would take time to heal.'

In spite of NEC warnings, however, the Area Committee refused to undertake to desist from such actions as making representations to the Scottish TUC, the Lord Provost of Glasgow and the Scottish Press, and the NEC dissolved the Area Committee on August 12, 1964. It was then reported that Campbell Christie of the National Assistance Board Glasgow branch had circularised other branches, proposing a meeting to discuss the future organisation of an area committee, methods of financing such a committee and how protests could be organised against the NEC decision. A motion to suspend Christie from membership was defeated, but there was more trouble to come.

On October 8, the NEC held a general meeting of members in Glasgow to discuss the position, but it proved stormy and the president, Joe Bryce, declared the meeting closed and left the hall. There were some fears of violence, but the meeting was resumed informally. The Press made much of the affair, however, and the general secretary, Len Wines, received letters calling for disciplinary action against Bryce. However, Bryce's explanation of what happened was accepted and a further meeting was held in January 1965, at which the Area Committee was re-formed. The transfer was finally completed in 1978. The affair was a remarkable example of the extent to which special local interest could conflict with Association policy.

The post-war changes in the composition and location of the CSCA brought with them changes in attitudes which were also affected by long periods of full or

*Joe Bryce, the CSCA
President who became
involved in the Glasgow storm*

over-full employment, which made security in the Service less of an attraction and produced a shortage of typists and some other grades. In spite of the high proportion of women, the Association remained mainly male led and Clerical Officer orientated, but the development of the welfare state meant an increasing number of members doing jobs which brought them into direct contact with the public, so that they were influenced by trends in popular attitudes, while dispersal resulted in the appearance of little provincial kingdoms within the Association. The great Newcastle DHSS branch became known for a time as the Newcastle Mafia. There was renewed vigour in the pressure for an end to provincial differentiation, under which provincial terms of employment were inferior to those in London.

Branches separated from London headquarters increased their demand for direct representation at the annual conference which remained, as it had always been, the Association's undisputed ruling body. The delegates decided in 1945 to increase the size of the conference from the ceiling of 350 adopted during the war to about 850, in spite of the increased burden on already tight finances.

Provincial branches demand direct representation at the annual conference

The more representative a conference, the more influential its decisions, but experience in other unions has shown that it is easier for the platform to control a big conference than a small one. It is more susceptible to emotional appeal and more likely to be impressed by the informed and carefully prepared speeches of leaders, particularly if they are allowed half an hour at the microphone while nobody else has more than three or five minutes. This is particularly true where the spokesman is a general secretary of exceptional and recognised ability such as Len White. Delegates found themselves agreeing to refer numerous resolutions to the Executive after listening to him for half an hour. It was decided that national officers and Executive Committee members would be subject to the same time limits as everybody else. This may be more democratic, but it can result in resolutions being passed without delegates having in their minds all the implications. The conference in 1956 abolished the rule limiting the term of office of presidents to a maximum of two years, which was adopted in 1937 to prevent any future president from becoming a rival in influence to the general secretary, as was Ross Wyld.

White was due to retire on November 12, 1952, when he reached the age of 55, but the conference invited him to stay on for another five years. This meant he was mainly responsible for the preparation and presentation of evidence to a new Royal Commission, under the chairmanship of Sir Raymond Priestley, which the Government set up in 1953 to advise them on what principles the remuneration of civil servants should be based, and also to inquire into hours, leave, overtime pay, extra duty allowances and superannuation. While the Commission was sitting, the National Staff Side unanimously invited White to succeed Sir Albert Day as its principal executive officer with the new title of Secretary-General and the CSCA Executive agreed to recommend his release. However, on May 11, 1955, before he had taken up the new job, White died at the age of 57.

CHAPTER TWELVE
Moderates v the Left

The CSCA, after all, is like a large, friendly, shaggy dog. It will scratch for so long but in the end it has to give itself a vigorous shake for a true cleansing.

This simile was used in a document issued by the Conference Campaign Committee (CCC) which, between the annual conferences of 1947 and 1948, challenged the power of Communists and their allies within the Association. The simile seems also to have appealed to their opponents for the next official reply to the CCC was called A Shaggy Dog Story and concluded with the suggestion that if ever a body stood in need of a vigorous shaking it was the CCC. Not a high level of debate, perhaps, but by that time the exchanges had been going on for some months.

Though he was so successful in restoring amicable relations with outside organisations, Len White could not avert the outbreak of an internal political battle which lasted for years. It began with a complex and interrelated conglomeration of struggles in which the National Executive was beaten by an anti-Communist revolt, Bill Brown was driven to resign before his time after hearings before a Commons Committee of Privileges, the NEC was at odds with its own general secretary and a Government Communist purge contributed to the conflict.

White did his best to ward off the explosion, warning the Executive bluntly of the dangers under existing conditions of the arrogance not uncommon among left-wing leaders. The General Purposes Committee minutes of November 8, 1945, recount that White deplored a tendency on the part of some members of the Executive Committee to speak of the necessity for educating the membership when what they really meant was engaging in propaganda in support of their own quite legitimate point of view. The Executive Committee had not been selected because of the special qualifications of its members to act as political tutors. It was not his opinion, White said, that the membership as a whole was necessarily less well educated on political matters than members of the Executive Committee, and he thought that anything which savoured of patronage or the assumption of omniscience on the part of the Executive might lead to consequences which those who favoured affiliation to the Labour party might regret.

Almost a year later he reiterated his warning, this time, according to the minutes, telling the full NEC that: 'There appeared to be an assumption that the political point of view which had been pursued by the Association and endorsed by conference necessarily represented the point of view of the majority of the membership. He would like to feel that this was the case but he had grave doubts. The last thing he wanted at the present time was a showdown on this issue. Circumstances might tend ultimately to convert the majority of the membership to the political viewpoint now held by the majority of the Executive Committee. But in his opinion this was not the case at present. If the issue were raised in rather dramatic circumstances at the present time, it might disclose that while a large section of the membership, as a result of apathy, would not challenge the political line of the Executive so long as there was no provocation to do so, if provocation was given there would be an unfruitful result.'

The Executive, however, does not seem to have been aware of the extent to which public attitudes were changing. After Russia had been attacked by Germany, she became Britain's heroic ally and some of the glory of Stalingrad descended upon the British Communists, who now did their utmost to stimulate productivity and prevent strikes. Many were elected to important positions in British unions and in a few, including the CSCA, secured with their allies a dominating influence. White became a member of the *Daily Worker* editorial board in 1945 and in the same year W J (Bill) Ellerby, an able left-winger, was made Deputy General Secretary. From 1945 to 1947, a succession of left-wing assistant secretaries was appointed. On the Executive, the most influential figure was E W McMillan, a quietly self-assured left-winger who had made his way up from the Post Office manipulative grades. He was an impressive debater who livened an intense and logical marshalling of his arguments with occasional sardonic flashes of humour. He was president from 1942–44 and again from 1946 to the middle of 1947, when he was promoted. He later became president of the Society of Civil Servants.

E W McMillan, twice president and a leader of the Left

But there were new forces at work in the country and the world. With peace had come growing suspicion and hostility between Russia and the West. Communists criticised British Government policy, particularly foreign policy, and the criticisms were resented by young men back from the forces and by Labour supporters in the unions, who wanted the first Labour Government with an absolute majority, returned in 1945, to be given every chance to fulfil its promises.

There were signs at the 1947 annual conference that the CSCA membership was revolting against the Communist-line attacks on the Government. In 1946, a resolution demanding a complete revision of British foreign policy was carried without difficulty, but in 1947 a similar motion was defeated by 3,172 votes to 1,449. McMillan said the conference was making a mistake. Much of his presidential address had been devoted to criticism of the Labour Government. Their task, he told the delegates, was to get inside the political movement and lend the full weight of their union to support those who, like themselves, sought to remedy the weakness of Labour's handling of their problems.

Many of the delegates were not anxious to affiliate with the Labour Party for this purpose, and the conference reversed by 2,855 votes to 2,002 the previous year's decision to support affiliation. 'If we affiliate to the Labour Party, whose views will be brought to bear on the Party, the views of the Executive Committee or of the membership?' one delegate demanded. 'The Communists and their fellow-passengers are cashing in on the position which exists in the CSCA and other unions today. They are attempting to get control of the trade unions and through the trade unions to take over the Labour Party. This attempt to secure the affiliation of the CSCA to the Labour Party is part of that policy.'

Evidently there was a spontaneous revolt against the Communist influence in the Association, but it was unlikely to achieve much without organised resistance. At this same conference at Prestatyn Holiday Camp in North Wales the seeds of anti-Communist organisation were sown. It began one evening when a delegate from the Official Solicitor's Department, A R (Gerry) Gerrard walked into the bar of the big dance hall and saw an empty chair at a small table. 'Is this place taken?' he asked, and joined a group of delegates who, like himself, represented non-section branches (branches in departments not large enough to justify the formation of a section). One was A J Walker of the Forestry Commission, another was Graeme Fallows of the Land Registry. They were young men who had come back from the forces to find the interests of their small branches, as it seemed to them, being neglected. Overtime was heavy and persistent and remuneration inadequate. They had been sent to the conference, mostly for the first time, to try to get someone to do something about it, and placed next to each other in a corner of the

Three Moderates: (from left) Bill Brough, Fred Houghton and Gerry Gerrard

conference hall, where they soon began to exchange grievances.

They were shocked to find the Association run by the big branches, under Communist control, who seemed to them to pay little attention to the small fry. As they talked they found that they also shared resentment at the Communist-inspired resolutions supported by the National Executive. So, in the holiday camp bar that evening a few young men determined to set rolling a campaign which in twelve months was to transform the political face of the Association.

They noted the names of those who made speeches opposing Communist-type motions and had their first meeting on the last day of the conference. As soon as the conference was over they got together to organise their campaign. As all four worked in London, contact was easy. They roped in Cliff Charles from the Ministry of Fuel and Bill Brough from the Public Relations Department of the same ministry, who was useful in preparing documents, and set up the Conference Campaign Committee (CCC). They found cautious support from George Green, the full-time officer responsible for non-section branches, and later from Len Wines, who, like Green, was to become general secretary of the Association, and Victor Feather, then TUC assistant secretary and appointed to lead the fight against Communists in the unions.

They received many offers of help, some of them embarrassing. One from the Tory trade union organisation was firmly rejected. The Civil Service Catholic Trade Union Group gave some assistance with the distribution of documents. The CCC declared it would not accept money except from CSCA members or branches.

The Committee welcomed support from any CSCA members who were opposed to the Communists. Some were probably Conservatives or Blimpish ex-officers back from the services, some were members of other left-wing sects. One, Arthur George, was a member of the Socialist Party of Great Britain, a much older extreme left organisation than the British Communist Party. George made a speech attacking the Communist international motion at the 1947 conference and came near the top in elections for the Executive for several years afterwards. The majority, however, were middle-of-the-road Labour supporters.

The first major problem facing the Committee was how to reach the CSCA membership. Perhaps it could get an occasional letter printed in *Red Tape* but it could not build a campaign on that. It decided to use the public Press and on October 27 called a Press conference to publicise what it was trying to do, though it knew trade unionists always resented outside interference. It got considerable publicity. Three days later the Ministry of Fuel and Power branch called a special meeting to denounce Communist infiltration into the union and adopted with only two dissenters a resolution supporting the Branch Executive in taking action against Communist infiltration.

On the date of the initial Press conference, Walker, who was chairman of the Committee, wrote to Len White saying there was a large and growing body of opinion within the Association that the majority of the National Executive Committee, because of their political beliefs, could not truly represent the economic well-being of the membership. So that all members could freely discuss this movement, he asked to be furnished with a complete list of branch secretaries. In White's absence, Ellerby replied that it was not the policy of the Executive to furnish individual members with addresses of branch secretaries but that any member had available the correspondence columns of *Red Tape*. But the CCC somehow got hold of a list of branch secretaries and their addresses. Exhaustive inquiries at CSCA headquarters failed to establish for certain how it had been done.

The CCC issued ten documents in all, the last one on the eve of the 1948 conference. Most of them were signed by Walker as chairman and Charles as secretary. From the beginning the committee insisted that Communist infiltration into the National Executive was the result of apathy among members. Asked for chapter and verse it said that three full-time officers of the Association had publicly declared their adherence to the Communist Party. A fourth, in its view, had made it plain that he was a fellow-traveller. Of the honorary officers and elected members, nine, in the Committee's opinion, followed the Communist line. For the rest, it could only say that the voting was always secure. It made a long list of Communist front organisations to which contributions had been made from Association funds. It stated that the *Daily Worker* convened a conference under the title 'Britain's Way Forward' in June 1947. A report on the conference was presented to the Executive by Frank Martin, one of the left officials, in July 1947, and it was arranged that a printed report be circulated. It was then agreed that a donation of £25 be made to the 'Britain's Way Forward' organisation.

On March 21, 1946, according to the CCC, the National Executive agreed to ask the TUC for information about the Women's International Democratic Federation, which had invited the Association to affiliate. The TUC replied that the conference which formed the Federation was Communist in inspiration and management and that, so far as Great Britain was concerned, it was not representative of any responsible women's organisation. On May 5 the NEC agreed to affiliate provided the affiliation fees were reasonable.

The CCC also published accounts by its supporters of Association schools at which, it was alleged, there had been much Communist propaganda. The introduction of one-week summer schools, in addition to the war-time weekend schools built up by Muriel Coult, now a full-time officer and Communist Party member, provided an opportunity for exerting political influence and for making

CCC insists Communist infiltration is the result of apathy among members

contact with potential supporters.

A fortnight after the CCC opened its campaign, Len White circulated a reply to branch secretaries on behalf of the NEC. The allegation that the Association was dominated by Communists, it said, was supported by a number of assertions and a notable absence of evidence. The Executive whole-heartedly agreed with the signatories to the CCC's initial document that there should be no discrimination against members on political, racial or religious grounds. Unfortunately the signatories, after enunciating this basic trade union principle, went on to contradict themselves by calling for a campaign to prevent members or sympathisers with the Communist Party from holding national office in the Association.

It was not good trade union practice, the NEC said, nor was it in line with the constitution of the CSCA that individual members, however strongly they felt about particular matters, should get together in this way to circularise branches in an attempt to determine Association policy. The NEC was democratically elected at annual conferences from nominations submitted by branches. The NEC asked members and branches to set their faces strongly against any attempt to introduce into the CSCA any kind of political discrimination against officers and members.

There was some evidence, it continued, that an immediate objective of the small group was to instigate and keep alive a constant state of disturbance inside the Association until the next annual conference. 'The National Executive therefore urges all branches and individual members to ignore all communications from this group and any similar attempts to foster internecine strife, and it is confident that the good sense of branch officials will tell them what should be done with such documents.'

Another official document, *The National Executive Committee and the Heresy Hunters* listed the achievements of the NEC in 1947 in securing improvements in pay, the establishment of temporaries and other matters, and added: 'Is the Executive Committee which produces these results being fairly criticised? Let your test be the real one, i.e. regardless of political convictions, have they produced the goods? The truthful answer is that no year has been more fruitful in the history of the CSCA than 1947 and that result has been produced against an economic background of great difficulty.'

Early in 1948, the CCC announced its intention to publish a list of recommended nominees for election who had a fine record and would serve the entire membership. The NEC expressed themselves shocked at the 'audacity' of this attempt to fix the elections. By this time it had become apparent that the CCC had attracted a large following. As the date of the conferences approached, the CCC published a detailed analysis of the voting in 1947 designed to show how plumping, the organised concentration of votes for particular nominees, had been used to secure the return of Communist group candidates. On the eve of the 1948 conference, again at Prestatyn Holiday Camp, the CCC published its own list of nominees and dissolved its organisation, which meant it ceased to make public statements and publish leaflets.

The 1948 conference was one of the most dramatic in the history of the Association and one in which delegates were least consistent in their attitude. No one could predict the result of any vote before the figures were announced. The CCC nominee, Walter Leftly (sometimes known as Wily Walter), was elected president with a big majority over G A Redding of the Left, 2,496 to 1,603. The CCC also got elected the senior vice-president, Fred Houghton, and about half the members of the Executive Committee. While to a large extent accepting the CCC's advice as to whom to vote for, the delegates passed a resolution deploring the

Dramatic conference at the Prestatyn Holiday Camp

Len White (left) with Walter Leftly (centre) and Bill Hicks, the Communist he replaced as president

activities of the Committee and condemning the disclosure to the Press of confidential NEC minutes (which the CCC had done), and yet another recording appreciation of the work performed by the NEC during the year and expressing confidence in Headquarters' officers. The conference decided to cancel its affiliation to the British Soviet Society but, by a narrow majority, to continue affiliation to the National Council for Civil Liberties, and deplored the contribution of £25 to 'Britain's Way Forward'.

Voting power on the NEC was now about equally divided. Sometimes members of one bloc or the other were recalled urgently from holidays or elsewhere to cast votes and a number of times Leftly used his casting vote. The moderates had behind them all the numerous pressures exerted by the Cold War through the media, the Government's Communist purge and the TUC, which was engaged in a world-wide struggle. The World Federation of Trade Unions split in two. The Communists captured the main French trade union movement. In Britain there was battle in many of the major unions. Some, like the Transport and General Workers' Union, adopted rules preventing Communists from holding office. The Communists gained control of the Electrical Trades Union and only a famous court case eventually dislodged them. A number of Civil Service associations besides the CSCA became involved. In the Post Office Engineering Union events presented a parallel to those in the CSCA, but there the moderates organised themselves at an earlier stage as 'the bloc' and made a practice of meeting on the eve of every conference to choose their nominees for election, a tactic which proved to be effective.

In the CSCA the conflict was more open than in most unions. In 1949 the moderates pulled ahead and within a few years they had a substantial and secure majority, though for a long time the left was liable to score an unexpected victory at the annual conference. Letters in *Red Tape* continually dealt with various aspects of the struggle, sometimes dying away a little and then reviving as a result of some provocation by one side or the other, with the editor always keeping a careful balance. Occasionally some theme was held to justify full-length articles on both sides. In October 1948, Ellerby defended the National Council of Civil Liberties (NCCL) against attacks made at the annual conference by moderates, who at that time regarded it as a left organisation. The following month, Bill Brough was given space to reply and the subject was taken up in the post-bag until the 1949 conference decided to break off its affiliation with the NCCL. At the end of 1948, the TUC attacked Communist infiltration in the unions in a document called *Defend Democracy*. The NEC decided to circulate it to branches, but by such a small majority that an article by Len White headed *The Red Scapegoat* was also published. On the opposite page, there was an article by Len Wines headed *The Red Menace*. The NEC decided to take no action on the document, however, and this decision was endorsed by the 1949 conference by 7,655 votes to 6,298. In October 1949, Communist Bill Hicks and George Green met in public debate at the Caxton Hall on the meaning of the words liberty and democracy, with cheering supporters on both sides. In January 1950, Len White wrote an article containing his reflections and questions for 1950, so Gerry Gerrard replied with an article containing his reflections and questions.

The CSCA rejects affiliation to the Labour Party

At the beginning of December it was announced that 55,569 members had voted against the setting up of a political fund and only 14,693 in favour, a result which ruled out affiliation to the Labour Party, and meant the CSCA could not spend money on any political objects. This did not mean, as White pointed out, that because the CSCA left party politics alone, politics in the wider sense would leave it alone. It certainly did nothing to halt the political in-fighting within the Association.

The left achieved one of its most spectacular *tours de force* at the next conference when Ann George secured the passing of a motion condemning 11 named moderate members of the NEC, including the two vice-presidents, for voting on the Executive for the adoption of a policy on pay contrary to an annual conference decision. The 11 members were instructed that the duty of persons elected to the NEC was to further Association policy, not to oppose it. However, the offenders were re-elected.

By the 1951 conference, the anti-Communists had a substantial majority on the Executive, but they opposed a series of four resolutions designed to secure the dismissal of Communist full-time officers and the motions failed. Legal problems would have resulted from such a course. The Executive supported, though with some moderate opposition, a motion inviting Len White to remain in office until he was 60, instead of retiring at 55, which was carried by 8,771 votes to 3,454. According to rule, White would have left in November 1952, and Ellerby, his deputy, the following year. It was felt that for the Association's two leading negotiators to retire within a year of each other would have seriously weakened the organisation. They had established throughout the Service a very high reputation as a negotiating team, with White as the man with imaginative and fertile mind working on a factual basis prepared by Ellerby.

After giving White another five years, the conference passed a resolution pledging continued opposition to Communism or any form of dictatorship which would curtail or remove the existing power and functions of trade unions. From this it went on to carry unanimously a resolution on freedom and democracy: 'Believing in the fundamental rights and freedoms of the individual, conference avers its determination to maintain the CSCA as a truly free, independent and democratic organisation. To this end it declares Association membership and officership open to all eligible persons irrespective of their race, colour, creed, religion or political beliefs, and rejects any theories of discrimination against members on such grounds. It states, however, that the pursuit of party politics, religious beliefs, dogmas and other forms of ideologies should be kept outside the Association sphere where there is ample scope for such matters to be ventilated and there is complete freedom for all to do so.'

'This is a resolution,' said Len White, 'which has to be implemented not only by the NEC but by every member of the Association.'

The conference has been remembered as an unusually good-humoured one but it is difficult to interpret the mood which produced the odd sequence of resolutions. President Fred Houghton referred in his opening speech to the mass meetings on pay which had been held in London and provincial towns in the preceding 12 months 'The same militant spirit prevailed throughout the country,' he said, 'a spirit of determination to end the petty quarrels in our own ranks and to unite in a common endeavour.'

Within a couple of months, however, the two factions were at each other's throats again. It began with a left-wing accusation that a list of candidates for election had been circulated, presumably 'the child of the successors of the Conference Campaign Committee', and four branches demanded a special conference to consider banning such lists. There was talk about other lists and about the NEC suppressing some list said to have been found in a Communist's wastepaper basket and it all went on in a vague, desultory way until the 1952 conference, when the NEC's refusal to call a special conference or change the voting system was endorsed. During this period, the moderates strengthened small holes in their defences by abolishing, after an inquiry led by Gerrard, the National Youth Advisory Committee, which they had sometimes found politically embarrassing, and by removing associate members (who included influential left-wingers) from the panels of lecturers at Association schools. There was a general desire to prevent the Association being influenced by experienced old colleagues who had been promoted. In addition Gerry Gerrard, now a vice-president and chairman of the Education Committee, persuaded White to replace Muriel Coult by Greg Challis as Secretary of the Committee.

In 1956, the NEC ran into a storm of trouble for adopting a resolution expressing grave concern about the Franco-British Suez adventure. This time, the storm did not come from the Communists, who were busy trying to maintain their membership after the shock of Soviet intervention in Hungary, but from the silent majority who occasionally played a part in the Association's history. The resolution they took to the 1957 annual conference was restrained in tone. The NEC, it said, had acted injudiciously and made an error of judgement and directed that in future it should observe principles which steered a middle course between isolationism and harmful controversy. George Green made a mild and thoughtful reply for the Executive, but while the first anger at the resolution had faded there was never any doubt that the critical resolution would be passed.

A storm over the Franco-British Suez adventure

With the appointment of George Green as general secretary and election of Tom Lillywhite as president, with no limit on the number of years he could hold the office, there was relative peace in the Association. The moderates were in full control but phrases like 'self-perpetuating oligarchy' began to appear in the letters' column of *Red Tape*, as did 'a plague on both your houses'. The 1959 conference opened with another row about the circulation of election documents, but Lillywhite dismissed it as 'a little spit and spat' and it ended with an apology. In the early 1960s there were letters about the H-bomb, re-armament, the TUC and politics. The subject of voting lists kept cropping up.

Getting a majority on the Executive was a comparatively straightforward job for the moderates in the post-war atmosphere. There were annual elections and all they had to do was to persuade enough branches to vote for their nominees. But there were still the full-time officers who had been appointed during the period of left-wing rule, for the most part experienced, able and tough men and women,

*Ian McPherson, Assistant
General Secretary and
Treasurer whose CSCA
career was cut short by
his early death*

who were not subject to re-election. It has been mentioned that the moderates held back from attempting to sack the Communists among them, but something could be done when promotions or new appointments were made. Some moved out of their own accord and some were affected by Government purges.

After White and Ellerby, whose positions were unassailable, the most senior full-time officers were Green, Wines, Charles Smith and Ian McPherson. Smith, an MP from 1945 to 1950, was then considered left-wing. He at one time hoped to succeed Ellerby as Deputy General Secretary but George Green told Len White he saw no reason to stand down in his favour and in due course Green was appointed. Smith accepted the position of General Secretary of the Post Office Engineering Union and eventually became Lord Delacourt-Smith and a junior minister. McPherson, a respected middle-of-the-road officer, was made Assistant General Secretary and Treasurer when Wines became Deputy General Secretary and he would have succeeded Wines as Deputy General Secretary had it not been for his unexpected death.

This meant the most senior remaining assistant secretaries had been appointed during the period of left domination. One of the seven appointees, Wilfred Fienburgh, had resigned earlier to take up a political career in the Labour Party in which he was expected to go far, but he was killed in a car accident. Muriel Coult gave notice that she wished to retire from the Association to take up teaching.

When Green was refused an extension of his period as General Secretary in 1962, therefore, the NEC had to decide whether to promote to deputy general secretary or treasurer any of the other left-wing appointees, all of whom had at least five years greater seniority than any of the officers appointed after the moderates took over. Frank Martin, George Jamieson, Margaret Leaver, Alan Ryalls and Greg Challis all applied for the jobs, but the Executive decided to pass them over and nominate moderates: Bill Kendall for the position of deputy general secretary and Gerry Gerrard for that of general treasurer. All the left nominees appealed to the 1963 annual conference except Challis, who as a matter of principle had ceased to be associated with any faction after becoming a full-time officer in 1947.

Martin, in his written appeal, referred to the comparative lack of seniority of the NEC members who made the recommendation. Not one of them, he said, took part in the original appointments of the appellants.

'That is true,' conceded the NEC. 'The CSCA was, in those days, in the hands of the Communist Party and its supporters. It was not wrested from the control of Communists and Communist sympathisers until 1949. For some six years prior to that date, the Communists and their supporters had misused the Association for the ends of Communism and brought it into close alignment with the policies and actions of the Communist Party. Appointments to many full-time posts in that era were conditioned by this circumstance.'

By the time of the 1963 conference, the situation had changed as a result of a new phase in the Government's Communist purge, based on the recommendations of the Radcliffe Committee. For the first time emphasis was placed not only on employing Communists and their supporters in the Civil Service but also on the risks involved in negotiating with Communist association officials in sensitive departments.

'We inquired,' the Committee said, 'into the penetration by Communists of the Civil Service staff associations and trade unions and were disturbed at the number of Communists and Communist sympathisers who were holding posts in those bodies either as permanent full-time paid officials or as unpaid officers or members of executive committees. We understand that there is no evidence the Communists have made any exceptional effort to get control of these unions, but they appear in fact to have achieved a higher degree of penetration here than in almost any other section of the trade union movement. No evidence has been brought to our knowledge that Communist trade union officers, whether serving on a paid or unpaid basis, have been detected in any form of espionage. Nevertheless we regard this presumably deliberate massing of Communist effort in the Civil Service unions as most dangerous to security, however one defines it.'

The 1962 conference had debated the report and adopted a resolution saying that, while all suitable safeguards should be available to protect the rights of members and officers who might be affected, the conference could not ignore the impact on the public of the report's references to penetration by Communists and Communist sympathisers of full-time and honorary posts in the Civil Service Staff Association movement and the possible threat thereby involved to the security of the country. The NEC was instructed to review the position and to take any steps that might be necessary in the interests of the Association.

Two of the full-time officers appealing against the NEC recommendations, Jamieson and Ryalls, had to retire, with lump sum compensation in addition to normal superannuation, after appearing before the committee set up to advise ministers. The Association's alternative was to confine those who failed to pass the test to jobs which could involve no security risk, but it was felt that since they could not perform the full range of duties, their continued employment was not in the interests of the Association, a view endorsed by the conference. So only Frank Martin and Margaret Leaver were left. She had taken the step, before the conference, of advertising in *The Times* that she had been cleared as a security risk.

Both made personal appeals at the conference against the non-recommendation for promotion. Martin, who was 52, would probably have been ruled out on age grounds in any case. Margaret Leaver made a long, eloquent speech which produced

The Radcliffe Committee reports on Communist penetration of Civil Service Associations

*Florence Bonsor, a Moderate
sometimes described as the
Queen Bee, who had two
spells as Association President*

a rousing reception. The case for the NEC was put by Florence Bonsor, one of the most formidable and able of all the moderates. She did not try to avoid the heart of the matter: 'The next consideration we had to bear in mind was the very delicate subject of what people believe and the attitudes they may strike. It is all too easy to say that these things should not matter and that all that did matter was the way people did their job. Our membership many years ago went on record against extremism and we believe that is still the mood of our members. One can say that individuals change and mellow with the years but I put it to you that old memories die hard and the NEC is bound to hesitate a very long time before taking chances with people appointed to these very important positions.' The Executive recommendations were endorsed by overwhelming majorities.

Martin retired in the autumn of 1965 and Margaret Leaver resigned in the spring of the following year. They had all gone and the NEC was now composed almost entirely of moderates. The old left wave had completely subsided. But here and there about the country there were signs that a new one was beginning to swell.

CHAPTER THIRTEEN
Brown's Last Stand

Before a House of Commons Committee of Privileges, May 13, 1947. Mr Winston Churchill, a member of the Committee, examines Mr Leonard Charles White, General Secretary of the Civil Service Clerical Association.

Churchill: *You spoke of the pressure that was put upon Mr Brown and you said that there was pressure from certain elements in your organisation?*

White: *Yes.*

Churchill: *That pressure related not to the discharge of the special duties he had with the Association, but to his general parliamentary conduct?*

White: *Yes.*

Churchill: *Parliamentary conduct and the political situation generally?*

White: *Yes.*

Churchill: *But, in particular, his parliamentary conduct is the only thing that involves us in the question of privilege. Did you consider yourself that this was a breach of the agreement they had made with Mr Brown?*

White: *I was in no doubt at all that a breach of agreement was involved, both in trying to stop him expressing freely his political views and in trying to get rid of him if he was not prepared to stop.*

Churchill: *It was a case of pressure put upon Mr Brown because of his discharge of his parliamentary duties in what he conceived to be a conscientious manner?*

White: *Yes, sir. It had nothing to do, of course, with his Civil Service duties.*

Thus Len White bluntly accused his left-wing Executive of breaking the Association's contract with his old leader and friend, Bill Brown. At the end White asked the indulgence of the Committee of Privileges to explain that he was in a difficult position. 'On the one hand, I disagree with Brown politically, but on the other hand I disagree with the Executive Committee in this matter. Therefore, I stand to be shot at from both sides.'

'We sympathise with you,' replied the chairman, Arthur Greenwood. 'A lot of us stand to be shot at, I am afraid.'

The episode was part of a long struggle by the NEC to get rid of Brown which, like the Conference Campaign Committee conflict, reached a climax at the 1948 annual conference. The controversy impinged on the CCC struggle without becoming a critical part of it. The left was accused occasionally of scheming to get Brown out and it sometimes referred to the CCC supporters as Brownites but he

Winston Churchill

*Brown with a bust of himself
made by the Russian sculptor,
Avram Melnikoff*

still had a following and probably neither side was sure that anything would be gained by making the issue a main one.

The origin of the affair was the contract signed between Brown and the Association when Brown was made parliamentary general secretary in 1942. This laid it down that: 'The said William John Brown shall deal with all questions arising out of the work of the Association which require parliamentary or political action and shall advise the Association from time to time on such matters,' but it also laid it down that: 'The said William John Brown shall be entitled to engage in his political activities with complete freedom.' So far as his work for the Association was concerned, he was as energetic and effective as ever and gave complete satisfaction. But his political activities caused increasing embarrassment. Apart from his Commons work, he built up a reputation as a broadcaster in the early part of the war and later as a journalist contributing regularly to the *Evening Standard* and occasionally to *Time and Tide*. Whenever he gave a series of broadcasts or wrote a series of articles, or went on a journey somewhere, a book would follow. There was one when he went to the United States, one when he spent Christmas with Lord Beaverbrook in Jamaica in 1946 and one when he spent Christmas with Beaverbrook again in 1947. He wrote a booklet about the Civil Service and one about Parliamentary procedure, and his autobiography, *So Far . . .*, appeared in 1943. There was also a volume called *Success – Your Birthright*, consisting of commonsense advice about everything from how to avoid constipation and insomnia, to the Good Law and how to add one's brick to the design of the cosmos.

All this gave Brown great scope for the expression of personal views which he used regularly to attack Russia and the Communist Party and frequently the TUC, the closed shop and the Labour Party. Members complained that this gave a false impression of the policies of the CSCA. The news that Royal assent had been given to the repeal of the Trade Disputes Act came through while the CSCA 1946 conference was in session and the Association at once reaffiliated to the TUC. It was hardly conducive to cordial relations with its new colleagues to have Brown attacking the trade union movement up hill and down dale. Brown supported repeal of the Act but was against CSCA affiliation.

The Labour Party situation was somewhat different. The NEC strongly favoured affiliation, the Communists seemingly more strongly than others because the Communist Party was working hard at the time to strengthen its base inside the Labour Party, with which it was still seeking affiliation. There had to be a ballot of members before the CSCA could affiliate because of the 1913 Act and the way Brown talked would hardly encourage them to vote for affiliation.

It all came to a head at the 1946 Trades Union Congress, when the CSCA nominated White for the new Civil Service seat on the General Council and he was defeated by Charlie Geddes of the Union of Post Office Workers by 3·3 million votes to 2·3 million. Since the Post Office Workers had had a long previous association with the TUC, Geddes was a strong candidate and White's relationship with the *Daily Worker* would hardly commend him to the right-wing TUC leadership of that period, the result was perhaps hardly surprising. But the Association's delegation, including McMillan, then President, was convinced that Brown's attacks on the TUC had adversely affected the voting and determined to propose to the next NEC meeting that if he was unwilling to discontinue his criticisms, his services to the Association should be terminated. White suggested a compromise solution under which Brown would give up the title of Parliamentary General Secretary and a public statement would be issued making it clear that the Association was in no way responsible for his speeches, actions or writings on general political questions. The NEC was overwhelmingly against this solution. Instead, it decided to seek negotiations with Brown with the object of arriving at agreed terms for ending the contract. 'There comes a time,' it said, 'when an agreement of this sort becomes so irksome in its operation that one of the parties is justified in asking for release from the obligations the contract imposes.'

The National Executive Committee seeks to terminate Brown's contract

White argued strongly against this course in the interests of the membership. Since Brown had no desire to leave the Association permanently, or to modify in any way the terms of his agreement, his departure could only be secured by buying him out. White warned the Executive members that 'they were going into negotiations without holding one single card in the pack.'

In January 1947, White proposed that the question of Brown's position should be deferred for three months so the ballot on affiliation with the Labour Party could take place first, but the President argued that if the ballot revealed the political viewpoint of the NEC was not shared by the majority of the members (both White and McMillan thought it was not), the Parliamentary General Secretary would be put in the position of saying that he had been right all the way through. White also pointed out that McMillan, in his 1947 presidental speech, had severely criticised the activities of the Labour Government. 'In view of the fact that one of the two declared reasons for proposing to terminate Mr Brown's agreement was his criticism of the Labour Government, the question arises whether the right to criticise the Labour Government is resident only in the President and is denied to the Parliamentary General Secretary who, by the precise terms of his agreement, had political freedom conferred upon him. Or is it that a particular kind of criticism of the Labour Government is permissible, and that Mr Brown's criticisms were of the wrong kind? I find myself quite unable to reconcile the action proposed against Mr Brown because of his political criticisms with the fact that the President of the Association indulges and, in my view quite rightly indulges, in political criticisms as emphatic and comprehensive as any that have come from the Parliamentary General Secretary.'

The NEC found the terms of agreement with Brown as costly as White had warned they would be. In addition to £3,243 for salary which would have accrued if he had remained until his normal retiring date of September 13, 1949, they provided for commuted pension and gratuity rights, continued use of the Association car, office and secretarial facilities, an *ex gratia* payment of £1,000 and the launching of a testimonial fund, with corresponding payments to Miss Cormack, Brown's secretary. The NEC gave way on every point raised by Brown but negotiations broke down because the parties could not agree on the terms of a joint statement to members conveying that it was an agreed solution to the problem. The NEC decided to put the question to the 1947 conference. But at this stage, on Brown's initiative, the question was raised in the House of Commons as one of Parliamentary privilege, and a Committee of Privileges was set up. Action within the Association was halted for the time being.

In his evidence to the Committee, Brown argued that there had been intereference with the complete political freedom to which he was entitled, culminating in an endeavour to get him to give up his post. The first approach was not to throw him out but to buy him out and, when he would not have that, to create a situation by the passing of a resolution which would have made it extremely difficult, if not impossible, to carry on. He was prepared to go to any reasonable lengths to reach a settlement, but, he added: 'I was not prepared to see myself driven out by a conspiracy which in my view originates with the Communist elements and their fellow-travellers on the National Executive Committee, and the parallel of which I have seen in other organisations. There is a wide trade union issue involved there.' He felt it was intolerable that a man's work in Parliament should be shadowed by this kind of thing. It seemed to him a negation of his conception of representative democracy and a breach of the rights and freedoms of Members of the House.

McMillan, supported by the two vice-presidents, Jimmy James and Bill Hicks, denied that the Executive Committee had at any time put pressure on Brown to change his political view or not to give expression to them. The Executive wished to secure a termination of the agreement because Brown's expressed political views were inconsistent with the policy of the organisation.

The Committee of Privileges decided there had been no breach of privilege and that the Executive Committee was entitled to bring the question of the termination of the agreement before the annual conference of the Association, as it had in effect been invited by Brown to do. The NEC, which had placed Brown on leave pending the Committee of Privileges' decision, now restored him to his duties and prepared a complex resolution for the 1948 conference, intended to terminate Brown's connection with the Association when he reached the retiring age of 55 the following year.

A couple of months before the conference, Brown made a speech in the House of Commons which may well have contributed to the result of the battle. He asked whether the Minister of Defence and the Air Minister were satisfied about defences against the cold war. 'How many members of the Communist Party are there serving in the headquarters of the Air Ministry today?' he demanded to know. 'I know at least one Communist who is serving there, because he is the President of my union. I have reasons enough to know both of his existence and of his unpleasant qualities. Is the Air Minister satisfied about the defences on the side of internal security? I have some reason for asking this question and we want to know the answer in respect of this department. There are cabinet ministers in Britain with Communists as their private secretaries; or at least one cabinet minister who has a Communist as his private secretary. Whether he knows of it or not, I do not know but I know of it. Are we satisfied about our protection against the internal enemy, the penetration and the erosion from within which delivered Czecho-

Bill Hicks

slovakia as a helpless corpse into the hands of the Russians last week?'

The acting president of the CSCA at this time was Hicks, who had taken over until the annual conference when McMillan was promoted. He was a friendly, self-educated extrovert who liked to go round in an open shirt and spend his holidays on such pursuits as cycling round Ireland or walking in the Cairngorms. He joined the Communist Party in 1945 because, he said, he found himself almost always voting on the same side, and has remained a Party member ever since. His unpleasant qualities in Brown's view consisted of moving anti-Brown motions on the NEC.

Probably no other speech by Brown had ever aroused more resentment in the CSCA, and nobody felt it more strongly than Stanley Mayne, still closely interested in Association affairs. For want of any stronger gesture, he wrote to Brown, resigning his chairmanship of the W J Brown Parliamentary Fund. 'The step you have now taken in the House means, if it means anything, that you have virtually called for the dismissal from the Service of the President, Bill Hicks. This is something I cannot stomach. As chairman of the fund I maintained over the years that your political wanderings were your own affair; support for the fund was on the basis of your value to the Civil Service. Now you use your position in the House to do the Civil Service serious hurt. Political discrimination in the Civil Service is a shocking proposal. It is one which would once have been as much anathema to you as it still is to me. Moreover it is a proposal you make specially to spite one who was over a number of years, to your knowledge as well as mine, a stalwart supporter of political freedom for you.'

Brown in reply denied that he called, either virtually or otherwise, for the dismissal from the Service of Hicks. He added: 'As regards Hicks having been a stalwart supporter of political freedom for me, he has been, as you must surely know, the prime mover in the events of the last year or two which led up to my complaint in the House of Commons.'

Brown made his speech in the House on March 4. Ten days later, the Prime Minister, Clement Attlee, made a long-awaited announcement on security. In future no one known to be a member of the Communist Party or associated with it would be employed in work vital to the security of the State. The State was not concerned with the political views as such of its servants, and as far as possible alternative employment would be found for those deemed unsuitable for secret work. A committee was set up to give advice to ministers on particular cases.

Hicks was suspended from his official duties on June 3. He had been Secretary of the Air Ministry Departmental Staff Side, and the full Staff Side sent a deputation to the Air Minister, Arthur Henderson, to express its belief in Hicks' integrity and loyalty and to ask the minister to reconsider his decision. Henderson said he accepted that Hicks' character and integrity were beyond reproach but he had to implement the policy laid down by the Prime Minister. Hicks was sent back to his former department, the Ministry of Health.

Meanwhile, the 1948 Association conference had taken place and a resolution carried with acclamation expressing strong disapproval of Brown's speech. Brown, unrepentant, replied: 'I will never accept the view that we owe any loyalty to people who are enemies of the country in whose House of Parliament I sit. I have made a statement which expresses my views of Communist methods, filth and political immorality. I have no apology to make for it.'

The private secretary mentioned by Brown in his speech was Ann George, who was assistant private secretary to George Tomlinson, Minister of Education. She was a forthright left-winger who later married Bill Ellerby. Miss George was

Ann George

asked to state whether or not she was a member of the Communist Party. After consulting the Association branch of which she was Secretary, she replied to Sir John Maude, Permanent Secretary to the Ministry of Education, refusing either to deny or admit the charge and insisting that no employer had any right to ask such a question.

'The Minister and those who know me intimately do not really doubt my loyalty,' she wrote. 'I find no difficulty at all in never allowing my trade union loyalties to interfere with my official loyalties, and I was most scrupulous in never allowing any knowledge gained in one field to become a guide to action in another. Like many thousands of persons, I have not dual but manifold loyalties, and if I ever found myself in a position in which those other loyalties came into serious conflict, then I should take steps to resolve the difficulty with full regard to my position as a public servant.'

To the indignation of her branch, which passed a unanimous resolution of confidence in her, Ann George was transferred to the Victoria and Albert Museum, but was promoted before long.

Hicks presided over the 1948 conference with such good-humoured impartiality that he drew a public word of appreciation from Cliff Charles, though he suffered the disappointment of not being able to stand for the presidency during the following 12 months. His own Air Ministry branch decided not to nominate him and declined to give approval to his nomination by 16 other branches. There were differences of opinion as to whether his branch's consent was necessary under the rules but the conference decided by 3,091 votes to 2,909 not to allow his nomination to stand. The rules were later changed to deprive a candidate's branch of an absolute veto.

Since White was against it, Bill Ellerby moved the motion to terminate Brown's position in the Association. He said the fundamental problem was that Brown and the union had been travelling along different roads. 'Today Brown is obsessed with the anti-red bug and has used labels like Communist and fellow-traveller to blackguard his opponents. Every Executive over the last 10 to 15 years has been accused of being political. Years before that, when Brown was an ardent socialist and a member of the Labour Party, this association was affiliated to the TUC and the Labour Party and at the time of the General Strike Brown was referred to as Bolshevik Brown by the reactionaries amongst our members. He was said to be leading the Association to destruction. Brown now claims that much of what he fought for in his youth was nonsense. I prefer the Brown of the General Strike – the Socialist Bill Brown . . . I prefer the Bill Brown who on the question of whether the Union should be political, said: "There has never been any other course open to us but to be political whether we want to be political or not. We cannot help being political because of the conditions under which we work." And by being political Brown meant being affiliated with the Labour Party as long as it was strongly socialist. We stand today where Brown stood then.

'Brown has rebutted all this now, but in the long run the workers will recognise those who truly represent their interest, as the Executive Committee is doing . . . I think that there are many of you who will not believe it, but your Executive Committee is a very mixed political group. It is not Communist dominated. It has tried to do a good job under very difficult circumstances.'

Brown's reply was as challenging as ever. 'Let me make it utterly plain that I renounce publicly and in front of you any rights of security of tenure which my agreements with the Association may give me. You may regard those clauses of the agreements, so far as I am concerned, whether I am entitled to stay until 55 or 99,

Ellerby says Brown is obsessed with the anti-red bug

as completely washed out. I do not want to stay unless it is made plain that I stay by the general desire of this conference. But I must also make it plain that I am not willing as a condition of staying to accept the slightest restriction on my political freedom whatever. I am not disposed to qualify my written or spoken utterances in any way whatever. I propose to live my life as I have always done on the basis of Emerson's "If a man would be a man, let him speak the truth as he sees it in words as hard as cannon balls. And tomorrow let him speak the truth of tomorrow in words as hard, even though they contradict every word he says today." ' If the speeches he made in the past, quoted by Ellerby, corresponded with the speeches he now made, he argued, the assumption would be that he was an unintellectual moron who had learned nothing from 40 years of life.

Brown moved towards one more of his famous perorations: 'In an hour's time I shall have been vindicated or I shall be free. I am not staying on for another year even on the basis that the Executive Committee would like to get rid of me now but think it hardly worthwhile since I have only got another year to go. I will only stay on on the basis that the vast mass of this conference desires, whether it agrees with me or not, that I should carry on the work I have tried to do in the last 35 years. I beg you to be clear in your decision, so that there shall be no doubt in the mind of Parliament or anybody else that when I speak on Civil Service matters I speak the mind of the organisation which I substantially founded, whose napkins I changed, which I put into long trousers and launched into adult life. The time has come you may think, for us to part. All right: I shall not quarrel with you if that is your view. You may think that I should carry on. All right: whatever your answer be, be it yea or nay, whatever is more than these cometh of evil.'

Brown seemed to be giving a rash hostage to fortune when he said he would only stay on if the vast mass of the conference desired it. He may have believed that he could sway the delegates even as he did in 1931, but he and they had changed. The Brown whose eyes once shone with missionary zeal seemed to many of the new generation of delegates just a vainglorious, middle-aged man whose appearance reflected his fondness for the fleshpots. The magic had gone. His old ally, Min Jackson, now a somewhat severe Controller of Typists, came to his aid with an amendment instructing the Executive to retain his services so long as he remained a member of the House of Commons, but her amendment was defeated by 2,990 votes to 2,486 and the Executive motion carried by 3,343 to 2,152.

Delegates, amid some excitement, asked for a statement from Brown in view of the categorical declaration he had made in his speech. Brown first said he would wait until the results of the Executive elections were known and then that in view of the destruction of the Communist domination of the Executive, he was willing to stay on until the 1949 conference. In the event, he did not stay so long. In October 1948, he wrote to Leftly, the President, saying he would like to give up his job at the end of the year. The NEC agreed and new terms of settlement were signed, including as before his salary to his retiring date, a sum in commutation of his pension rights, the office car and some furniture, with an additional £4,000 to Brown and £1,000 to Jean Cormack from the WJB Guarantee Fund. This was the fund set up in 1919 to ensure the future security of himself and his secretary. No one quite knew to whom it belonged.

Brown negotiates his departure terms

The furniture Brown was to have, it had been agreed, consisted of a few articles of sentimental value. The Finance and Organisation Committee was rather surprised to receive a list which included a carpet and rug, desk and fitments, desk armchair, leather armchair, lounge armchair, six armchairs, roll-up front cabinet, steel bookshelves, hat stand, electric fire, wastepaper basket, clock, table, standard

lamp, four filing trays, one everlasting calendar, one pair of curtains and pictures, and an equally long list from Jean Cormack's room. The NEC realised that in the aftermath of the war office furniture was both difficult to obtain and expensive, and parting tributes showed that the members were still conscious of what Brown had done for the Association. Nevertheless there was some feeling that the term sentimental value had been illegitimately stretched.

Some delegates to the 1949 annual conference treated the matter lightly At one social occasion Bill Ellerby featured Brown addressing his office furniture in a ditty which went:

> *I couldn't bear the parting,*
> *I'll need you all once more,*
> *But I've left the paint upon the walls*
> *And the varnish on the floor*

But others reacted more strongly and passed a vote of censure on the Executive Committee for disposing of the bulk of the Guarantee Fund and of office furniture and equipment to Brown without the consent of the annual conference. The motion also asked for legal opinion to be obtained on the possibility of regaining for the CSCA the value that had been lost. It was a mean end to an outstanding career in the Association.

Brown lost his parliamentary seat at Rugby in the 1950 general election but continued his political and journalistic activities for some years. He also continued to occasionally champion break-away unions against the big battalions. One of these was EOTA, the Engineering Officers (Telecommunications) Association, whose claim to recognition was opposed by the Post Office Engineering Union. In 1950 Brown became the EOTA national negotiator. When the Postmaster General, Ness Edwards, suggested a truce, Brown insisted that EOTA must first be recognised and the POEU unaffiliated from the TUC which was 'not entirely a non-political organisation'. Edwards appointed a committee under Lord Terrington to examine the problem of trade union recognition in the department, but Brown said the committee's report might have been 'drafted by a committee of the Nazi party concerned with the setting up of a Nazi Labour Front.' Brown resigned his position with EOTA in 1953.

In later years Brown worked from a flat in London but spent much of his time at a house in the quiet village of Wittersham in south Kent, not far from Rye. He provided a cottage round the corner for Jean Cormack, who remained faithful to him to the end and lived there until her death, while this history was being written, in the self-sufficient solitude she always loved. Brown bought some farmland a few miles away and his friend Lord Beaverbrook gave him a prize bull to develop his herd of cattle, but he does not ever seem to have been really absorbed in farming.

Brown's last years

Eventually, after a long illness, he died in 1960, at the age of 66, surprising everybody by leaving a fortune of £232,000. During the Second World War, Brown started keeping a journal, spending half an hour on it before breakfast every day, and after five years found it had already amounted to more than two million words. He wrote that it would not be published during his lifetime, and Jean Cormack was convinced that no one ever saw it but himself. Before his death he ordered that it should be destroyed, and it was duly burnt by his housekeeper.

His continued mistrust of officialdom was reflected in a clause in his will which set aside a sum to make sure he was not buried alive.

(Opposite) Brown in his middle age

CHAPTER FOURTEEN
Women on the March

The Civil Service presents as regards its non-industrial and common grades the conditions relevant to the application of equal pay in a highly simplified form. Such conditions include exact gradation of jobs, perfect interchangeability of men and women employees within each common grade, and again within each common grade, presumptively, equal efficiency of the two sexes, at least during the period when each is actively at work. Here over a big field are men and women doing identical jobs, doing them well, and doing them on unequal pay.'
Royal Commission on Equal Pay, 1946.

Simple though it appeared, it took many years and one of the most powerful, united and sustained political campaigns in Civil Service history to persuade the Government to make the concession to women of equal pay for equal work.

In contrast, the Government had almost to force on the associations in 1946 the removal of the marriage bar which compelled women to leave the established Service on marriage because the unions could not agree among themselves on removal of the bar. The bar had been introduced in the 19th century and was given less attention than equal pay, though some women regarded it as hardly less important. However, it was one of the subjects on which the Tomlin Royal Commission of 1929–31 was asked to express a view.

While the Tomlin Commission was sitting, Stanley Mayne initiated a crusade to get rid of the bar, supported by a number of active women members but few among the rank-and-file. When women retired to get married, they received a gratuity related to their years of service, regarded as a dowry and attractive to young men in a period when males were in short supply. The CSCA balloted its women members on the subject, the only Association to do so, and the leaders were disconcerted to find not merely that an overwhelming majority were against removal of the bar if the gratuity was forfeited, 4,795 to 138, but that a big majority were against its removal even if the gratuity was retained, 3,537 to 1,396. So although a number of associations representing higher grades opposed it, the Staff Side, with the backing of the CSCA, gave evidence in favour of preserving the bar. The Official Side also wanted to keep it and the Commission came down in favour, though exceptions were to be allowed where retention was considered advisable because of a woman's special qualifications. This loophole was rarely used.

The marriage bar controversy

In the two years before the Second World War, the subject was continuously debated in *Red Tape*, and at Branch and Youth Advisory Committee meetings between those who regarded the marriage bar as a constriction on the freedom of the individual and those who considered a married woman's place was in the home. It was decided to hold another ballot, for which ballot papers had actually been prepared when war broke out and put a stop to it. The bar was suspended during the war and at the Association's reconstruction conference in 1944, the Executive submitted a motion that it should be abolished. There were still strong feelings on both sides and the debate was the liveliest one of that conference. The bar was opposed by Len White on the grounds that it was 'anachronistic, illogical and antisocial'. He added: 'Marriage is the only sort of relationship which a woman may have with a man which the Government will not tolerate. She may live with him. She may have a child by him, in which case she is given three months special leave and still retains her job. But if she dares to marry him, she is thrown out.' He thought that so long as the bar remained, it would be impossible to get equal pay for men and women. Over and over again the Treasury had used the argument against equal pay that women had to leave on marriage and had not the same continuity of experience. In reply to the argument that if married women stayed on, it would reduce the opportunities for promotion and for establishment for others, White replied that most female civil servants would leave on marriage but there was no justification for compelling them to go.

Opponents said the abandoned ballot should be held before reaching a decision, they should consider children, who should have the care of their mothers in their early years, and if there was large-scale unemployment after the war, they did not want to be faced with the problem of pin-money married women as well as pin-money girls. An amendment in favour of retention of the bar was defeated by 2,490 votes to 1,818.

In 1945, because of manpower problems, the Prime Minister and other ministers appealed to married women to remain in employment and to employers to keep them at work. At the invitation of the Official Side, a joint committee was set up to discuss the implications of abolishing the marriage bar but the Staff Side was so divided that it could express no representative opinion. Six associations, including the Union of Post Office Workers, the Inland Revenue Staff Federation and the Ministry of Labour Staff Association, wanted to keep the bar. Four, including the CSCA, the Society of Civil Servants and the Institution of Professional Civil Servants, wanted to remove it and four had no declared view.

Quoting arguments for and against, the report of the joint committee mentioned support for removal on the grounds that the bar might discourage marriage and depress the birthrate, which was socially undesirable, and might encourage immorality. Against this was the argument that the married woman who carried on with her career might be disinclined to have children and her career might come into conflict with her husband's and prejudice the happiness of the family. Another argument against removal was that where there was a large amount of routine work to be done, it was a real advantage to employ women who stayed only a few years. The Service could not provide adequate careers for all the young people recruited to the lower grades so that a fairly rapid turnover was essential. The answer again was that most women would resign on marriage in any case so turnover would not be much affected.

On October 15, 1946, Hugh Dalton, Chancellor of the Exchequer, announced the immediate abolition of the marriage bar in the Home Civil Service. The change reflected a new attitude of the population towards working wives. In 1931, only one wife in ten was working. By 1951, the proportion had risen to more than one in five and is now more than one in two. Experience of the Second World War, smaller families, aids to housework, and expectations of a higher standard of living are no doubt among contributory factors.

The bar is abolished by the post-war government

The drive for equal pay had subsided somewhat after the disappointing end to the 1935 campaign, but during the war, when everybody was working together and women were demonstrating their abilities, there was a strong feeling, as there was with the Trade Disputes Act, that transparent injustices should be righted. After all, it was 20 years since the House of Commons had first come down in favour of equal pay and it had done so several times since. In a debate on the Education Bill in 1944, the Government was defeated on a motion for equal pay for teachers but Churchill, repeating Baldwin's tactics of 1936, got the decision overturned. The same year W J Brown tabled a House of Commons motion asking for the immediate application of equal pay in the Civil Service. He managed to get 180 signatures to the motion and was promised a debate, but a week later the Government announced it would set up a Royal Commission on the subject. Brown said the object of this was to dispose of the motion, on which the Government feared a decisive defeat, and put the question out of the way for a long time to come. A demonstration was held in Trafalgar Square supported by the Civil Service Equal Pay Committee and by some of the largest unions in the country. The terms of reference of the Commission, presided over by Sir Cyril Asquith, were not limited to the Civil Service but included the relationship between the remuneration of men and women in the public services, industry and other fields of employment, and the social, economic and financial implications of equal pay for equal work. Albert Day gave evidence for the Staff Side in favour of equal pay, which the Treasury opposed.

The Commission reported in October 1946. Although it could not make formal recommendations, the passage quoted at the beginning of this chapter was helpful to the campaigns of public service unions. Some 400 delegates from trade unions and women's organisations met shortly afterwards. Len White warned them that the Labour Government was 'just as unprincipled in its attitude to women as any private employer', but said it was apparent that the public service unions must be the spearhead of any campaign. In February, 1947, the Staff Side sent a deputation to see Hugh Dalton, Chancellor of the Exchequer, who described the report as a very poor one, long-winded, niggling and handicapped by its terms of reference. In June he accepted in a Commons statement the justice of the claim on behalf of the Government's own employees, but said that it could not be applied at that time because of the economic situation, costly developments in social policy, and because the principle, once adopted, could not be confined to public employees.

James Callaghan, MP, and Leah Manning, an MP sponsored by the National Union of Teachers, pressed the Chancellor to consider a plan to give women the male increments, thus reaching equality over a period of 12 to 18 years. This was the first public suggestion of an instalment system and caused considerable indignation among female members – particularly older women in the higher grades who had long campaigned for equal pay. The National Staff Side, however, followed up the MPs' suggestion and a scheme was prepared and discussed with the next Chancellor, Sir Stafford Cripps, in February 1948. He refused to consider even the modified form because it conflicted with his White Paper on Personal Incomes, Costs and Prices. The TUC supported the Chancellor's policy of restraint and informed the Association that the General Council was not prepared to press for equal pay at that time. The Association was thus faced with the problem of converting the TUC as well as winning public and parliamentary support.

A CSCA resolution carried at the 1949 Women's TUC, an advisory body, urged the TUC to press the Government for equal pay, but only elicited a reply from Vincent Tewson, TUC general secretary, to the effect that at the 1948 Trade Union Congress it was decided that in the present economic situation the Government should not be pressed for implementation of the principle and since then the economic situation had made it even more necessary to exercise restraint.

However, the general election of 1950 provided an opportunity to campaign among Parliamentary candidates. The Staff Side did not think this a suitable activity for itself, so the Association called a meeting of interested unions, who agreed to take over the job. The 1950 Trade Union Congress carried by 4·5 million votes to

James Callaghan as a young MP

2·4 million, against the advice of the General Council, a CSCA motion instructing it: 'To secure the practical application of equal pay for equal work and, in particular, to urge the Government to give a lead to other employers by applying their declared policy on this issue to their own employees forthwith.'

In the light of this change in TUC policy, the Staff Side sent a deputation to see a third Labour Chancellor of the Exchequer, Hugh Gaitskell, though it rejected suggestions for a poster parade to accompany it. Gaitskell's reply came in a statement to the House of Commons in June 1951 which caused such indignation that the nature of the campaign changed until an agreement was finally won.

Gaitskell not only repeated his predecessors' arguments about the cost to the public services and the effect on outside industry but added a new twist of his own. Since the majority of male employees had families dependent upon them, while the majority of female employees had not, the introduction of equal pay would mean that the standard of living of a married man with a wife and children to support would compare unfavourably with that of an unmarried woman with no dependants. This would give rise to demands for much larger family allowances, either by an extension of the national scheme or through special arrangements in particular occupations. These allowances were no doubt very desirable but the cost to public funds and the burden to industry would be very heavy. Prices would go up further and taxes would have to be increased. The Government did not consider that it could extend the principle until the full consequences to the economy as a whole, including any necessary increases in family allowances, could be accepted within a relatively short time.

The Staff Side described this as the biggest blow the cause of equal pay had ever sustained. 'If the decision is allowed to stand on the grounds advanced by the Chancellor it is clear that the introduction of equal pay will be deferred beyond any foreseeable period,' it said. Albert Day, in an unusually emotional finish to a speech at a mass meeting in Central Hall the following month, gave expression to the frustration felt by the associations: 'Defying the repeated decisions of the House of Commons; defying Labour Party policy; defying the Declaration of Human Rights; defying the considered judgement of the Royal Commission; defying the views of the Treasury; defying, I venture to suggest, the trend of public opinion; defying the claims of justice, and last, but not least, defying the women in the Civil Service, what the Government have said is this: that when the world at long last has settled down from the turmoil into which it has been thrown by the events not just of the last ten years, but of the last 20 or 30, so that the burden of armament once more becomes bearable; when world shortages have been overcome and widespread price increases cease to harass our economy; when we no longer need to worry too much about the balance of payments; when Chancellors of the Exchequer have ceased to utter gloomy warnings against the fear of inflation under which we have lived for ten years past; when the budget situation has permitted some alleviation of the crushing weight of taxation; when some remote Chancellor of the Exchequer, consequent upon all this, can spend a lot of money on substantially increased family allowances as well as the full cost of equal pay in the Civil Service and other public services, and the national economy can bear all the heavy burdens which, it is alleged, equal pay in the Civil Service will directly or indirectly impose upon it; when in short, the millennium, comparatively speaking, is in sight, then equal pay shall be adopted. But not until then.

'It is against this monstrous doctrine that all who, like the Government, believe in the justice of the claim for equal pay, but unlike them believe that justice should be done, must now campaign. And it is to call the rank and file of the Civil

Gaitskell administers a blow to the cause of equal pay

Service movement to take their part, as the National Staff Side will do, in that campaign, that this meeting has been called.'

After the meeting, hundreds of civil servants, mostly women, went to the House of Commons to lobby Members, taking the authorities by surprise. After about 20 had gone in, the doors were shut and the remainder left outside.

The National Staff Side set up an equal pay co-ordinating committee which, using a motion in the House tabled by Douglas Houghton as a rallying point, planned a campaign from October to February 1952, thus spanning the October general election which returned a Conservative government. In the autumn of 1951, mass meetings were held in 13 provincial towns and a thousand London members lobbied their MPs. In February 1952, another thousand civil servants, mainly from the Home Counties, lobbied their Members. The Staff Side went to see yet another Chancellor, this time a Conservative one, R A Butler. It found him more disarming than the Labour ones, though no more ready to make promises.

In April, Charles Pannell, MP, was successful in the ballot for private Members' time and put down a resolution for discussion on May 16. The Co-ordinating Committee backed this with a Press conference and mass meetings in the three halls of Church House, Westminster, with open-air overflow meetings in Deans Yard and speakers on the steps of Church House. Pannell's resolution calling for a definite date for the application of equal pay for women in the Civil Service, teaching, local government and other public services, was passed without need for a division as there was no dissent.

January 1, 1953, brought New Year greeting cards to all MPs from the new committee. Provincial committees organised competitions to select equal pay queens. On February 11, the first debate on the subject in the House of Lords was initiated by Lord Pethwick-Lawrence (who had played a part in the suffragette agitation 40 years earlier). On February 14, Muriel Coult, the chairman, and two others from the Staff Side committee delivered a huge valentine to the Chancellor of the Exchequer.

Douglas Houghton during the post-war period

The Staff Side now linked its campaign with those of the teachers and local government officers for immediate equal pay. The budget promised nothing. Deputations went to see all the main party leaders before their autumn conferences and the equal pay committee prepared a winter campaign which was to take the form of a monstrous petition to Parliament. 'Petitioning the House of Commons is an old democratic right going back to 1675,' said *Red Tape*. 'For the first time we shall take our campaign out to the general public for their support.' The petition ran as follows:

The Humble Petition of citizens of the United Kingdom Sheweth

(1) *That Her Majesty's Government has accepted the principle of equal pay for men and women in all public services.*

(2) *That the House of Commons on May 16th, 1952, called upon Her Majesty's Government to announce an early and definite day by which the application of equal pay for equal work for men and women in the Civil Service, the Teaching Profession, Local Government and other Public Services will begin.*

(3) *Wherefore, your petitioners pray that steps be now taken to meet the wishes of the House expressed on 16th May, 1952, by implementing the principle of equal pay in the Civil Service, The Teaching Profession, Local Government and other Public Services without fail during the year 1954.*

Muriel Coult urged members to collect signatures in homes, offices, special meetings, factory gates, shopping centres and anywhere else. The aim was for more than a million signatures. In the event, they got 600,000 from the associations and 80,000 from a group of women's organisations.

On Equal Pay Day, March 9, 1954, the petition was presented bundle by bundle in the House of Commons by Douglas Houghton and Irene Ward. Outside, flags were flying bearing the old suffragette colours of purple and white. There were purple and white buttonholes, and purple and white stickers and purple and white handbills, all bearing the slogan 'Equal Pay on Budget Day'. Inside, there were 25 questions on equal pay on the Order Paper and 33 supplementaries and Houghton sought leave to bring in a Bill on the subject which was granted without dissent. The Chancellor said he had no new statement to make that day, which, it was hoped, implied he would say something later. In the evening, about 6,000 people attended a rally which filled Central Hall and three smaller halls and overflowed into the open air. Afterwards, a crowd trooped over to the House of Commons and formed a queue to enter the lobbies, occasionally chanting, 'Oh why are we waiting for equal pay.' 'The tune,' observed *Red Tape*, 'though perhaps not too well chosen for female voices in concert, brought to the precincts of Westminster the atmosphere of a carol service on a winter's evening.'

Equal Pay Day may have given Butler the final push. To make sure he would not forget, a group of members were present when the traditional photograph was taken of him holding up the red box as he left for the Commons to present his budget. At the last moment they pulled out banners from under their coats and got into the pictures, a demonstration which was delightedly picked up by the television cameras.

That day the women knew that they had won at last. In his budget speech, Butler said he wished to have a talk with the Staff Side as a preliminary to Whitley Council discussions; and in May he met the Staff Side and authorised negotiations on the National Whitley Council for equal pay to be introduced on a gradual and agreed basis. A special joint committee was set up and after months of detailed discussions reached agreement on February 18, 1955, 35 years after the House of Commons first approved the principle. It was to be introduced by stages, which

Lord Pethwick-Lawrence, veteran campaigner for women's rights

meant that it would be in full operation on January 1, 1961. The fears expressed by chancellor after chancellor that it would quickly spread from public employment to outside industry proved quite unfounded. Most women working in the private sector had to wait until the Equal Pay Act of 1970, half a century after the original Commons resolution.

Women often blamed the slow progress, with some justice, on apathy among their male colleagues. It was natural enough for family men to regard without enthusiasm the idea of single women earning as much as they did, but the women owed a good deal to men like Douglas Houghton and Len White. Doubters among the men could usually be convinced that it was a folly to allow the Treasury a supply of cheap labour by which they could be replaced. At the time of the Tomlin Commission, when unemployment was very high, it was pointed out that women on low rates of pay had monopolised typing and writing assistant work.

Typing and machine grades revolt

An issue which occupied the joint committee for months was how to apply the principle of equal pay to the typing and machine grades, composed largely of women. This led to what later became known as the Typists' Revolt.

Some years earlier a few men had been appointed for the first time to these grades and had been paid 25 per cent more than the women. The Associations claimed the women's rates should be raised to those of the men. The Treasury said the rate for the job was that of the women and in theory the men should be brought down to the women's level. However, it was willing to compromise and eventually the CSCA had to agree in order to get the equal pay settlement. The 25,000 typists and machine grades lost by comparison with Clerical Assistants. The aggrieved girls were encouraged to hope that relativities might be restored as a result of the report of the Priestley Royal Commission, which was then sitting.

The typing and machine grades made up the first group to have its pay investigated by the Pay Research Unit (PRU) set up on the Commission's recommendation. The Unit's report on these grades was delivered on January 1, 1958, and a report on clerical officers and assistants three months later, but the CSCA and the other members of the Clerical Alliance, for tactical reasons, took the Clerical Class first. They had to go to arbitration and eventually got an award, a reasonably satisfactory one, at the end of 1959. So it was not until almost 18 months after completion of the PRU report that the Treasury and associations began talking about typists and machine grades.

In July, the Treasury made an offer which included some improvements at the lower end of the scale, generally less than Clerical Assistants received, but cut the scale off at 25, which meant that future staff would never reach even the existing maximum. By the end of the month negotiations had broken down.

It was the last straw. Two days after August Bank Holiday the typists marched in protest. More than a thousand assembled on the Horse Guards' Parade and, not allowed to meet there, moved through the archway into Whitehall and along to Horse Guards' Avenue. They were addressed by a speaker standing on a rickety table. They passed two resentful resolutions with which they marched to Treasury Chambers, singing and chanting as they went. The newspapers were delighted at the unexpected and photogenic copy to brighten the August doldrums provided by the excited, indignant but good-humoured girls, with pleated skirts swinging and banners held aloft, marching in the sunlight. The Press dubbed them the Cinderellas of the Civil Service. 'Clickety-click went two thousand angry heels,' wrote one scribe. 'Bowler-hatted senior civil servants stared horrified as the girls surged into Whitehall,' wrote another. A third described it as 'the prettiest procession seen in London for many a long year.' The girls got a lot of useful publicity out of it.

There was a crowded demonstration in Central Hall at the end of the month, followed by another march, and many protest meetings up and down the country, culminating in a final Central Hall meeting at the end of September. At least two groups of girls took direct action. Some in Newcastle stopped working overtime and some in Bournemouth refused to get the senior officers' tea, but this was discouraged since it had been agreed to take the dispute to arbitration. The eventual arbitration award did prevent the Treasury from reducing the maximum but did not give the typists the relativities with clerical assistants they thought were justified, and in general was regarded as disappointing.

One result was that the typists were treated with a new respect at the 1960 annual conference. 'The days when typists' affairs at conference were poked into one afternoon later in the week have happily gone for good,' commented Evelyn Cutler, chief commentator on typist matters for *Red Tape*. 'What's more, the delegates no longer slope out to the tea bar in a hurry every time a typing motion comes up.'

A year after the revolt, George Green was writing of smouldering discontent in the typing pools and a fantastically high wastage, both during and after training, of new entrants in London. The Civil Service Commissioners were successful in recruiting school leavers, he said, and gave them free tuition at government training

Civil Service typists demonstrate in Whitehall

*Evelyn Cutler, commentator
for 'Red Tape' on
typists' matters*

centres. As soon as the girls were proficient, however, outside firms were after them and many were ready to take employment where they did not have to wait 15 years for the top rate. Green wrote another article about machine operators being in a ferment and in both articles he warned about what would happen if the girls concerned were to work to rule.

By the end of 1964, a shortage was reported of from 700 to 900 typists in the London area. Again there were Pay Research Unit delays which provoked a new outburst of feminine wrath. Typists were still waiting for an agreement on new scales which should have operated from the beginning of the year and found that because the scales had not been fixed they could not draw a general 3·5 per cent increase due on January 1, 1965. Once again there were protest meetings and demands for drastic action. There was also a spate of letters and telegrams addressed personally to the Chancellor of the Exchequer, James Callaghan, whom many senior staff had known as a tax officer and as assistant secretary of the Inland Revenue Staff Federation. The Treasury found this embarrassing and protested to Len Wines in his capacity as secretary of the Civil Service Alliance, but negotiations were speeded and a quick settlement followed. The agreement not only improved pay at all levels, shortened scales and provided increased opportunities for additional allowances, but introduced a career structure in the typing field with two new grades, personal secretary and senior personal secretary. Towards the end of 1967 there were yet again negotiating delays and the NEC warned typing and machine grade members that it might have to ask for militant action. One December 18 talks were renewed and on December 29 a settlement was reached providing some of the biggest increases ever obtained for that section of the membership.

CHAPTER FIFTEEN
Fair Comparison

The immediate reaction of the Civil Service to the report of the Royal Commission was like that of a swarm of bees smoked out of a tree — the air was filled with a puzzled, plaintive, angry buzzing. Headquarters received a sudden influx of letters and telegrams with appeals for 'leadership', demands for 'action', indignant protests and emphatic instructions to reject the Report forthwith. As members read beyond the headlines, the temperature dropped and the flow of correspondence subsided. The General Secretary's circular describing the meeting with Treasury officials calmed the fearful and damped the excitement. People now began to realise that their pay and leave would not be cut next week. There was time for second thoughts and more critical examination. Perhaps, after all, the recommendations were not wholly bad.

Thus commented *Red Tape* on first reactions to the report of the Priestley Commission published in November 1955. It was a complex document containing both welcome and unwelcome recommendations, but it also set a pattern for pay settlement which the CSCA and the Staff Side have since fought again and again to preserve.

National Whitley Council negotiations began almost immediately and with unusual speed an agreed package was approved for submission to the 1956 annual conferences of the associations. A formal agreement was signed in June. The five-day week, now common outside the Service, was conceded with unexpectedly little difficulty. Another welcome concession was to give temporary staff pay parity with established staff, something for which the CSCA had been pressing for years. But annual leave allowances were reduced for new entrants to the Service on the grounds that they were over-generous as compared with those of other employees. A storm of protest had been roused by the Treasury's proposals to the Commission on leave and hours because they were contrary to the Government's war-time promise to restore pre-war practices unless otherwise agreed. But the cuts in leave were eventually accepted as part of a package which contained much that was attractive.

From the long-term point of view, by far the most important outcome was acceptance by both sides of the principle that Civil Service pay should be based on fair comparison with the current pay of outside staff. This was contrary to the old trade union view that the State should be a model employer, setting standards for others, but it was an important advance on the Tomlin formula in that pay would be related to current remuneration outside rather than to 'long term trends and the economic conditions of the country', an essential change in an inflationary era when wage increases were being constantly negotiated. For the first time there were practical proposals as to how the comparisons should be made. The aim was no less than to take the settlement of Civil Service pay and conditions out of the political arena and it could have succeeded if successive governments had not felt it necessary to break the agreement in the national interest.

'We believe,' the Priestley Commission explained, 'that the State is under a

The Priestley Commission produces a new pay formula

categorical obligation to remunerate its employees fairly. We do not regard wastage as a reliable indicator of the fairness or unfairness of rates of pay. We see very considerable danger in the assumption that Civil Servants are fairly paid and the Service is in a healthy state because its members appear to be carrying out their duties "efficiently". The process of deterioration arising from a sense of grievance on the part of the staff may be a very slow one, particularly in a Service with the high traditions of the British Civil Service . . . The end to be served by principles of pay in the Civil Service may be stated as the maintenance of a Civil Service recognised as efficient and staffed by members whose remuneration and conditions of service are thought fair both by themselves and by the community they serve. A correct balance will be achieved only if the primary principle of Civil Service pay is fair comparison with the current remuneration of outside staffs employed on broadly comparable work, taking account of differences in other conditions of service. If the Civil Servant's remuneration and conditions of service taken together approximate to those prevailing in the outside world he cannot legitimately complain of injustice.'

A unit was to be established to ascertain the facts, on which comparisons would be made, based on the pay and conditions of comparable workers employed by 'good employers' outside the Service. 'The good employer,' in the view of the Commission, 'is not necessarily the one who offers the highest rates of pay. He seeks rather to provide stability and continuity of employment, and consults with representatives of his employees upon changes that affect both their remuneration and their conditions of work. He provides adequate facilities for training and advancement and carries on a range of practices which today constitute good management, whether they be formalised in joint consultation along Civil Service lines or not. Such employers are likely to be among the more progressive in all aspects of management policy. Their rates of remuneration will compare well with those of the generality of employers, will move readily but not atypically upward when the trend is in that direction, and will be rather more stable that most when the trend is downward.'

The Pay Research Unit (PRU) to do the fact-finding was set up under a joint Whitley steering committee with an assistant secretary from the Ministry of Labour, Norman Singleton, as the first director. The unit would make its comparisons separately for the various classes or grades. As it would obviously take several years to cover the whole Service, it was agreed that when outside wage movements were particularly marked and rapid the pay of the lower and middle ranks would be adjusted on an interim basis by means of central settlements. The unit began its work on October 1, 1956, but for six months or so was largely occupied with Post Office claims. By the time of the 1957 CSCA conference, however, the Staff Side was engaged on a central claim and the CSCA had referred to the unit the position of clerical officers and of typing and machine grades, which was discussed in the previous chapter.

With Len White gone, the CSCA moved into the new world of pay research and fair comparison with a new team led by George Green, chosen unopposed as White's successor, with a formidable character, Len Wines, as his deputy. Green was a thinker and an idealist, less of a schemer than any of the other general secretaries. The son of a London fishmonger and a domestic servant, he was educated at a modern secondary school and continued his studies at the Working Men's College in Mornington Crescent. There, at about 19, he was recruited by a German missionary from the Internacio Socialialista Kunbatalo (Esperanto for Militant Socialist International), a group formed to build up an elite whose

George Green

members would set an example in their personal life to socialists everywhere. They did not drink, smoke or swear, and were pledged to set up no permanent personal relationships so they could be free to serve the movement wherever they could be of most use. Green took up active trade union work as his contribution to the aims of the organisation and became a CSCA assistant secretary before he was 30. The war killed the organisation, which was strongest in Germany, but Green retained many of the aspirations which led him to become a member. Slightly built and normally quiet in manner, he was unpredictable. 'At times icy, detached, remote, at times right in the thick of it, stung to anger and fighting hard,' *Red Tape* once observed. A *Times* correspondent wrote: 'Mr Green has a way of making a pay claim sound rather like one of the more abstruse fields of metaphysical inquiry.' Pay research exercises based on volumes of details about similar jobs collected by the unit and the need to give every variation in conditions a 'true money' value, had become something like metaphysical inquiries.

Tom Lillywhite, a President popular with conference delegates

Green was less dominating in his relations with the Executive than most other general secretaries, though he was capable on occasion of making decisions without thinking it necessary to consult it. Generally, he had the backing of the President, Tom Lillywhite, who in 1956 defeated the moderate choice, Joe Bryce, with the support of the left, and retained the office through the remainder of Green's eight years as Secretary. Lillywhite, once a Post Office boy messenger, recognised that he was not Green's equal intellectually, but that did not imply any lack of self-confidence. He had complementary qualities; ability to rouse or pacify the conference, quick repartee and an easy sense of humour. The delegates loved him and when necessary he could get the NEC to think again about some disputed issue by threatening to appeal to the conference. He also had a powerful following in the Post Office. In the latter part of his time he became something of a prima donna, assuming an authority which set executive and full-time officers against him, and part of the growing resentment rubbed off on Green. Lillywhite was supported by

The National Executive Committee, with Lillywhite in the chair

the left in preference to an alternative which it thought would be worse and he tried to calm the internal struggles. Green was with him in this. Although Green had been an active supporter of the Conference Campaign Committee behind the scenes, he took the view that when you are winning is the time to be generous rather than to dominate everybody and call all opponents reds. Green became the first CSCA chairman of the Staff Side in 1958, in succession to Douglas Houghton. Partly as a result of skilful manoeuvres by Lillywhite and the efforts of a family friend of Frank Cousins of the Transport and General Workers' Union, whose votes were vital, Green was elected the first CSCA member of the TUC General Council in 1960.

Another new member of the CSCA team was the first full-time editor of *Red Tape*, T J (Jimmy) O'Dea, one of those who had entered the service as a temporary during the war and stayed to make his mark. He had been a vice-president and in 1956 received easily the highest vote in the Executive elections. For some years he had been a regular contributor to *Red Tape* in *Talking Shop*, a delightfully humorous commentary. When he took over the editorship on January 1, 1957, he brought to the job not only a light touch but also enterprise and judgement. Though he was a moderate and a Catholic, in a period when the left was complaining of the number of Catholics in the voluntary leadership, it was accepted that he allowed freedom of expression to members of all political shades, from

Jimmy O'Dea

Tories to Trotskyites, and he had the strength of character to stand up to any top official who thought his tolerance went too far. 'The editor is left free to get on with the job without interference,' he declared in one editorial which was partly a challenge. O'Dea also found time to act as Press Officer, building on the good relations with industrial correspondents established by Len White and gaining their confidence through his frankness and accuracy.

Negotiations on the first PRU report on the Clerical Class showed how differently exactly the same massive assembly of facts could be interpreted. The Civil Service Alliance, led by Green, argued it would justify increases costing £20 million a year. The Treasury estimated it would justify increases of £3 million. The Treasury attitude was blamed on the Chancellor of the Exchequer, Peter Thorneycroft, who as part of the latest incomes policy had ruled that all pay increases in the Service must be met by compensating economies. There were countrywide protest meetings and demands for a strike to which George Green replied at a big London demonstration: 'You are hog-tied by the Civil Service tradition that whatever happens you do not let the public down.' But he wondered how long the civil servants would retain their patience. The case went to the Arbitration Tribunal, which ruled that the facts justified increases which would cost £7·5 million, more than twice as much as the Treasury's estimate but less than half as much as that of the Alliance. The increases were awarded in February 1959, and back-dated to July 1957, which meant record lump sums in back-dated pay, and the result was greeted as a great victory.

After this a new Clerical Class claim could not come quickly because the Pay Research Unit could not get around to everybody in less than four or five years. To keep pace with inflation, the Staff Side agreed with the Treasury that there should be an annual examination of the general index of wage rates to see if it had risen sufficiently to justify an interim general increase.

On August 10, 1961, the whole system was reduced to chaos when Selwyn Lloyd, Chancellor of the Exchequer, to meet a new economic crisis, ordered that there should be a 'pay pause' at least until the following spring. Awards by the Civil Service Arbitration Tribunal could not be put into effect until the pause ended, and even then there could be no back payments.

The whole Civil Service was up in arms. R A (Dick) Hayward, Secretary-General of the Staff Side, wrote to Sir Norman Brook, chairman of the National Whitley Council, accusing the Official Side of a flagrant breach of agreement which

Civil Service leaders on their way to the Treasury to cross-examine Selwyn Lloyd about the 'pay pause': Dick Hayward, Secretary-General of the Staff Side, is at the left of the front row; the head of Len Wines of the CSCA is just visible behind him

The mass protest in Central Hall

the Staff Side bitterly resented. The Staff Side organised country-wide protest demonstrations along now familiar lines. George Green told a rally in Central Hall in August that if members were denied pay increases, 'one might expect some display of emotion and heat in a more practical way than protest meetings.'

In the autumn, the CSCA Executive called for direct action by the Association in the form of working to rule and a ban on overtime, which was fixed to start on January 17, 1962. Similar action had been taken by the main Post Office unions. It was the first time the Association had ever decided on national industrial action, reflecting bitterness about the pause, the reasons for which were summarised in that month's *Red Tape* editorial:

'It is grossly unfair. Civil Service pay is rigidly frozen. Pay increases are gained by other workers whose unions have used or threatened to use the strike weapon.

'The Government insists that pay increases withheld from civil servants during the "pause" cannot be claimed retrospectively when the "pause" ends. What you lose now you lose for ever.

'The irrecoverable loss means that Civil Servants' pay may never catch up on outside pay rates. In this way the "fair comparisons" principle has been casually abandoned by the Government which solemnly accepted it.

'The Government has also wantonly broken the Civil Service arbitration agreement – a vital agreement meticulously honoured by successive Governments for the past 36 years.

'Pay claims have been rejected by the Treasury for all our grades – for Clerical Officers, Clerical Assistants, Typists and Machine Grades, and for Higher Clerical Officers through the rejection of the Executive Officer claim.

'The CSCA is barred from going to arbitration on these claims, an essential of which is a retrospective operative date, because the Government applies a veto on the operative date. The CSCA flatly refuses to submit to such dictation.

'Claims for better conditions of service such as improved leave, shorter hours, higher allowances, are also completely frustrated.'

The biggest rally in the Association's history took place on the eve of the day of action. There were 7,000 members, it was claimed, in the Royal Albert Hall and 3,000 in an overflow meeting in Central Hall. As banners waved outside and seats began to fill, there was an atmosphere of intense excitement. An orchestra played contemporary music. Gradually, all the seats in the Albert Hall were taken. Then came a period of expectant waiting.

George Green was not there. He was in a taxi, accompanied by Jimmy O'Dea, on the way from a Staff Side meeting with the Treasury. When he arrived he hurried in and had a short talk with Lillywhite. They came on to the platform and the President moved to the microphone to accompanying cheers. But his opening words startled his audience into silence, followed by thunderous applause. 'I have come to tell you,' he announced, 'that instead of inaugurating a work-to-rule, we can translate this meeting into a victory campaign.' Green followed him to the microphone, bearing, according to *Red Tape*, 'a particularly uncanny resemblance to the man who started it all, Selwyn Lloyd.' He explained that the Government had said that afternoon the pay pause was to end on March 31 and there was to be a return to unfettered arbitration. Someone rushed to tell speakers holding the fort at the Central Hall to stop giving pep talks about working to rule and explain about the victory instead.

In the Albert Hall, as Green, still and upright with his arms hanging loosely in front of him, continued his reasonable, unemotional explanations, the mood of his audience changed. There were cheers but also some boos and heckling. Many in the hall felt as if they had received a douche of cold water. Some wondered whether a great deal had been gained. It had been expected that the pay pause would end in the spring. They had got the thing they had demanded most vociferously, a return to unfettered arbitration, but back-pay was still ruled out. It was also known that Selwyn Lloyd intended to move on to a second stage of his incomes policy, which turned out to be a guiding light of a 2 to 2·5 per cent maximum for pay increases which the Civil Service would certainly be expected to observe.

Green calls off the national overtime ban and work-to-rule

Among members of the National Executive, there was strong resentment that Green had taken his decision without consulting them. At a special meeting the next day, a motion of censure on him and Lillywhite was defeated by one vote. Looking back in later years, Green conceded that he had made a mistake in not deferring acceptance until he had consulted the NEC. Up and down the country, inquests were held. Was the work-to-rule properly prepared for? Could it have succeeded? The annual conference at Margate in May endorsed the decision to work to rule but complained of lack of co-ordination by the Staff Side and of vague and inconclusive work-to-rule instructions. It rejected a proposal to instruct the NEC to adopt a strike policy, but decided by 75,052 votes to 45,648 that future benefits obtained by the Association should be enjoyed by members only, though Green and others pointed out that this was completely impractical. Delegates were anxiously waiting for an arbitration award on a Staff Side all-Service pay claim which would show whether the Tribunal felt itself bound by the guiding light.

This conference, only four months after the Albert Hall episode, had to decide whether Green should retire in August the following year, when he would reach the headquarters officers' age limit of 55, or whether he should be given the extension he badly wanted. The Executive had taken the view that there were not

exceptional circumstances which would justify waiving the rule and submitted a motion to this effect. There was strong opposition and the show of hands at the end was so close that a card vote was called and Green lost by 68,239 votes to 63,359.

That same evening, the Arbitration Tribunal Award was published in London and it was arranged that Green would announce the result on the lower promenade at 9 p.m. In the fading light, 800 delegates made their way to hear it. Green appeared calmly above them and, with the tall figure of Lillywhite at his shoulder, raised a megaphone to his lips and announced that they had got 4 per cent, twice as much as the Treasury had offered. The cheering delegates scattered about the town to celebrate. Green sat by himself in a corner of his hotel lounge appearing to read. The majority against him had been small. If the award had become known earlier in the day, it might have made all the difference.

Later in the conference an executive recommendation that Green should be succeeded by Len Wines, the deputy general secretary, was approved by 76,644 votes to 53,888 (for Ian McPherson, the assistant general secretary and treasurer, who appealed against the recommendation).

The 1962 conference also made a decision which meant that Lillywhite would have to step down from the presidency the following year. In future, presidents and vice-presidents would not be eligible for election for a continuous period exceeding three years. Lillywhite had been returned unopposed in the five years since his first election. In 1962, Bryce again ran for the office, but Lillywhite won by 69,201 votes to 59,713.

The conference reiterated its support for what had become known as the Green Plan, a far-reaching long-term scheme for the reallocation of duties in the clerical and executive classes which Green believed could restore to clerical officers and assistants something of the status and purchasing power they had enjoyed before the war, but which had since sadly declined in comparison with those of other workers. The scheme, as he saw it, would produce economies in manpower which would justify the higher pay levels. He had first put it to the Treasury in February 1957, and had further developed it in a booklet on pay policy in 1960. The Treasury's initial reception was friendly but the large users of clerical labour, the Service, Supply, Social Service and Revenue departments, and the Post Office, had not been convinced of its value. Moreover, Green had not been able to get the other unions in the Civil Service Alliance to go along with him, and the Society of Civil Servants, whose membership would have been affected, would have nothing whatever to do with it.

Nevertheless, Green persevered, and annual conferences repeatedly backed him. Whenever Governments imposed pay restrictions, Green pointed out how much better it would be to make economies through a restructuring of the Service. They were always talking about the importance of increasing productivity, he complained, except among their own employees. The Treasury finally had another look at the plan and agreed to try pilot schemes in the Post Office and the Ministry of Pensions and National Insurance (MPNI), working through the sections, but the Post Office showed no inclination to co-operate and progress with the MPNI was slow. 'We shall continue to press on with this,' Flo Bonsor, speaking for the Executive, told the 1962 conference, 'because there is a growing feeling in our membership that this is the way that is necessary to improve the lot, not only of the clerical officer but also of the clerical assistant.' It never came to anything, although the ideas behind it were more than once revived in later years.

Another issue now petering out was a dispute, which aroused strong feelings, over a vanished differential between post and telegraph (manipulative) officers (P

George Green is refused an extension to his period as General Secretary

(Opposite) Green at the Albert Hall meeting

and TO) and clerical officers. The P and T officers had traditionally got less than the clerical, and had often sought promotion to the Clerical Class, but at the end of 1960 the CSCA was infuriated by an agreement between the Post Office and the Union of Post Office Workers that in future P and TO pay would be aligned to that of the clerical officer. The CSCA immediately put in a claim for restoration of the differential, held a Central Hall rally, and took the claim to arbitration. There was rejoicing at the 1961 conference when Green announced that the claim had succeeded. The Post Office proceeded to operate its agreement, so the P and TOs got exactly the same amount and the differential had gone again. There seemed nothing left for the CSCA to do but to censure the NEC, which was duly done at the 1963 conference.

This was the last conference for both Lillywhite and Green. Soon afterwards Lillywhite was made an executive officer and disappeared from the CSCA scene. Green, the 55-year-old idealist with more than a quarter of a century of practical experience as an Association officer, became Secretary of the National Association of Launderette Owners.

Len Wines, who started his career in the Welsh Board of Health, succeeded George Green with only four years of office in front of him. He was clear-headed, strong-willed and hard-working; the amount of time he spent on the job was a wonder to everybody. He was a stickler for detail and, though generally respected, was never a popular figure. His intellectual strength enabled him to exercise a dominating influence on the Executive, now composed almost entirely of moderates, and the annual conference. A 'practical believer in social democracy', he was relentless in his opposition to Communists and those with similar views. Opponents complained that he would look at them from beneath his over-hanging brows as

Len Wines, the new General Secretary, looks suspiciously at the photographer from beneath his heavy brows

if he were planning some deadly plot against them even when his intentions were of the most innocent. He had experienced unemployment in his youth and showed a strong sympathy for the under-privileged.

When he took over, Wines had already achieved a Staff Side reputation as a master of the intricacies of superannuation. He had also, during some years' responsibility for members at the War Office, become a leading exponent of the case for civilianisation – the increased use of civil servants for suitable clerical work in place of forces personnel. It was, and is, a continuing part of the Association's job to preserve jobs and career prospects for their members. They argue that civilians are less costly to employ, that civilian organisation has advantages in dealing with such things as pay, records, supply, administration and training and that there should be reasonable career prospects for civilian staff employed by the defence ministries.

Contrary arguments were that training for the Forces in pay, supply and administrative techniques was essential to meet the exigencies of war, that a reasonable ratio of posts was needed to enable officers and men to enjoy some home postings and that security and freedom from dislocation by industrial action had to be secured. A new committee on the subject, the Wilson Smith Committee, reported at the end of 1967, but the Staff Side rejected the report and since then there has been a long succession of meetings with secretaries of state and with the Ministry of Defence Official Side, occasional pressure in Parliament, with some gains here and some losses there, and an unending series of inquiries, the most recent of which conducted in 1978 a study of the Army and RAF supply organisations. Such work will no doubt continue in the foreseeable future.

Wines believed in negotiation, at which he was expert, rather than campaigns or threats of action as a means of attaining his ends and was helped in this by an easing of pay problems during his first couple of years. He contributed to Staff Side negotiations for a long-term agreement which would provide general increases of 3·5 per cent in three of the next four years with a PRU exercise for each grade every four years. A favourable London Weighting agreement was made at the beginning of 1964. London Weighting had been introduced in place of provincial differentials as a result of a Priestley recommendation. The associations which had constantly attacked the old system of paying Civil Servants in the provinces less than those in London, seemed quite happy with the new system of paying Civil Servants in London more than those in the provinces, but other urban areas also wanted weighting. At the end of November, a Pay Research agreement for the Clerical Class brought Wines a flood of appreciative telegrams. There was also the typists and machine grades settlement mentioned in the previous chapter. 'We have gained, between the 1964 conference and today, more hard cash than in any year within the active experience of any of us,' asserted Wines at the 1965 conference.

In this rosy period, *Red Tape* sponsored a CSCA Personality Girl contest which attracted 600 entries, with clerical officers and typists dividing the prizes. A motion submitted to the conference expressed disapproval, but one of the successful girls claimed the contest had shown the CSCA was not composed of 'ancient, antiquated fuddy-duddies' and the motion got little support.

A new incomes policy had been introduced by George Brown, Minister for Economic Affairs, after a Labour Government had been returned to power in October 1964, but it did not at first cause the CSCA serious difficulties. Since the 2 to 2·5 per cent Tory guiding light had been replaced by a 3 to 3·5 per cent norm, the third 3·5 per cent payment under the Staff Side's long-term agreement went through without difficulty. By the autumn of 1965, however, the CSCA was

Wines' negotiating successes

The CSCA Personality Girls

feeling some anxiety about how the Government's policy was going to develop and Wines wrote an exceptionally lucid exposition of unanimous NEC views on fair comparison.

'This method of settling pay, if it works properly, ensures that the Civil Service reflects what is happening in respect of comparable work outside the Service. If outside wages go up for a particular kind of job or skill, then, on the evidence, Civil Service pay for comparable work or skills is revised. If, e.g. because of the operation of a general Government policy the "outside" wages move more slowly or not at all, the Pay Research report evidence will point against any bigger movement of the Civil Service grade's pay. This – inherent in the "fair comparison" principle – we accept.

'So, to the degree that the Government's general policy "bites" in the matter of outside pay movements, Civil Service pay movements will be affected as a reflection of this. What would be grossly unfair, however, would be any action by Government specially directed against the pay of a Civil Service grade irrespective of, or on top of, what may be happening to its outside analogues. That would be a double dose of Mr George Brown's medicine, and would represent discrimination against the Civil Service . . .

'The clerical side of the Civil Service would – and this needs to be said plainly – react sharply and dramatically against any attempt to impose a double effect of policy upon us – once by comparison with the outside workers, who had been subject to that policy and, on top of that, by direct application of that policy.'

The Government's voluntary 3·5 per cent norm proved a failure and the Government moved to an early warning system under which employers were expected to give advance notice of proposed price increases and negotiators to give advance notice of wage claims. The TUC responded by setting up their own vetting machinery under which unions were asked to give notice of intended claims to a special committee of the General Council. The CSCA went along with this somewhat reluctantly and wrote to the TUC explaining the special position of the Civil Service.

In the summer of 1966 came a sudden balance of payments crisis and the Government imposed a wage freeze until the end of the year, backed by legislation, to be followed by a period of severe restraint. The TUC General Council reluctantly acquiesced and the Executive of the CSCA, after a long, tense special meeting, decided to support the General Council's attitude with provisos that there should be no discrimination against civil servants, that control of prices would be a reality and that special priority should be given at the end of the stand-still period to the lower paid workers. The Government had envisaged special consideration for lower paid workers but had not said what they meant by lower paid. The NEC took the view that they included a considerable proportion of CSCA members. The Staff Side successfully resisted a suggestion at a National Whitley Council meeting that incremental scales should be frozen. They maintained that the rate for the job in the Civil Service was the whole scale and said that if the Government and the TUC really wished to set the Civil Service ablaze they would conspire to stop the granting of annual increments. There was also agreement that genuine negotiations could continue during the stand-still and that Civil Service negotiating machinery would be preserved.

This was very important to the Civil Service unions. Charles Garrick, the CSCA President, in his report to the 1967 conference, emphasised that in all the confusions and frustrations they had endured, 'for the first time in any such crisis conditions, Government measures, so far, have not discriminated against Government employees. To put it simply, we are all in the same boat or, as some would prefer to say, in the same soup together.' He also said that not only had they succeeded in preserving the principle of fair comparisons but had maintained the right to pursue fruitful negotiations on a broad front. They could report useful successes on such things as starting pay on promotion, overtime, Bank Holiday attendances, subsistence allowances, progress with London Weighting and tele-printer operators' pay and had begun work on a PRU report on the machine and typing grades. Len Wines, speaking at his last conference, recorded that in the past four years the standard working week of members had been cut by more than 4 per cent and their pay had been improved by a general average of 20 per cent. The CSCA had accepted in principle that wise planning was more sensible than the jungle of the free-for-all. There had been few comparable spans of time in earlier CSCA history, in the free-for-all days, which showed as good a position. He moved a resolution on the same broad lines which was carried by a large majority.

The worst of the Labour Government policy was still to come, but a different General Secretary, Bill Kendall, would have to handle it.

PART FOUR

A FIGHTING UNION
1968-1978

CHAPTER SIXTEEN
The First Strikes

The 1968 Annual Conference:

Emergency
Motion 8:   *Preparation should be made for direct industrial action by
            the Association if there is a breakdown in Clerical Class
            pay discussion. The National Executive Committee is
            instructed, if necessary, after urgent consultations with
            branches, to plan for limited withdrawal of labour – initially
            on a selective basis.*

Motion 812: *This conference instructs the NEC to formulate a strike
            policy immediately.*

Motion 802: *This conference instructs the NEC to implement the
            sentiment that compulsory membership of the appropriate
            association becomes a condition of service for civil servants.*

Motion 303: *Conference instructs the NEC to ban compulsory overtime
            being introduced at any date.*

Motion 36:   *This conference instructs the NEC to withdraw our
            support from the Government's prices and incomes policy.*

Motion 828: *Conference calls for the promotion of a competition to select
            a new name for the CSCA which is more suited to the
            present wide-ranging membership and allows for further
            development later.*

With this series of resolutions, the Association's 1968 conference prepared to enter a new stage in the Association's history. It was to have a new industrial policy, a new name and would no longer be prepared to accept even a Labour Government's incomes policy. The title Civil and Public Services Association was chosen the following year.

The occasion was skilfully stage-managed. The heart of the matter was Emergency Motion No 8, of which the key sentences are quoted above, because it suggested immediate crisis. The debate on it was held in strict secrecy. Credentials were carefully examined and the doors locked. 'Everyone was in his seat dead on time,' wrote Jimmy O'Dea in *Red Tape* in a picturesque account of the affair. 'The Press table was bare; the photographers absent. There was an air of suppressed excitement. In dead silence the president [Charles Garrick] rose to begin the session. Prosaic but practical, he announced that tea would not be available [a sad blow]. No one could enter or leave the hall in any circumstances. For those who might be in distress, he pointed out where the toilets could be found without leaving the hall.'

Bill Kendall, attending his first conference as general secretary, made a rousing speech in which he explained why the Executive had decided publicly and irrevocably to reject a pay offer at a time when to get a pay offer at all was an achievement. There was some vigorous opposition, based on delegates' knowledge

The case for industrial action is debated behind locked doors

Preparing posters for the march through Blackpool during the 1968 conference

of their own members, but in the end the motion was carried by 736 votes to 62, with about 100 abstaining. After other militant motions had been adopted, the delegates left the hall to march through the streets of Blackpool as a gesture of solidarity and held a short meeting on the promenade.

The motions were perhaps not as aggressive as they first sounded. The Clerical Class negotiations had not broken down and the leaders had reason to think that a better offer was coming. The NEC had emphasised the difficulties in the way of getting the closed shop and had actually opposed the motion to ban compulsory overtime. But the instruction to formulate a strike policy gave Kendall his opportunity to build for the future and the delegates had been roused to an enthusiasm they had not shown for years. *Red Tape* commentators described the 1964 conference as 'efficient, bland, tranquil'; the 1965 conference as 'lacking opposition in the best sense'; the 1966 conference as 'orderly, painstaking and business-like', and the 1967 conference as having 'little excitement but a lot of solid work'.

The left wing had been reduced to a few scattered voices crying in the wilderness; there was not one left-winger on the Executive in 1968. Behind the scenes the moderates, now known simply as The Group, were in full control. In the branches, where contact with the membership had rested to a large extent on collectors, deduction of union dues from pay had rendered them unnecessary. On the National Whitley Council, relations between the Official and Staff Side leaders had remained close. A build-up of frustration, resulting from the Government's continually more oppressive incomes policies, found no outlet.

Kendall was determined to change all that. 'Members are getting bored and baffled by the complications of top-level negotiations,' he said in a *Red Tape* interview on his appointment. 'I would like to see more controversy, more argument and debate about the union's affairs. The voice of dissent should not be stifled.' Perhaps in the last sentence there was implied criticism of The Group, or of Len Wines with whom at the end he had strong personal and policy differences.

Kendall, who later became the secretary-general of the Staff Side, is a complex character. He once described himself as 'a human being in the shell of a technocrat', which is in itself a little puzzling but as explained by a colleague meant that 'he was a sensitive, friendly chap who had to don an armour of toughness and remoteness in order to succeed at his job.' Born in 1923 in South Shields of working-class parents with a Methodist, socialist and trade union background, he left school before he was 15, spent a period on the dole and educated himself through varied reading at the local public library. He has remained a voracious reader, perhaps more influenced by books in his later life than most people.

Kendall joined the Young Communist League in 1937, keeping it secret from his father, and left it in 1941, having found its imperialist war period hard to take, but remained sympathetic to its aims. After the war, in which he became a fitter-armourer, he entered the Civil Service in the Ministry of National Insurance (now the DHSS) in Newcastle and by 1949 was secretary of that branch, even then one of the largest. In the same year he rejoined the Communist Party, which he had supported in the post-war CSCA struggles, but this time remained in it for only a year. In 1951 Kendall and his wife were received into the Catholic church and he

Bill Kendall, 'the mildest revolutionary in the business'

became a fierce critic of his former associates. The following year he was elected to the National Executive Committee and in December was appointed an assistant secretary. He was chosen deputy general secretary at the bitter 1963 conference.

He was a militant Catholic. He described himself at the 1968 conference as 'the mildest revolutionary in the business', and with his near bald head and spectacles, his habitual neat dark suit and tie, his quiet manner and tolerant attitude, he seemed a thoroughly respectable one. In the eight months of his general secretaryship before the conference he had done his best to rouse a militant spirit in the Association. 'It is not our intention to adopt a docile attitude,' he declared, 'and there is every need to develop an aggressive and militant attitude.' A little later he wrote: 'There is more anger and resentment among basic grades in the Civil Service now than at any time since Selwyn Lloyd's pay pause. The Government can, of course, ignore it, but they do so at their peril.'

Nevertheless, it had not been a bad year, with satisfactory settlements for teleprinter operators and typing and machine grades; something for the low paid, and a London Weighting settlement which substituted flat rates for allowances varying with salary levels, something for which the CSCA had long been pressing.

The trouble over the Clerical Class arose out of the Government's White paper for 1968–69, which fixed a ceiling (instead of a norm) of 3·5 per cent except for productivity agreements. Since the clerical grades had had no increase since January 1966, they would be allowed a maximum of 7 per cent from January 1968. If the Pay Research exercise produced any figure above 7 per cent, staging had to be applied, which meant they would have the difference deferred until 1969 without retrospection. Moreover, interim increases obtained for the low paid would have to be deducted from the 1968 settlement. Almost immediately after the 1968 conference, negotiations were resumed and by the middle of June an agreement was reached which improved increases and shortened the scales, to which the Association attached much importance, and allowed the ceiling for low paid to be based on existing rates, but otherwise left the staging proposals unchanged.

While the negotiations were going on, branches were consulted about their readiness to participate in stoppages of anything from an hour to a full day, with the following results:

In favour	273 branches – 43%
Against	178 branches – 20%
Doubtful	27 branches – 3%
Did not reply	292 branches – 34%

Members ballot in favour of limited stoppages

This was considered satisfactory in view of the fact that negotiations were still going on when the inquiry was made.

During the following winter, Kendall drafted the report on strike policy, running to more than 10,000 words, which was accepted by the NEC with minimal alteration, and became known as 'the little red book' because of the colour of its binding. It outlined the theory of collective bargaining and discussed the pressures which could be brought on governments through mass protests, political activity and industrial action short of a strike, such as working to rule, going slow and banning overtime. It was a realistic document. It concluded that an Association strike policy was necessary because collective action was an essential part of the bargaining process. Strikes were not a substitute for normal bargaining machinery. Various methods of action would complement each other. Collective action was not only appropriate for issues of general and national concern, but also to protect and promote the interests of groups of workers.

The report emphasised the practical problems and limitations associated with strikes in the Civil Service. 'The problems are related to the strong position which the Government as employer occupies and the functional difficulties with any action which affects the machinery of Government and can be interpreted as a significant challenge to the authority of Government or to policies which the Government pursues from time to time which it is alleged are intended to apply to the community as a whole. In current circumstances a completely nationwide strike of the membership of a prolonged nature must be ruled out. Apart from constitutional difficulties such a strike, given the nature of work on which CSCA members are employed, would not necessarily have maximum coercive effect – the substantial cost to union funds would be prohibitive. A sizeable strike fund would require years to build up and a formidable increase in membership subscriptions. A strike fund could be wiped out in a short time by a general stoppage. For the immediate future CSCA strike strategy must be directed to the development of short stoppages – the withdrawal of membership services on a selective basis in areas where such stoppages will have a maximum effect.'

The report warned members that no action could be taken without approval by conference or the NEC, which would be responsible for binding settlements and would exercise discretion in the payment of benefits from the Fighting Fund. The NEC would continue to make allocations to the Fighting Fund and already had power to impose a levy on the membership in support of authorised action. Presenting the report to the 1969 conference, which enthusiastically approved it, Bill Kendall warned the delegates that endorsing the document would not itself have any magical significance. 'Nobody worries about a strike policy which is never activated.'

The policy was first activated in January 1970, by the CPSA Posts and Telecommunications group. Since the Post Office had become a public corporation two years earlier, the 25,000 strikers were no longer civil servants but, as members of an association without experience of such action, they were exploring new ground, testing the reaction of CPSA members when the call for militancy affected them directly. A claim for a productivity increase had been made the previous September and industrial action was called because of delay in making an offer. It began with a ban on overtime on January 19, followed by a one-day strike, claimed to be 95 per cent effective, three days later, and a series of guerilla strikes in key offices in large towns from early February. A Post Office offer was refused and the action lasted seven weeks. Victor Feather, TUC General Secretary, helped to bring the two sides together and the action was called off on March 7 on terms which were accepted by a massive majority in a ballot. The increases obtained averaged 9·5 per cent and agreement was reached on a formula for a review of clerical productivity by the end of the year. 'Nobody can doubt our ability to fight in future, either on our own or with other unions,' Kendall wrote in *Red Tape*. The strike put an end to the Corporation's hope for a situation where all the unions with which it bargained would be Post Office only, demonstrating that the CPSA was deadly serious in its intention to retain its Post Office presence.

The policies of the Tory Government from 1970 to 1974 were calculated to provoke a militant spirit in the Association, and other unions, if it had not already existed. In 1969, the Association had been an active supporter of the TUC in the opposition to Barbara Castle's White Paper, *In Place of Strife*, proposing legislation to restrict the right to strike in some circumstances, and it was now even more bitterly opposed to the Tory Industrial Relations Act. It resisted the Government's initial de-escalation (or N–1) pay policy, which attempted gradually to reduce the level of settlements from the 14 or 15 per cent which had been bequeathed to them

The Post Office members demonstrate their ability to fight

by the Labour Government to 12 per cent, 10 per cent, 8 per cent and so on. In the private sector the White Paper relied on indirect pressure on employers to resist demands regarded as excessive. As regards the public sector, Robert Carr, secretary for employment, declared: 'We are not going to treat our own employees in any way unfairly but we are going to set an example.'

But the brunt of the policy fell on the public sector and it was from there that the main resistance came. The first official country-wide strike of local authority workers came in the autumn of 1970 and was settled at about 15 per cent as a result of an award of a committee of which Professor Hugh Clegg, chairman of the Civil Service Arbitration Tribunal, was a member. Prime Minister Edward Heath was infuriated and Professor Clegg's contract as chairman was not renewed the following year, to the intense indignation of the CPSA and other Civil Service unions.

After a major struggle in the electricity supply industry, the Union of Post Office Workers called out 180,000 members in January 1971, in its first continuing national strike; in support of a claim for increases of from 15 to 20 per cent. The Post Office offered 8 per cent, which Kendall said was intended to be a pace-setter for the whole public sector, and the CSCA contributed £2,500 to the UPW hardship fund. After two months, the Post Office union had to accept an award of 9 per cent. There was some criticism in the CPSA of the donation, as there was of a donation to the miners the following year, but the critics found little support at the 1971 annual conference. A motion urging the CPSA to re-affirm its non-political status also received little support. The mover complained that *Red Tape* got redder and redder and the general secretary's notes seemed more and more like the thoughts of Chairman Mao.

The mood of the majority of delegates was very different. They were infuriated by Government delay in dealing with Pay Research negotiations, which now came round every other year, and there was, in the words of a *Red Tape* commentator, 'a clamour for militant action on a scale and intensity not previously encountered in Civil Service circles.' There was a resolution calling for selective industrial action unless there was an immediate reply. 'We cannot go on year after year crying "wolf" and not doing anything about it,' Kendall said, and the delegates started singing a battle song. There was a also a resolution instructing the NEC to look into the best way of building up a strike fund of £5 million in the next five years.

The next month a Pay Research settlement was reached giving clerical

Robert Carr, Secretary for Employment, who introduced the Industrial Relations Act

The 1971 conference, at which delegates demanded the Association build up a £5 million strike fund

assistants an average of 11 per cent and clerical officers an average of 11·6 per cent, as well as an incremental advance scheme providing those entering the Clerical Officer grade before they were 25 an accelerated increment after three years. A central pay arbitration award gave other CSCA grades from 9·5 to 13 per cent.

The miners' strike in the spring of 1972 finally destroyed the Government's de-escalation policy and Heath decided the Government must find a more sensible way of settling differences. However, a long series of talks with the TUC and the Confederation of British Industry failed to produce an agreed method and in November the Government announced the introduction of a new statutory incomes policy beginning with assumption of powers to freeze prices and incomes for 90 days. The second stage, announced in January 1973, was to start at the end of March. It limited pay rises to less than the sum of £1 a week plus 4 per cent of the current pay bill of the group, with a maximum increase of £250 for everybody.

A new statutory incomes policy

Negotiations had already begun for a new Clerical Class Pay Research increase effective on January 1, 1973. Nothing that came out of the negotiations would be paid before the end of the freeze. There would be no retrospection and payments would be restricted to Stage II limits. Again, the fair comparison principle was to be breached by the Government. The time had arrived, said CPSA leaders, to implement their five-year-old threat of industrial action, if possible in conjunction with other Civil Service unions.

After the freeze was announced, on November 6, the National Staff side sent deputations to see, successively, the Lord Privy Seal, Lord Jellicoe; the Head of the Civil Service Department, Sir William Armstrong, and the Prime Minister, Edward Heath, to press the case that as Civil Service pay reflected changes which had already occurred in outside employment, it was unfair and a breach of the pay agreements to withhold overdue increases. Deputation members, including Kendall, spoke of the danger of industrial action if nothing was done to remedy their position under Phase II of the incomes policy. In each case the deputation members were given a sympathetic hearing but were promised nothing.

On December 14, the CPSA Executive called on branches to co-operate in protest meetings, and in hammering the facts into MPs, and undertook themselves to step up publicity, to set up liaison machinery with other unions and to consider selective strike action. On January 1, the CPSA published press advertisements saying that pay increases approaching 20 per cent were due to civil servants and that the Government was defaulting. On January 10, the CPSA and the Society of Civil Servants co-operated in nation-wide protest meetings during working time and, on January 16, the CPSA launched a series of regional rallies at the Central Hall, Westminster. When the Phase II White Paper was published on January 17, the Executive decided to consult other Civil Service unions with a view to early industrial action, organise a public sector conference and seek a special congress of the TUC. The Civil Service Department announced that if anomalies remained after study of Pay Research reports they would then be considered in relation to Phase III.

A one-day strike was fixed for February 27, but before that management action had provoked some stoppages. About 2,000 DHSS employees staged an official one-day strike. On February 22, Sir William Armstrong sent a personal but unsigned letter to civil servants which resulted, according to *Red Tape*, in a walk-out of about 30,000 staff. *Red Tape* recorded that, on the previous day, duplicator operators at the Ministry of Defence in Donnington had been asked to leave their machines so that army personnel could produce a top secret document, which turned out to be Sir William's letter. The CPSA branch protested to the head of the office against the use of military personnel to do a purely Civil Service job and, when the letters were delivered, ceremoniously burnt them in the official incinerator.

The strike itself, on February 27, was supported, the CPSA claimed, by about 75 per cent of its members in the Civil Service sector, but of the other Civil Service associations only the Society of Civil Servants and the Customs and Excise Group took part. Roger Willson-Pepper, assistant secretary of a CPSA Somerset House branch, received much publicity when colleagues persuaded him to dress up with a bowler hat and 'brolly', after the manner of a civil servant of earlier years, carrying a banner demanding 'Fair Pay for CPSA'. Some members were not happy about this revival of the old Civil Service image, but the newspapers were delighted.

On March 8, selective strike action began with employees who worked on the Customs and Excise Southend VAT computer, who then received threats of disciplinary action. It was continued by branches in agriculture, National Savings, employment, environment, health and social security, defence and the Stationery Office. At the end of March, following a decision at a special TUC congress to assist unions which found themselves in disputes arising from the Government's incomes policy, the CPSA had a series of meetings with the TUC General Council, but, as none of the other Civil Service unions would undertake to support the CPSA action, the General Council merely noted it and called upon affiliated unions to render what assistance they could. At the beginning of April, the Association suspended the selective strikes in order to negotiate a Phase II settlement.

Kendall was disillusioned by the attitude of the other Civil Service unions. 'Although I am firmly in favour of united action,' he told the annual conference in May, 'I have to say that after our experience this year of trying to organise co-ordinated militant action in the Civil Service, we shall be most careful in future about restricting our freedom to take action ourselves unless we get guarantees of

A few of the 1973 strikers

more fighting spirit than most Civil Service unions have shown. It is a melancholy fact that when the TUC General Council met representatives of affiliated Civil Service unions we presented a spectacle of dismal disunity which contrasted sharply with the solidarity demonstrated by the four unions representing the hospital ancillary workers. . . .

'The CPSA is the only organisation which has fairly and squarely met the challenge of the situation where the Government as employer ratted on Civil Service pay agreements. For great numbers of our members, industrial action was something of a traumatic experience, but they rose to the occasion and whatever their reservations, one way or the other, CPSA members gave a heartwarming surge of support on the vital days and in the programme of selective strikes.'

Kendall defended the Executive against critics who said it had not gone far enough and those who said it had gone too far. To the former, he replied: 'We have had to ensure that we did not commit CPSA membership to an indefinite solo struggle – heroic but unproductive – where you take on the Government single-handed. Our job is to bring home the bacon, and not merely to indulge in an emotionally gratifying exchange of black eyes and broken noses.' To the latter, he replied: 'It is pleasant to talk about the delights of civilised negotiation and arbitration, but it is not real. The CPSA has relied upon negotiation and arbitration for half a century, and where has it got us? It has got us into the ranks of the new poor – the white collar paupers. It has got us into the position where our employer, the Government, has had the colossal bloody nerve to override even the parsimonious pay agreements which have held us in check ever since the Priestley recommendations became Parliamentary policy seventeen years ago.

'I am absolutely convinced that, in the long run, what we have done will have lasting effect. I am sure that the demonstration of the ability of the CPSA to withdraw labour and, where necessary, to escalate industrial action rapidly, will improve our prospects in all future negotiations and not only those relating to pay. It is now understood, as never before, in official and political quarters that the CPSA means business. What we have done on one occasion for one purpose we can, and will if necessary, do on other occasions for other equally legitimate purposes.'

As it turned out, the inquest on the first national Civil Service strike was overshadowed at the conference by a bit of over-enthusiastic militancy which resulted in what *Red Tape* described as 'the biggest, costliest, noisiest and most-publicised annual assembly in the Association's history.' The journal said: 'One decision taken in the heat of the moment and against the advice of the NEC, secured a blaze of headlines and produced a week of such heartache and heart-searching for officials, delegates and the membership at large that its like is difficult to recall.'

'The biggest, costliest, noisiest and most publicised annual assembly in the Association's history'

Delegates from the Department of Health and Social Security, at their sectional meeting on the Sunday before the conference, passed a resolution, in spite of opposition from their committee, asking for authorisation to refuse to do the preliminary work on the uprating of social security benefits, due on October 1, until CPSA members had received the full amount of pay increases justified by the findings of the Pay Research Unit. This appeared as an emergency motion for the national conference. The NEC decided unanimously to oppose it. Its spokesman was a young officer, Peter Thomason, who was secretary of the DHSS Section. There was an outbreak of jeers and catcalls mixed with cheers when he announced that the NEC was opposing the motion. DHSS delegates seemed to regard him as a traitor to the Section and in a continuous stream of heckling and interruptions it

Peter Thomason, who spoke through a mixture of cheers, catcalls and jeers

took him 15 minutes to deliver his three-minute speech. 'This motion,' he said, 'is asking for an assembly of trade unionists to deprive old age pensioners, the chronically sick and the severely disabled of increases in benefit. I suggest anyone in this hall who describes himself as a trade unionist and has any conscience whatever should not support this.' A show of hands gave a majority for the motion of 365 to 348. A card vote was asked for but could not be taken because it was an emergency motion.

The papers were full of it the next day and soon telegrams of protest began to arrive from members, branches and pensioners' organizations. One from the CPSA Posts and Telecommunications Group, which now held a separate conference while the main conference discussed Civil Service matters, declared itself appalled by the decision. Victor Feather, the general secretary, who was present as a guest speaker, condemned the resolution.

On the Wednesday morning, the Post Office group delegates joined the conference and demanded that the resolution be discussed again but Len Lever, the president, ruled this out of order. The Post Office delegates challenged his ruling but the conference endorsed it by a five to four majority. Uproar followed. A woman delegate presented the president with a wreath 'for the pensioners'. The P and T Group members, led by a delegate with a large open umbrella, filed past the top table to the accompaniment of cheers, boos, whistles, exchanges of abuse and gestures of contempt. Along with Alistair Graham and some members from other departments, all but five walked out. Posters and banners condemning the decision

Delegates mill round the hall while Alistair Graham looks down philosophically

were displayed and pickets appointed to cover every entrance. 'CPSA Day of Shame' said one provocative banner. When the remaining delegates emerged for the lunch interval there were exchanges of violent abuse. Kendall had a hurried meeting with Thomason and Graham, the Post Office group Secretary, and eventually they persuaded the Post Office delegates to rejoin the conference in the afternoon, but they did so still carrying their banners and placards. But on the Thursday morning, Kendall reported that the NEC had considered the position in view of the fact that the DHSS motion was in conflict with others and decided that a special meeting would be held the following week. He added to loud applause: 'I am confident that whatever happens the pensioners will not suffer at all,' and the DHSS spokesman said they had decided to recommend that the terms of the resolution should not be implemented. 'The moment of mean bloody-mindedness among civil servants is over,' commented the *Daily Mirror*. 'It is over because the vast majority of trade unionists are not really bloody-minded at all.' On the station platform on Friday afternoon, Thomason was spat at by some delegates.

The final outcome of the incomes policy struggle was that the CPSA civil servant members, in addition to the Phase II interim settlement in April, got increases based on the Pay Board's report on anomalies dating from November 7, and Phase III increases from January 1, 1974.

A couple of months later they found themselves facing a new, Labour Government and ready for whatever pay restrictions that government might feel were necessary.

CHAPTER SEVENTEEN
Discontent–and the Search for Remedies

From time to time we have to tell the Official Side that there is 'grave discontent' in the Service. I honestly do not believe that this has much impact. I suspect, very little. The top brass of the Civil Service is fairly well insulated from the thinking and feeling of basic grades. Their social provenance, education, and class situation cuts them off from the lower orders. They share the ideas, prejudices and outlook of similar social groups, and this influences their approach and effectively limits their understanding of worker grievances.

Of course this is a generalisation. There are individual exceptions. If the exceptions are so rare it is because an heroic act of imagination is required to leap out of an administrative spectrum of thought of which blinkered orthodoxy forms one extreme, and a milky conservative reformism the other. I am not highly critical about this because I very much doubt – given the same background and social compulsions – very many of us could produce the necessary heroic mental agility.

To generalise is therefore legitimate. The top brass of the Service is intelligent, honourable, industrious and matey – they are also committed to the status quo, *defenders of the 'national interest', insulated from popular pressures, and, whatever their individual liberal pretensions, tough employers.*

The Civil Service is organised in a class structure. There are the people who work at the base and – above, beyond, out of reach and in many respects out of touch – the top brass who control. It is absurd to pretend that a gap does not exist. It is nonsense to think that Fulton Committee mythology will close the gap – it will grow wider as the Civil Service becomes less and less of a sheltered occupation and adopts more and more commercial techniques and outside business practices. The conflict between those who control and those who work will become sharper; the liberal pretensions of management less evident.

These were the opening paragraphs of a piece by Bill Kendall in *Red Tape* in December 1969, the year after the report of the Fulton Committee set up to examine the structure, recruitment and management of the Service. With not a word changed it was reprinted as the leading article in the *Red Tape* of May 1973, not long after the strike which led to a Wider Issues Review (wider than pay) undertaken by the Official Side. Taken together, Fulton and the wider review led to almost continuous examination of Service discontents in the early 1970s and removed some of its major causes, notably by the superannuation settlement of 1972 and the facilities agreement of 1974. The 'top brass' certainly tried. But the heart of the trouble was pay – the continued relative decline in the living standards

Lord Fulton

of white-collar workers and the discrimination against public employees under successive incomes policies. About this the Official Side could do little, sandwiched as it was between governments determined to make their own employees an example and associations growing increasingly frustrated and militant. Consultation remained close, and in spite of financial limitations, progress was made in other fields. Some ministers as well as permanent secretaries were disturbed by the evidence of restlessness among the staff.

In the CPSA's evidence to the Fulton Committee, as in Kendall's article, it is possible to hear echoes of the attacks on the caste system made by the Assistant Clerks' Association at the time of the MacDonnell Commission nearly half a century earlier. The system lingered on in Britain, especially in the Civil Service, and remained a source of resentment to the men from working class homes who for the most part led the CPSA in the 1960s and 1970s. The old gulf remained between the 'O' level people at the bottom and the university people at the top. To *Red Tape* the division evidently seemed as relevant in 1973 as in 1969. Fulton had not effected a cure.

The CPSA leaders hoped for much from the Fulton Committee and were deeply disappointed by the report, mainly because it concentrated attention on the higher Civil Service and relegated the clerical grades to an appendix and a report commissioned from a management consultancy group. 'The vast bulk of the Civil Service is treated as a sort of ghostly chorus applauding a battle between two heroes – the man with a degree in the humanities and the man with a degree in the sciences,' wrote Greg Challis. Kendall deplored 'the absence of a thorough analysis and the proliferation of emotive phrases' though he thought some good might result. Irritation was increased when, at about the same time, the Government set up a panel of 'experienced people' under Sir Robert Bellinger, ex-Lord Mayor of London, to examine the organisation of the larger areas of Civil Service employment – a move which produced an angry protest from the Staff Side, which the CPSA dismissed as a political gimmick and seems to have had little result.

The Fulton report was, however, treated seriously. The Staff Side set up a co-ordinating committee and was represented on teams sent to examine the Civil Services in the United States and Canada, on which the Fulton Committee had modelled some of its recommendations. The CPSA Executive had a special two-day session and arranged open general meetings of members in a number of places which were addressed by NEC speakers.

The first major outcome of the report was the transfer of responsibility for the central management of the Service from the Treasury to a new Civil Service Department. To get away from control by the Treasury, with its financial preoccupations, was one of the vain hopes of Brown and his colleagues at the end of the First World War, but it had its disadvantages. The Lord Privy Seal to whom, under the Prime Minister, the new department was made responsible, could never have as much influence in the Government as the Chancellor of the Exchequer. There was some compensation for this in the choice of Sir William Armstrong, a man of exceptional ability and personality, as the top civil servant for the new department, with support from a second Permanent Secretary, Sir Louis Petch, who had earlier done much to improve relations between the Official Side and Staff Side.

Sir William was the first head of the Civil Service to visit the Association annual conference, which he did in 1969. 'The boss of the Service has hitherto been a remote, unknown figure orbiting in the Civil Service stratosphere,' observed *Red Tape*. 'But this year he expressed a wish to meet the ordinary members at our

Sir William Armstrong, accompanied by Lady Armstrong, addresses the 1969 conference

annual jamboree. And meet them he did. Around midnight, I saw him in a hotel bar having lively arguments with various delegates. His charming wife was being whirled around the dance floor by other delegates. Clearly both Sir William and Lady Armstrong were having a whale of a time.' The next day Armstrong spoke to the conference in a friendly way, gave a solemn assurance that he was totally committed to genuine consultation and received a standing ovation.

The Fulton Committee's most valuable recommendations, from the point of view of the CPSA, were those concerning superannuation. Ken Thomas, then Deputy General Secretary, described them as wide-sweeping and progressive.

Leslie Williams, Secretary-General of the Staff Side

Thomas had become an expert on the subject under the guidance of Len Wines and was appointed vice-chairman and chief of the Staff Side team on a joint review committee. Previously, the job would probably have been assigned to a Staff Side official but the Secretary-General at that time, Leslie Williams, preoccupied with the many aspects of Fulton, and believing in letting the work go round, adopted a policy of leaving more to his colleagues from the Associations.

Agreement had been reached on many aspects of the subject by the time of the CPSA's 1970 conference, but it was planned to dovetail reforms with the Labour Government's national insurance pensions plan devised by R H S Crossman. This went out of the window when Labour lost the election shortly afterwards and the joint review had to go back almost to scratch. The Tories were encouraging occupational pension schemes, as an alternative to higher national pensions, and Thomas was able to exploit this by urging that the Government should set an example to the rest of the country. Many difficult issues and a lot of detail were involved, however, and talks dragged on. At last John Herbecq, chairman of the joint committee, took them to the Russell Hotel and kept them there for three days, from 9 a.m. to 10 p.m., until they finally hammered out a settlement.

Hailed as the most significant superannuation reform of the century, the agreement was enthusiastically approved at conferences of the various associations. The CPSA gave Thomas a standing ovation and the other association leaders made him a presentation.

In future the pensions of established civil servants would be a right instead of a privilege which could be withdrawn or abated – though it rarely was – but they remained non-contributory. They had never been a free gift since pay negotiations always took account of their value, usually estimated at about 6·5 per cent of pay. It was now accepted for the first time as an accruing benefit which could be preserved or transferred if a Civil Servant resigned on his own initiative at any time after he had been in the Service for five years. There would be short service increments for those leaving after between two and five years. Moreover, the basis for determining pensions would be the last year's pay, or the best of the last three years, instead of an average of the last three. Many other changes were designed to benefit widows and children and those retiring as a result of ill-health or injury.

A provision that the pension scheme should be extended to unestablished staff formed part of major reforms affecting temporaries. Another agreement based on a Fulton recommendation made establishment possible after a year's service and automatic after five years to all temporaries, covering immediately about 50,000 employees, or 10 per cent of the non-industrial Service. It had always been a puzzle to commissions, committees and observers that someone could be employed in the Civil Service for 20 years or more and still be a temporary without pension rights and with pay and conditions inferior to those of permanent staff, a problem accentuated by both world wars. The MacDonnell Commission objected to it. Members of the Tomlin Commission wondered about it and suggested a five-year limit. The Priestley Commission produced equality in pay scales. In 1964 a 'safety-net' agreement provided that staff who reached the age of 60 with 20 years or more service without becoming established would be treated for pension purposes as if they were established. It was agreed in 1972 that all staff would be placed on a permanent and pensionable footing as rapidly as possible.

Superannuation had also been improved by legislation in 1971 which linked public service pensions, including those of the Civil Service, to the prices index, with a promise of annual reviews. This was rare in outside industry and was frequently brought up in subsequent campaigns against the Civil Service by the

Press and others, but such critics were always handicapped by the knowledge that it was a Tory government which did it.

One of the main proposals of the Fulton report was for unified grading in the Service based on job evaluation, but in the end it produced little change at the clerical level. A Clerical Work Review Team had numerous meetings over several years trying to redefine the duties of clerical and executive grades. It came to nothing because the Official Side wanted to transfer a band of work from Executive to Clerical Officers for monetary compensation so small as to have no attraction when weighed against the loss of promotion posts. Some improvements in the structure of the machine grades were achieved. The Fulton Commmittee criticised the working environment in some Civil Service offices and a joint team visited about 50 offices to determine the best way available money could be used to improve conditions.

In 1971 an agreement was made on compensation for premature retirement, for example as a result of redundancy or inefficiency. It also set up an independent Appeals Board to deal with complaints of unfair dismissal made by permanent or temporary employees. The first chairman was Jock Shaw, for many years one of the most trusted Official Side negotiators, and he was followed by Sir Leslie Williams after his retirement from the secretary-generalship of the Staff Side. In 1978 Sir John Wilson became the third chairman. A feature of the agreement was the explicit recognition that the clerical grades were no longer completely mobile geographically. Since then it has been possible to transfer staff compulsorily from job to job within reasonable distance of their homes but not beyond that, a concession made desirable by the increasing proportion of wives in the clerical grades. In 1977 the Board heard 166 appeals of which 42 were decided in favour of the appellant. Compensation was paid in 11 cases where reinstatement was not practicable or the Board's recommendation was not accepted.

Another CSD working group, which reported in the autumn of 1971, considered how far women might be given part-time employment in positions of responsibility, how it might be made easier for a married woman to combine looking after a family with a Civil Service career and what retraining might be given to make it easier for a married woman to return to Civil Service employment after a long period of absence. It produced 22 recommendations proposing special treatment in respect of leave and hours to meet domestic responsibilities and an experiment with a day nursery. This was followed in 1974 by the introduction of flexible working hours, which allowed employees, within limits, to decide their own starting and stopping times, so long as they put in the agreed total working hours. This proved highly popular and soon became widespread. The CPSA had regularly urged the establishment of more day nurseries but little progress was made because of the cost and the incentive for the CSD to start them was reduced when unemployment made recruitment of staff easier.

Making it easier for married women to further a Civil Service career

A minor CSD concession was that departments in future would avoid using the term sub-clerical grades as applied to Clerical Assistants, Typists, Machine Assistants and Sorting Assistants. 'The term has rather been felt to have some kinship with sub-human and sub-normal and other categories below the line,' Kendall explained.

The idea of extending productivity bargaining to the Civil Service was vainly discussed in this period as a means of increasing pay. The Labour Government, in its incomes policy in the late 1960s, laid emphasis on productivity agreements as a justification for pay increases above the norm and consultants were busy trying to apply the principle to white-collar staff.

The Official Side had started experiments in various forms of clerical work measurement before the Fulton Committee reported. The CPSA was at first suspicious and critical but in 1970 agreed to become members of a joint working party on the subject. At the same time the introduction of productivity bargaining for industrial workers in a number of departments, notably defence and technology, had so reduced the differentials enjoyed by clerical and typing grades, some of them with the job of calculating and issuing these pay increases, that they bombarded the NEC with demands that they should be included in such exercises.

Progress in clerical work measurement was nipped in the bud at the 1970 annual conference by a motion condemning the idea as an attack on the dignity and well-being of members for which a marginal productivity payment would not be sufficient compensation, and instructing the NEC to withdraw from working parties, experiments and negotiations and take direct action if the need arose. Ken Thomas, Deputy General Secretary, protested indignantly that the joint working party had not had time to report and had not even got down to talking money but the motion was carried decisively. The NEC had to pull out and instruct branches taking part in the experiments to do so. 'It summarises the reactions of our members,' wrote Kendall after this was done, 'to say that they object to stopwatches, they object to having the Civil Service run by outside consultants, they object to individual performance rating and they find self-recording of daily output an irritating extra burden.'

At the following year's conference there was a warm debate on a motion asking for authority for sections or groups of the Association to negotiate departmental or local improvements in pay based on contributions to improved efficiency and productivity. Kendall described it as potentially dangerous. There could not be a system of national pay determination by comparability and departmental or local productivity bargaining as well. 'There is no case for COs and CAs to get productivity pay in some areas and not in others,' he added. 'Are not all of us making a contribution to productivity and improved efficiency whatever department we are in?' Again the idea was decisively rejected.

The NEC took up the problem of the reduction in differentials with the Official Side, but the latter did not want to disturb, any more than the associations did, the primary principle of fair comparison and argued that Civil Servants were getting the benefit of productivity bargains in outside industry when the pay of the two was compared.

By and large, considerable efforts were made after the publication of the Fulton report, in small matters as well as larger ones, to remove staff grievances but restlessness remained and increased, as the republication of Kendall's 'grave discontent' article shows. On May 23, 1973, not long after the strike of that year, Kendall took a deputation to see the Lord Privy Seal, Lord Jellicoe, to tell him of discontent over a long list of issues including pay and pay research, incremental scales, starting pay on promotion, substitution rules, annual leave, general hiving off, dispersal of offices throughout the country, career problems, working conditions, facilities for branch officials and departmental problems. Already disturbed by the extent of support for the CPSA's industrial action, the CSD set up in July the Wider Issues Review team to try to tackle the troubles. In consultation with the Associations, the team had talks with management and staff representatives at a large number of offices.

Some reforms did not wait for the team's report. Before the end of the year a new agreement was reached on substitution. It was not wholly satisfactory to the Staff Side but improved the pay and conditions of officers who temporarily replaced

Lord Jellicoe, one of the initiators of the Wider Issues Review

others in a higher grade who were absent. Increases were made in allowances for officers permanently transferred from one part of the country to another. Experiments in job satisfaction were begun to relieve the tedium of routine employment. An office improvement programme was launched. On the advice of the Fulton Committee a start was made on new personnel management and training systems.

Most welcome of all was the Facilities Agreement of 1974, intended to stimulate the further development of the Whitley System at departmental and local level. The *Whitley Bulletin* considered it one of the most important developments in the progress of Civil Service trade unionism and *Red Tape* said it was a branch officers' charter. It gave national backing to departmental and local arrangements for Staff Side representatives to have the use of rooms, furniture and equipment, and typing, telephone and other services, and for them to be allowed time to carry out their staff relations work. It provided for annual branch meetings, at which officers were elected, to start in working hours to encourage attendance. It removed the 2·5 per cent charge for deducting union subscriptions under the check-off system. It extended special leave for union schools to cover those dealing with industrial relations. Departmental Whitley councils were left to work out the details of the agreement.

At the end of the same year, the Staff Side, on the initiative of the CPSA, negotiated a new National Pay Agreement which, while still based on the fair comparison principles, revised the old 1956 agreement to take account of the

Ken Thomas, architect of the 1972 Superannuation Agreement, who later became General Secretary

unprecedented rate of inflation. It introduced annual Pay Research negotiations in place of the existing biennial cycle, reflecting the private sector practice of full pay reviews every 12 months and eliminating the need for the old 'unsatisfactory and divisive' central pay settlements. Formerly, Pay Research negotiations were finalised up to six months after increases were due on January 1. The increases were backdated in full but the real value of these back-dated payments was reduced by inflation. After prolonged negotiations, including several meetings with the Prime Minister, the agreement introduced a new system devised by Ken Thomas, known as the time lag formula, which would increase outside pay rates by the equivalent of the movements in the Retail Price Index between the time the rates were agreed and the operative date of the Civil Service settlement. The CPSA made a transitional pay settlement based on the new agreement in 1975.

The Wider Issues Review team found just cause for many of the complaints made, but in its final report in February 1975, reiterated that pay was the most important single cause of staff discontent and notably aggravated other discontents. 'The effect of various national incomes policies,' the team wrote, 'has been that in the last ten years the implementation of comparable pay rates has more often than not been delayed. As a result civil servants have – at least for a time – lost pay increases due to them. They have also lost confidence that their pay will in practice be determined by the due process. More and more feel that successive periods of incomes policy have borne more severely on the public service than on other employment. As inflation continues at a higher rate than before, civil servants' fears about their future pay are compounded by their bitter experience of the pay pauses and pay freezes of the past.'

The report also emphasised the unsettling time the Civil Service had had in the previous ten years or so: 'Successive governments have tended more and more to adjust and change their predecessors' policies – and even their own. Sometimes the alterations are radical; they are always required quickly; and too often a change in the system of taxation or social security can alter the everyday work of tens of thousands of Civil Servants. Departments have been created, merged and abolished. [The report included a diagram to illustrate this.] These changes undermine valuable traditions and old loyalties. The consequent institution of new working procedures and the assimilation of new people cut across ongoing efforts to improve a department's performance and they distract central and line management from what they see as their proper work. From time to time staff shortages, high turnover or the operation of manpower ceilings have made it more difficult to staff offices as the work requires and to provide enough experienced staff to do it properly.'

Senior civil servants advise governments how to avoid staff difficulties

So the team of senior Civil Servants spoke frankly to governments: 'If they want to help the Civil Service out of its present difficulties and help keep it out of difficulty in future:

– they can avoid discriminating against the public service in the application of their economic and social policies;

– they should, in a desire to get things done, and quickly, still duly consider what it is possible for their staff to do and to do properly.'

The Labour Government of the day failed to follow either piece of advice.

CHAPTER EIGHTEEN
Shifting Boundaries

If the Civil Service trade union movement is to emerge from the present period of challenge not merely unweakened, but positively strengthened, it is essential that all constituent associations should reassess the existing arrangements from the point of view not only of their own immediate membership interest, important though this will obviously be to them, but also of the need to secure a unity of purpose greater even than that which has been developed over the past 50 years. The development of incomes policies by governments of both major political parties has revealed cracks in our defences precisely at the time when there was the greatest need for unity against the divisive policies of the employer. Unless that unity of purpose is both achieved and maintained, there is a very real danger of a situation developing in which inter-union rivalry and competition could so accentuate the strains and stresses inherent in the whole field of trade union activity as to call in question the effectiveness of the Whitley system of negotiation and consultation through which the work not only of the Staff Side but also of its constituent organisations is conducted'

Staff Side discussion paper: *The Future of the Civil Service Trade Union Movement*, published in April 1974.

That warning was given when the divisions accompanying the 1973 strikes were fresh in everybody's minds. Four years earlier, in the aftermath of the Fulton report, the then Secretary General, Leslie Williams, had produced a paper advocating a single union for the whole Service, but all the associations turned it down. Now his successor, John Dryden, recognising the problems inherent in attempting to represent everybody from messengers to permanent secretaries, put forward the alternative of federation. So long as the Post Office unions were members of the Staff Side, probably no one would have thought of such a development, but they had gone when the Post Office was hived off to a public corporation and the composition of the Staff Side was now more homogeneous. Nevertheless, federation would have meant a loss of individual association sovereignty which none was prepared for. The CPSA totally rejected it at its 1975 conference. In 1978, when the associations were preparing for what they expected to be the biggest struggle with the Government in Civil Service history, the old hampering divisions reappeared. Whether some form of closer structural unity would have prevented that or eased its impact is debatable.

CPSA rejects plans for a staff federation

There had been no major change in the structure of the Civil Service trade union movement in the previous decade, but there had been a series of bilateral discussions about closer unity or amalgamation involving every association. Few had been wholly successful. The CPSA, however, had undergone important changes resulting from the separation of some parts of the Service and new amalgamations. Some, particularly the transfer of the Post Office to a public corporation, caused periods of sharp conflict with other unions. The Savings Bank was not included in the Post Office transfer, but some 30,000 Association members ceased to be Civil Servants and there was danger that they would be absorbed by Post Office unions. This would have meant much more to the CPSA than a decline in numbers. The Post Office Section had from the creation of the CSCA played a leading part in its development, provided many of its most effective voluntary officers and contributed a certain balancing element through its representation of members who were employed by a commercial, although publicly-run concern.

The struggle to retain these members, against a united front of the corporation and Post Office unions, began as soon as the Government announced its firm intention to make the transfer, more than two years before vesting day on October 1, 1969. The Union of Post Office Workers (UPW) at once made a take-over bid to which the NEC replied that it was for its members to decide what union they wished to belong to. There was some division of opinion inside the Section but at the 1967 conference the majority voted to remain in the CSCA and this was endorsed by the CSCA conference. 'If there is intimidation by other unions or, as is more likely, intimidation by the Corporation who may say, "This is the type of union we want to deal with", then we can promise one hell of a row,' declared Bill Kendall.

On August 9, three months later, the UPW, the Post Office Engineering Union and two smaller Post Office unions decided to form a joint trade union council and declared their intention 'to represent all the staff employed by the new Post Office Corporation.' They were convinced, they said, that the Corporation would refuse to recognise any organisation which was not exclusive to the Post Office. Kendall described their agreement to carve up the CSCA as a cheerful piece of butchery which was worthless and meaningless. 'They are not in a position to carry out the threat,' he said. 'What they are in a position to do – and *they* have started the terrible process – is to divide the Post Office staff into hostile camps, create controversy that will weaken trade union organisation and strengthen the employer at a time when maximum trade union strength is essential.' The Post Office, Kendall said, would be told that the Association had always had many thousands of members in the Post Office and had unchallengeable negotiating rights for them. 'We will acknowledge the right of management to express views about trade union organisations but assert the management has no right to instruct people, as if they were so many unthinking units, about the type of organisation which should represent their interests. This is old-style "company unionism" with a vengeance.'

The Section and main conference reaffirmed their attitudes in 1968 and during the year both sides abandoned recriminations and prepared for the trial of strength. The UPW, POEU, Post Office Management Staff Association, Association of Post Office Executives and National Federation of Sub-Post Masters formed the Council of Post Office Unions (COPOU) with a full-time Secretary. The CPSA turned its Post Office Section (excluding the Savings Bank) into the Posts and Telecommunications Group with its own semi-autonomous Executive, a new journal, *The Link*, and a vigorous new officer, Alistair Graham, as Secretary.

When the Corporation took over, it found waiting for it a productivity claim for clerical grades and Executive Officers. The Corporation delayed negotiations and the P and T Group, with CPSA support, threatened industrial action unless the Corporation named January 1, 1970, as the operative date for any settlement and increased subscriptions. When informed that its claim would probably be considered with other Post Office claims at a meeting of ministers on January 22, the Group called a one-day strike for that date and began the seven-week industrial action described in Chapter 16. This proved its power to enforce recognition. The

The CPSA fights for recognition by the new Post Office Corporation

(Opposite) Alistair Graham, first Secretary of the Post and Telecommunications Group and later CPSA Deputy General Secretary

following year, when the UPW had its first great national strike, the CPSA not only sent a donation but was represented by the P and T Group at national and local COPOU meetings and joined in a UPW march. Alistair Graham was invited on to the platform with other Post Office leaders at a Hyde Park demonstration. The following year peace was made with the Post Office unions and the CPSA was accepted into COPOU.

P and T Group granted increased autonomy

The P and T Group's position within the CPSA was uneasy, however. Though it negotiated pay and conditions directly with the Post Office, it was inevitably a junior member of COPOU. On the other hand members were no longer concerned with Civil Service conditions. So it was agreed that for two days during the conference week they would meet on their own while the remaining delegates discussed Civil Service matters. The P and T delegates would join the others to consider such things as finance, administration, constitutional amendments and organisation and would take part in the national elections. They were disappointed that they did not benefit, like Civil Servants, from the 1973 Anomalies Report and were unhappy about being excluded from Civil Service decisions which affected the public attitude to the organisation, as they demonstrated at the 1973 conference, and entered into discussions with the Post Office Engineering Union about the possibility of joining it. However, in return for increased freedom to run their own affairs and increased secretarial and financial support, they eventually decided to remain with the CPSA.

The CSCA changed its name to CPSA in recognition of the transfer of the Post Office members to another employer, but it differed from other hivings-off, such as those to the Atomic Energy Authority and the Civil Aviation Authority, only in the numbers and importance of the membership involved. The position of the P and T Group, with its own executive and conference and independent negotiations, was characteristic of a federation, and opened the possibility of the expansion of the CPSA on a federal basis. The Civil Aviation members, after their successful ten-week strike in 1977, discussed the possibility of breaking their pay links with the Service. Both they and the P and T Group were free to negotiate productivity agreements and experiments in industrial democracy. There was even talk in the CPSA at one time of the possibility of joining forces with other public sector unions outside the Civil Service.

The CPSA was always against hivings-off, which a government was likely to carry out not so much, according to the Association, because it thought that a transfer to autonomous bodies would increase efficiency, as to enable it to claim it was reducing the size of the Civil Service. When sections of the Department of Employment were separated, the Association pressed hard and long, and eventually successfully, for staff members to remain civil servants. This created intricate problems of organisation. The staff had different direct employers – the Manpower Services Commission and its agencies, the Advisory, Conciliation and Arbitration Service and the Health and Safety Executive – and were scattered over the country.

Mergers with the Ministry of Labour Staff Association and Court Officers' Association

The problems of organisation were accentuated by the fact that the Ministry of Labour Staff Association had recently merged with the CPSA, bringing in some 15,000 members, mostly working in employment exchanges, and in itself creating organisational problems. In 1978 efforts were made to find a satisfactory basis for reorganisation of the Section.

The mergers with the MLSA in 1973 and the Court Officers' Association in 1974 were the first since the early 1930s. They were partly the result of the Fulton Committee's recommendation to abolish departmental grades but in any case would probably have come before long. The CPSA had for a long time been impatient with the Civil Service Alliance, which included these three unions and the Inland Revenue Staff Federation. It regarded the Alliance as sometimes useful as a means of burying embarrassing conference resolutions, which had to go through the Alliance to the Staff Side, but for little else. The CPSA looked after practically all the work involved in running the Alliance. The Association had several times previously discussed with other members the possibility of amalgamating, including once in Len Wines' period of office when the TUC was actively encouraging union mergers, but without success.

The post-Fulton period was more propitious. John Tindall, the MLSA General Secretary, was older than 55 (the CPSA age limit for full-time officers) but he was hard-worked and not in the best of health and accepted lump-sum compensation for loss of office. Ray Shuttleworth, the honorary part-time Secretary, joined the CPSA staff.

The situation of the Court Officers' Association, one of the oldest Civil Service organisations, had changed because recent legislation had resulted in a unified court service and the absorption of clerical and executive staff into general grades. There seemed no point in the continued existence of such a small, non-professional, departmental union. Its honorary General Secretary, Frank Humphries, also joined the CPSA staff. An approach was made to the IRSF but it still had its specialist grades and saw no reason to give up its independence. The Alliance was wound up and the CPSA and IRSF set up a co-ordinating committee to ensure the closest possible future co-operation.

An important part in the concluding stages of the negotiations was played by John Raywood, the son of a regular soldier turned civil servant, who had been appointed the youngest ever full-time CSCA officer when not quite 22. He was now chosen at the request of the members as first secretary of the new Section. Four years later he became CPSA Assistant General Secretary.

The mergers with the MLSA and the COA were important for the CPSA in two main ways. One was the absorption of a new large block of officers at the Employment Exchanges whose attitudes, like those of local officers in the Department of Health and Social Service, were influenced by constant direct contact with the under-privileged. The other was that the CPSA acquired its first substantial group of Executive Officers, who were organised by both the other unions and had played an important part in them.

There were also a few in higher grades up to that of Principal. Some of the Executive Officers, then and later, transferred to the Society of Civil Servants since it held national negotiating rights for the grade, but an appreciable number preferred to go with the majority of the MLSA into the CPSA.

John Raywood, first secretary of the Department of Employment Section and later Assistant General Secretary

The 1973 annual conference promptly instructed the NEC to open discussions with the Society with a view to recruiting Executive Officers and to ask the Civil Service Department for joint negotiation powers for Executive Officers. The NEC had deprecated this, on the grounds that there was no possibility of securing joint negotiating rights across the board, suggesting instead that these should be more limited talks about representation of the Executive Officers who had opted to join or remain with the CPSA. One delegate said what was proposed was poaching, but the conference as a whole was undeterred.

At that time, however, Clive Jenkins' Association of Scientific, Technical and Managerial Staffs (ASTMS) made a foray into the Society's territories and the Society hurriedly affiliated to the TUC – which made it impossible under TUC procedures for either ASTMS or the CPSA to recruit Executive Officers except by agreement. The NEC could only report in 1974 that it would not miss any opportunity to enter into discussions with the Society – and was censured and told to start talks immediately.

Bill Kendall reported to the 1975 conference a warning by the Society that anybody who tried to woo the Executive Officer grade away from it would be taken to the TUC under the Bridlington Agreement which covers relationships between affiliated unions. But the Society had added that, while its right to represent the executive grade was unchallengeable, it was conscious of the facts of membership and was willing to talk about some form of closer relationship. The CPSA began talks with both the Society and the Inland Revenue Staff Federation, which also had some Executive Officer members. The IRSF soon dropped out, but in six months the Association and Society representatives agreed on a joint document advocating a complete merger. It was to be presented to both annual conferences, leaving the details, if it was approved, to be worked out afterwards. It all came upon delegates too suddenly and the CPSA turned it down out of hand at the 1976 conference.

'Like it or not,' said one delegate, 'SCS members hire and fire our members. It would be a bosses' union.' 'The Society could not swamp the CPSA numerically,' said another, 'but it does not require numbers to have influence.' In vain Bill Kendall defended the proposal. 'Conference has told the Executive to get EOs into membership,' he pleaded, 'and there is no way you can do so without some form of structural rearrangement with the Society. Our turnover in CPSA is enormous. We lose key workers every year. Moreover, in the final analysis, negotiating strength cannot be divorced from organisation. The fears of a bosses' union ignore the size and nature of the EO grade which contains some of the best and most militant trade unionists the CPSA has ever had. Surely the CPSA has the numbers, the character and the sheer bloody-mindedness not to be submerged.' The delegates were unconvinced. The majority of the left were against it. Some moderate members apparently opposed the proposal because they suspected a plot by the two strong deputy secretaries, Campbell Christie and Alistair Graham, to form a dominant left block in the Staff Side (though all the chief officials were in general support). However that may have been, the deal was off. The Society did not have to take a decision. 'A pity!' said one observer, 'It would have been interesting to see which of the two "young Turks" came out on top.'

The make-up of the Staff Side had been radically changed by the withdrawal of the Post Office unions. The CPSA had become the largest member union and its representation had risen to seven, as a result of the MLSA and COA mergers, out of a total of 24. The Society had three representatives. A table published in the *Whitley Bulletin* in 1974 gave the CPSA 215,702 members out of a total of 528,092 in the 11 constituent associations. (Of these 178,951 in the CPSA, out of the Staff Side membership of 459,478, were employed in the Civil Service or the near 'fringe'.) The largest of the other constituent associations were the Institution of Professional Civil Servants (98,403 members), the Society (66,686), the IRSF (53,085) and the Civil Service Union (42,716). The CPSA and the Society had together considerably more than half the total membership and slightly more than half the Civil Service and fringe membership but less than half the Staff Side representation. The CPSA had had merger talks with the Civil Service Union at an earlier stage but they had fallen through mainly because of the difficulty of fitting together the very different structures of the two organisations.

The IPCS followed the Society into the TUC in 1976 and the First Division Association followed in 1977, so almost all the Civil Service was affiliated. The motive for joining in most cases was not defence against outside TUC unions but the desire to play some part in an organisation whose negotiations with governments on economic matters affected everybody. In earlier days, no one would have believed that the First Division Association, representing top civil servants, would ever affiliate to the TUC.

The CPSA was the largest association in the TUC group which lumped together the Civil Service and Post Office unions. It was larger now than the Union of Post Office workers and the 12th largest in the country, but it had had no member on the General Council since George Green's days. Frank Cousins, General Secretary of the Transport and General Workers' Union, was upset by Green's moderate attitudes with the result that his union ceased to give its massive vote to the Association. As far back as 1967, the Association had pointed out to the TUC, with no result, that the Civil Service and Post Office group was under-represented on the General Council as compared with other groups and that no one person could speak adequately for the three divisions of Civil Service membership: the Treasury, departmental and Post Office grades. In 1971 the CPSA submitted a motion to the annual Congress expressing the view that every union above a certain size should be entitled to a seat on the General Council but that also failed. Bill Kendall returned to the subject in 1975 but again the TUC rejected arguments for greater representation of the group.

Cyril Plant, whose seat on the TUC General Council was coveted by the CPSA

The Civil Service seat had been held by Cyril Plant of the IRSF since 1963 and when he retired in 1976 it was hoped that Ken Thomas would take his place on the Council, but instead Plant's successor at the Federation, Tony Christopher, was elected with 2 million more votes than Thomas got. *Red Tape* reacted angrily. 'It is regrettable that TUC leadership remains unrepresentative of unions within the Civil Service. The seats reserved for Civil Servants on the general Council (restricted to two) are annually the cause of growing discussion and controversy. CPSA has long maintained that it is nonsense that because of grouping arrangements and allocations made many years ago, prior to changes in the status of some former Civil Service unions, of these two seats one should inevitably be filled (since that is what vote-trading dictates) by a representative of a non-Civil Service body, the UPW, with 190,000 members, and the other by an IRSF nominee representing a small, departmental union within the National Whitley Council. For us, and for Civil Service colleagues, there is a mounting sense of exclusion and frustration, particularly when issues as vital as national economic salvation are being discussed and decisions presented as a joint production. CPSA and some other TUC members have no party affiliation. Nevertheless we find ourselves subjected to fraternal and moral pressures as a result of commitments to which, in the absence of General Council representation, we have not been a party.'

At the Blackpool Congress the following year, however, the group was allowed three members and Thomas got on, defeating Brian Stanley of the Post Office Engineering Union for the third place by 6·9 million votes to 6·2 million. The CPSA once more had a member of the 'cabinet' of the trade union movement.

The narrowness of the majority appears to have been due to abstention by the TGWU because the CPSA delegation walked out when suspension of the TGWU, for failing to carry out a Disputes Committee award, was reversed. The CPSA arranged a party for its friends at Blackpool to celebrate its victory – and was censured for it by the next annual conference, which the previous year had given instructions that no money was to be spent on parties at Congress.

CHAPTER NINETEEN
Membership and Money

Today a large proportion of the staff in the Civil Service were born and brought up in the post-war world and naturally their values, assumptions and attitudes have been shaped by the existence of the welfare state and the security it provides, by the changes in our educational system which encourage a more questioning outlook, by the wider horizons of the television age and the greater awareness of what is happening in the outside world.

Civil Service and Change, the final report of the Wider Issues Review Team.

The Association's membership grows younger and younger

This was probably more true of the CPSA in the 1970s than of any other association. Its membership was always young and had been, on average, growing younger. It had become more volatile, more independent and critical of the leadership and more reckless in its internal struggles. Since the experienced Higher Clerical Officers disappeared from the scene, the union's stability was increasingly dependent on the influence of the able full-time officers which it continued to find, recently more frequently from outside the Association. But their job was constantly complicated by the alternation of moderate and left majorities on the Executive in recent years.

In 1977, about 45 per cent of the 36,000 male Clerical Officers in the Civil Service and 41 per cent of the females were under 30. Among the 30,000 Department of Health and Social Security Grade 2 Officers, nearly three-quarters of whom were female, the proportion of both sexes under 30 was 60 per cent. The National Executive Committee, the Association's controlling body between conferences, was almost entirely drawn from these grades. Since grade representation on the Executive was abandoned, Clerical Assistants and typists and machine operators had rarely found a place on it.

There was still a large proportion of Clerical Officers over 50 in 1977 – 36 per cent of the men and 31 per cent of the women – but comparatively few between 30 and 50. In the quarter of a century of near-full employment after the war the clerical grades of the Service did not greatly attract school-leavers and it became necessary to recruit tens of thousands of older people, many of them temporary clerks who gained establishment. In 1956 the age limit for establishment was raised to 60. These older groups were retiring year by year in large numbers and were replaced by youngsters who were easier to recruit and retain as heavy unemployment was back, though wastage was still high in some areas, particularly the southeast. As soon as these young men and women got their first promotion, for example to Executive Officer, they had to leave the union. This contributed to a disturbingly large turnover among active workers in the branches. On average, it was thought, branch secretaries changed every two or three years. In a union which relied more than most on voluntary workers, this contributed to volatile and unpredictable policy attitudes.

Partly because of the scarcity of young recruits in the 1950s and 1960s, the CPSA devoted much effort into attracting as many as possible into Association work, and with considerable success as was apparent to anybody who attended an

CPSA delegates at the 1977 TUC youth conference

annual conference. After the TUC started an annual Youth Award in 1970, CPSA members won it twice in six years. The first of the two in 1971 was Sid Platt, 23, of the Post Office Group, who had become secretary of his branch at 18 and led a membership drive which built it up to 95 per cent of its potential strength. He had been made editor of *The Link* and elected a member of the National Executive. The second, in 1976, was David Luxton, a 22-year-old member of the DHSS Section who joined the Association when he was 16 and had become a branch chairman and an area secretary.

The increasing proportion of women in the Association reduced the number of members from whom active Association workers could be drawn because the spare time of so many was tied up by domestic responsibilities. At the end of 1978, there were 146,250 female members out of a total of 225,000 – 65 per cent. Of the 29 members of the National Executive, including the President and two vice-presidents, only seven were women, and that was one or two more than was usual. None of the senior officers and only four of the 14 assistant secretaries were women. An analysis of the 1960 conference in *Red Tape* showed that 145 men and 22 women took part in the debates. It might have been that the proportion of women voluntary workers was higher at branch level, where the demands on their time were less and where there were reports that an increasing number of married women, returning to the Service after getting their families off their hands, were taking up local Association work.

After 1948, when Association membership stood at 153,000, it remained stagnant for 17 years, never again reaching 150,000 and twice falling below 140,000. But between 1966 and 1976 it surged up to 231,000, in the following two years falling to 225,000. Membership naturally reflects to some extent the rise and fall in the number employed in the grades which the Association covers, but there were two independent factors which pushed it up from 1966–76: the introduction of the 'check-off' (the deduction of union dues from pay by the employer) and the mergers with the Ministry of Labour Staff Association and the Court Officers' Association, which together brought in about 21,000 new members. The loss of membership from 1976 to 1978 was thought to be due partly to public expenditure cuts, partly to the subscription increase of July 1978, and partly to resignations in protest against internal policy decisions.

The check-off and the growth in membership did much to ease the chronic financial problems and avert the periodic crises which had been a source of trouble

TUC Youth Award winners: Sid Platt (top) and David Luxton

since the CSCA began. The annual conference was a hard paymaster. Asked for a 6d (2½p) increase on the monthly subscription, it was as likely as not to allow 3d (1½p) – or nothing.

Len Wines warned delegates on the subject at his first conference as General Secretary in 1963. They had succeeded in reducing the current account overdraft from £54,000 to £24,000 in a year, he said, but only as a result of a modest increase in subscriptions and a frugality in expenditure which could not continue if they wanted maximum efficiency. The General Fund balance had fallen by £14,000 and in budgeting for the following year they had to raid the Fighting Fund to avoid a further fall. The subscriptions of the main group of members had gone up by 7d (3p) in 40 years. Younger members were paying only 1½d (½p) a week more than, as a 17-year-old, he paid when he joined the CSCA in 1929.

Two years later, on the initiative of the CPSA, the Staff Side persuaded the management to deduct union dues from pay if requested and, after taking 2·5 per cent for its pains, pay the remainder to the Association concerned. For the CPSA this started on January 1, 1966. The arrangement had obvious advantages for both sides over the old system under which more than 3,000 branch and sub-branch collectors went round 150,000 members every week or month, interfering with office work while arrears built up and members dropped out and occasionally some collector would pocket the cash. The first year, 80 per cent of the members accepted the plan. Membership grew, lapsings practically disappeared and contribution income rose from £307,000 to £380,000. By 1978 the proportion of members using the scheme was 99·8 per cent.

The check-off, introduced during Wines' period of office with A R Gerrard as Treasurer, was a major step towards financial sufficiency, but the most important move of all, automatic increases in subscriptions in line with pay, had to await a

Tony Baker, who, in spite of inflation, put the union's finances on a basis which made a strike policy possible

new Treasurer, A J (Tony) Baker, who succeeded Gerrard in 1972. Baker, made responsible for the finances of an organisation which in 1978 was to have assets of more than £5 million and an income of more than £4 million, was a Croydon milkman's son who left school at the age of 14 in the confusion of war, but was later sent to college for two years under a Post Office education scheme. When he took over, the finances of the Association were based on a review of future needs made at the end of 1970 and endorsed by the 1971 conference. Almost immediately he ran into a period of mounting inflation which made nonsense of the 1970 projections. At the same time, the idea that the massive Fighting Fund needed to back the new strike policy could be obtained by a voluntary levy proved illusory.

Baker set himself with determination to put the Fighting Fund on a sound basis and revise the estimates of future needs. 'If we are to have a Fighting Fund it must be financed properly,' he told the 1973 conference. 'The only answer is to stop all the gimmicks of raffles, dances, bingo tickets and so on, to stop trying to achieve an impossible target of £5 million, and to face reality by imposing a subscription increase.' If they did not accept that, he warned the delegates, they might as well forget their Strike Policy document and forget they ever had a Fighting Fund. The conference accepted his arguments and agreed to allocate £1·20 a year to the Fighting Fund for each member.

But in 1974 inflation reached unprecedented levels and Baker had to go back to the Conference with a new review, endorsed by the NEC, which estimated the Association would need £2 million a year by 1975–76, twice the estimate made in 1970. He put forward two important new principles. The first was that subscriptions, which in the past had varied according to grade, would in future be the same for everybody except those under 20 and part-time and associate members. The second was that 10 per cent of all contribution income should go to the Fighting Fund so that the fund would grow automatically as contributions increased. The conference accepted it all, coupled with a rise in the basic contribution to £1 a month, by an overwhelming majority. More than that, the Conference instructed the NEC to investigate the possibility of relating increases of subscriptions to increases in pay.

Subscriptions are automatically related to pay increases

Two years later the NEC somewhat anxiously asked the conference to approve a sliding scale of subscriptions along those lines. People tend to be reluctant to relinquish control of the money bags and the CPSA conference seemed more likely to be difficult than most others. But Tony Baker was persuasive. The Executive was confident, he said, that rather than continue *ad hoc* arrangements, members would prefer a system of small increases each time they received a pay rise – on the clear understanding that if there was no pay increase there would be no subscription increase either. He added that part of the proposed increase would go to branches, sections and groups by way of higher rebates and per capita allowances. In future subscriptions would be 1 per cent of the Clerical Assistants' maximum. Again the Conference agreed with comparatively few dissenters.

Things seldom turn out exactly as planned. In 1976 and 1977 the Government's incomes policy only permitted increases in the form of supplements which, it was considered, did not rank as pay increases for the purpose of the new rule. When allowances were consolidated in 1978, on top of a pay rise of 9·5 per cent, the automatic increase in subscriptions was embarrassingly large – 14p a week. There was some talk of imposing it by stages, but eventually it was done all at once and most members accepted it.

Another factor in increasing income was the acquisition of a computer at Tolworth which in 1974 started building up a central membership record. The computer found that many branches exaggerated their membership and it also identified non-paying members. One example of the effect of this, quoted by Baker at the 1978 conference, was that the number of fee-paying members of the DHSS rose from 37,000 in 1974 to more than 50,000 in 1977. A new and larger computer was installed at Balham in 1978. As a result of these various developments subscription income rose from £424,000 in 1968 to £4·1 million in 1978 and the Fighting Fund from £106,000 to £1·2 million. The value of the Association's assets increased from £622,000 to £5 million.

The increased resources meant the headquarters staff could be increased to meet the new and expanded demands of a larger membership, more could be spent on education and social services, and money could be set aside for projects such as an overdue new headquarters, a residential education centre and possibly a convalescent home. The Association's officers and staff numbered 70 when it moved to Balham in 1961, expecting the premises to be adequate for 50 years. By 1978 the complement was 200. The office of Assistant General Secretary (in addition to General Secretary and Deputy General Secretary) had been created, the number of assistant secretaries had risen from ten to 14 and a second rung of six deputy assistant secretaries (HEOs) had made its appearance, all with supporting staff. A

The Balham headquarters

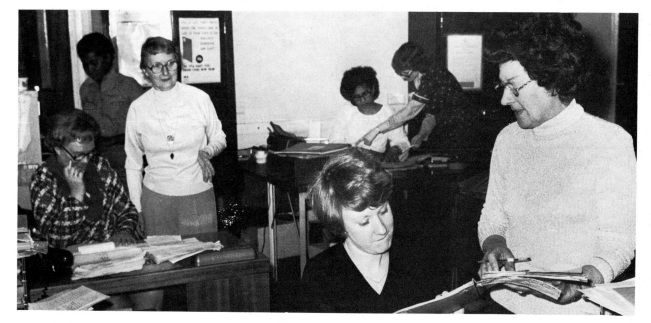

Girls at work in the finance department

research department and library were built up from 1965 onwards. The National Organiser, Alex Ritchie, had been given a deputy and four assistants. To accommodate all this, the headquarters at Balham had been supplemented by a new building at Nightingale Lane, not far away, to which the chief officers moved, the computer centre at Tolworth and other offices.

The amount spent on trade union education rose from about £20,000 in 1969 to £100,000 in 1978, when it was estimated that about a thousand students went through the weekend, mid-week or full-week courses arranged by headquarters and Sections. Most of the money went on hotel bills. The CPSA grudged this and wanted the proposed residential centre started as soon as possible. It was envisaged that the Nightingale Lane premises might be converted into a college when the new headquarters was established.

Baker paid a lot of attention to the improvement and expansion of the Association's Friendly Benefits. 'We get what we pay for and let us ensure we *do* get what we pay for,' a delegate said when increased contributions were discussed at the 1976 conference. Improving benefits went along with Baker's inclination and at the same time demonstrated, at comparatively small cost, the Association's ability to help members over the problems of their lives outside the office. In the environment of a welfare state and with employers providing comparatively safe employment and their own range of social services, there had not been demand from the membership for costly sick pay or unemployment benefits.

There was a death benefit scheme, dating back to the inter-war years, under which next-of-kin benefits were raised from £40 in 1973 to £265 in 1978, and a small benevolent fund used to supplement the first-class employers' schemes. The Association's old under-utilised convalescent home in Hayling Island had to be closed in 1965 but £10 a week for two weeks was contributed to the costs of members who entered a convalescent or rest home. The Association offered free initial advice on any legal problem and helped with personal accident claims. It had an insurance scheme for victims of assaults while on duty by members of the public – a not uncommon occurrence in social security and employment offices – and for personal accidents while on duty outside normal office hours. There was a holiday

Alex Ritchie, the national organiser, was given a deputy and four assistants

guide, a new holiday travel scheme and a popular motor insurance scheme introduced in 1973 and, from the autumn of 1978, a shopping guide to cut-price facilities. The Association diary was issued 'at a very modest price'. In 1978 it sold 100,000 copies and made a profit of nearly £20,000.

The most expensive item was the free issue of *Red Tape*, which cost more than £200,000 net in 1978. A charge of 3d (1½p) a copy used to be made but the 1961 conference decided it should be free on request. Circulation immediately rose from 40,000 to 120,000 and in 1978 was more than 200,000. Since it was free, branches tended to order enough copies for all their members but it was supposed that many unread copies went to be pulped. There was a motion at the 1978 conference that it should be replaced by a tabloid newspaper type of publication, but after powerful resistance by Clive Bush, the editor, it was easily defeated, as similar motions had been before.

Since the Second World War a monthly magazine called *Braille Tape*, consisting mostly of extracts from *Red Tape*, had been provided for the Association's 70 or so blind members, mostly typists and shorthand typists but including some telephone operators. At the end of 1978, the CPSA was considering the production of a new rule book by cassette recording for these members, for whom the Association had done much good work.

Blind CPSA members at the 1962 Albert Hall rally

The check-off had been invaluable in maintaining a stable paying membership, but it also had one serious disadvantage. It meant the disappearance of the collectors who, listening to grievances and explaining union policy on their rounds, had always been the first line of contact, often the only line of contact, between individual members and the Association. Much thought was given to alternative ways of maintaining communications, but the problem was not fully solved. The Association membership was spread all over the United Kingdom and there were still some groups in Gibraltar and elsewhere abroad, though these were much fewer than in the days of the British Empire. At home, the CSD and the ministries had their headquarters in London so the headquarters of the union and the various sections also had to be in London. When Government departments split or coalesce, the structure of the Associations must follow suit. But 75 per cent of the CPSA membership is not in London. When large parts of a department have been dispersed, large branches have been created to negotiate with them. Apart from such groups of Government employees, many departments, such as the DHSS and the Department of Employment, have offices all over the country where small groups of men and women are employed, and the CPSA had to cater for them as well. It had about 1,100 branches and 4,700 sub-branches in 1978, but it was estimated there were 32,000 workplaces in which its members are employed, many in small numbers and often at a distance from the nearest branch. Some were not even able to get to their branch to record votes, so that for practical purposes they were not only isolated but also disenfranchised.

The Association therefore had a double problem: how to maintain communications with large branches without collectors and how to enable all the little scattered groups of members to play a part in its life. The CPSA had always been among the most open of unions. The amount of paper it circulated to Sections, groups, branches and members was colossal. In 1978 it used internally 45 tons, which does not take into account the large amount distributed by outside printers. Hardly a week passed without a member receiving some circular, report or journal. But paper can never be a satisfactory substitute for personal contacts.

There was practically nothing an active member could not know about the running of the Association if he wanted to know. Since the 1977 conference, National Executive minutes were sent free to any branch that asked for them and they record how the various members vote on contentious issues. Only about one-fifth of the branches asked for copies in 1977–78. The ample letter columns of *Red Tape* were always available for upward communication. There remained the apathetic mass of members who did not find time to read documents or go to branch meetings. A hundred or two often took decisions in the name of thousands.

The proportion of members who attend meetings of small branches is usually larger than that of big branches and in recent years there had been a trend to break up some of the biggest. For instance, one branch of the London Post Office Telecommunications Region was split into ten. The 4,000 members in the Metropolitan Police staff were divided into eight branches. In the north-east, the child benefit section was separated from the Newcastle DHSS branch, which nevertheless remained the largest.

Inevitably, there was resistance to this carving up. Most of the big branches worked out their own systems of communication, adjusted to their special problems. The Newcastle DHSS branch, for instance, was mainly housed in premises originally designed for a hospital. They consisted of 13 single-storey blocks, one of five storeys and one of three storeys surmounted by a tower, all spread over one very large site. In addition, there was an office in Hebburn-on-

Problems of organising a scattered membership

Tyne and one in Central Newcastle. This Branch replaced collectors by appointing block agents, and floor agents in the multi-storey blocks. The block agents were responsible for distributing *Red Tape* and other literature and for representing the interests of the block members to the Branch Executive, of which they were all members. There was something similar to an embryo shop steward system here but the agents were elected at the annual general meeting, attended at most by a few hundred out of the 8,000 members, not by their block membership. The branch tried out pilot schemes for block committees. It had its own journal, *Headway*, printed for it by the management every two months, and a regular day school for rank and file members. General meetings of members were held every quarter. In one block the branch had three rooms at its disposal along a corridor which also provided a room for the Newcastle DHSS Staff Side and one for the Society and one for the Civil Service Union. Several of the chief branch officers were engaged full time on Association work and two or three others 50 per cent of the time, the remainder getting time off as required.

Expanding branch consultation

The National Association developed an extensive system of branch consultation before major decisions were taken, such as the calling of industrial action or the acceptance of a pay offer. Branches were required to consult their members, either at a general meeting or by ballot. At the 1977 Rules Revision Conference, two new bodies were established: the Northern and Southern Departmental Assemblies. They enabled representatives of branches in fringe bodies and small Government departments to discuss common problems, listen to Association leaders and explain their own attitudes, but it was difficult for the employees of the wide variety of fringe bodies to find common ground.

The appointment of four assistant national organisers under Alex Ritchie in 1977 was the most interesting attempt to develop contacts with the membership scattered about the country. By the autumn of 1978 they had visited more than 100 branches, the majority of which covered many locations over a wide geographical area, holding meetings with members and non-members to stimulate union activity and aid recruitment, apparently with some success. 'It is obvious,' it was reported, 'that branches with a large ambit find communications with members on a regular basis very difficult, and it is quite understandable that members in this situation feel isolated. The danger of this situation, of course, is lack of participation by many members in the management of their branches and, as a consequence, we have found disillusionment and a poor knowledge of union affairs in many areas. Coupled with this we have a high turnover of branch representatives and officers, many on promotion, and the insoluble problem of apathy. We have found a number of branches which would be in a state of demise but for the untiring efforts of some CPSA stalwarts who strive to keep the CPSA alive and operable.' In 1978 it was decided to separate the organisation and education departments.

As 1978 drew to an end there was talk of two major changes to improve the place in the Association of the scattered pockets of membership. One was a new voting system which would enable every member to cast a vote at his place of work instead of having to attend a branch meeting. The other was the creation of a regional organisation which would reflect the fact that the bulk of the membership no longer lived and worked in London.

In 1974, in response to a conference resolution, the NEC made a detailed report on the case for setting up regional offices. They found against it, at least for the time being, and the 1975 conference accepted the verdict. The only function the report could find for regional officers was to advise branches in their area, but it would be impossible for them to have detailed knowledge of all the branches or of all the sections to which they belonged. The cost would be formidable. It would be more economical and convenient to make use of departmental facilities than to set up their own in every region.

Moreover, the report continued, the CPSA was exceptionally fortunate in its supply of volunteers able and willing to undertake branch officer work. 'The CPSA is in a position of having large numbers of members whose potential capacity is being under-utilised. Even those trade unions which represent executive grades often have more difficulty in getting competition for branch officer jobs than does the CPSA. The reason is plain. A man or woman who does executive work for a living is less likely to be ready to do it as a hobby than a clerical worker who finds in it a welcome opportunity to stretch his wings and develop his potential abilities. For these reasons, the CPSA can claim to have a higher average quality of voluntary activist than the majority of trade unions, and this is confirmed by the very efficient branches in the Association – branches who would be resistant to the idea of yielding up any of their autonomy to any professional officers whatsoever. Where our branch officers are good they tend to be very good because they have a local knowledge and relationships with their members and their management which a professional officer, calling in only occasionally, could not hope to rival.'

The assistant organisers did not find it all like that and the case for a regional structure was vigorously revived. In his address to the 1978 conference, the President, Len Lever, said the difficulty had reached a point where he was not satisfied with the service obtained by branches and his fellow senior officers shared his view. The basic weakness would need 'some novel and drastic changes in our HQ establishment and in the regions outside London.'

The case for a regional structure is revived

The Association was constructed in the days when there was no strike policy. The weapons were negotiation, arbitration and political pressure and consequently negotiations were given a higher priority than organisation and the CPSA did not adjust to the new priorities. Central negotiations affected members at all levels so it was natural for authority to be centralised. All contributions went to the headquarters which paid all conference and educational expenses and provided the professional officers who acted as secretaries for the sections and groups. It received all subscriptions and made allocations to meet their needs. From an income of £4·2 million in 1978 it distributed £259,000 to the sections and groups and £160,000 to the 1,100 branches.

There existed area co-ordinating committees, supposed not to be concerned with policy matters, though some of them transgressed occasionally, but with the local co-ordination of educational programmes, national campaigns, etc. They did not have the trouble-shooting and organising role which was played by the assistant organisers and which, it was suggested, would be better played if there were more of them and if they were stationed in the regions. There were 70,000 non-unionists in the Civil Service grades for which the CPSA catered. The more of them that could be brought in, and the stronger the services provided for them, the stronger would be the case for a closed shop, for which the Association had pressed for several years.

While in 1978 the CPSA was considering the case for a regional structure, it was also trying to make up its mind about Sectional developments which threatened the Association's traditional policy on clerical pay. It began in the Department of Health and Social Security six years earlier when there was growing unrest in local offices about inadequate staffing, increased complexity of work and frequent changes in benefits. About the same time, Peter Thomason, who had been active in the Post Office Group, was made an assistant secretary and given responsibility for the DHSS as his first job. Trouble began in September 1972 when, to test member reaction, an overtime ban was imposed in Scotland. It was so successful that the Section Executive declared an overtime ban to cover all offices throughout the country. Within six months the Conservative Government had provided between 4,000 and 5,000 more officers and set up a joint working party to look at the system of fixing staff complements, of which the employees had until then known little. It was agreed that instead of determining complements annually and covering unforeseen demands by overtime they would be fixed quarterly, thus making possible quick adjustments.

The result was to inspire a new self-confidence and militancy in the DHSS Section, which with more than 50,000 members was the largest in the Association. It was in this period of growing activity and influence that, in the aftermath of the 1973 national industrial action, the Section caused so much excitement at the annual conference by proposing to refuse to pay benefit increases.

In 1974, Mrs Barbara Castle, Secretary of State for Social Services in the new Labour Government, announced in Parliament, without prior consultation with the unions, that proposed increases in benefits were to be put forward from November to July. There was an immediate outcry from the staff who complained it was impossible to make the necessary preparations in time and imposed a ban on overtime. Urgent meetings followed as a result of which Mrs Castle confessed in the House of Commons that she had acted precipitately. Eventually an agreement was reached on the work to be done, including a provision that anybody who worked 25 hours overtime should be granted an extra day's annual leave. A demand for a bonus payment of £50 was rejected but instead the staff, after much persuasion, agreed to the establishment of a joint committee to undertake a job evaluation exercise to see if local staff were entitled to a special allowance. Eventually they were offered £80 a year, later raised to £100. There was sharp division within the DHSS. The evaluation had shown the case for extra pay for local officers but not for the big blocks of DHSS staff at Newcastle, Blackpool and the London headquarters. At a section conference, Newcastle and Blackpool voted against the agreement but it was approved by a narrow majority, a favourable vote from London turning the scale.

Barbara Castle, who as Secretary of State for Social Services initiated far-reaching negotiations on the pay and conditions of members of the Department

At the 1974 annual CPSA conference, the DHSS made a motion instructing the NEC to negotiate a departmental allowance not only for the DHSS but for every other section of the membership for which a case could be made. Bill Kendall pointed out that the conference had already approved an NEC document on future pay policy which recommended a strengthened and improved Pay Research system. Delegates would have to consider, he said, how they could integrate this particular demand into their policy objectives and in particular the possibility of preserving the national rates of pay for everybody at a rate sufficiently high to satisfy those grades, or parts of grades within departments, that would have to make do with the nationally determined rate of pay. 'The strength of our union lies in the ability to unify membership pressure,' he concluded. 'In relation to the issue before us we must devise a method of approach which avoids fragmentation, which avoids division within our own ranks.' The motion was carried, the offer accepted and from April 1, 1975, two new grades came into being in DHSS local offices – Local Officer I (formerly Executive Officer) and Local Officer II (formerly Clerical Officer). Among the justifications for the special allowance were the skill needed to handle applicants across the counter, many of them immigrants, the need for familiarity with complex legislation, frequent pressures of work and the growing risk of assault by aggrieved members of the public.

Inevitably other departmental claims for special treatment followed. The Ministry of Defence Section revived the case for increases for all their Clerical Officer members on the grounds that internal pay differentials had been disturbed by productivity agreements for government industrial workers, a claim rejected by the CSD and abandoned when the 1971 CPSA conference decided against departmental bargaining. The Department of Employment Section also asked for a pay and grading review similar to that which proved successful in the DHSS, but with resulting gains pooled to provide something for all CPSA grades. The DHSS proposed an extension of the Local Officer II allowances to its other members. The work done at headquarters, regional offices, Blackpool and Newcastle was interdependent, it said, and involved similar problems and pressures. A fourth claim was proposed for County Court Clerical Officers based on the quality and complexity of the work done. Attention was also drawn to the long-standing lead over the Clerical Officer scale enjoyed by Tax Officers.

There were thus claims for allowances on top of the CO scale from four Sections, including the three largest in the Association: the DHSS with (at the end of 1978) about 55,000 members; the Ministry of Defence with 32,000, and the Department of Employment with 26,000. Together they covered more than half the Association's Civil Service membership and about half its total membership. If the claims proved successful, it was impossible to believe that other sections would not try to catch up. The Civil Service Department was naturally anxious to know the CPSA's attitude to such claims before considering them.

Other big sections try to catch up with the DHSS

At the end of 1978 headquarters officers, committees and research officers were pondering over the problem, a problem made harder because the Ministry of Defence claim was on different grounds from those of the others. They could hardly turn down claims from so formidable a mass of members, but were they to destroy the national Clerical Officer grade which Bill Brown had fought so hard to establish and later leaders to preserve? If better quality work was to be split into departmental grades it could undermine the position of the basic Clerical Grades under Pay Research. The minds of the leaders were moving towards the creation of a new grading structure which would allow higher pay for more responsible work in all sections and branches. It was thought this would in some ways ease PRU negotiations since in many outside organisations the work done by Clerical Officers encompassed more than one grade.

At the same time Alistair Graham was preparing a paper on the possible repercussions of new computer technology, thinking in terms of revising the Association's opposition to all forms of productivity bargaining. Perhaps it would be possible to bargain for efficiency payments in return for co-operation in technological advance. And perhaps the Ministry of Defence claim could be fitted into the arrangement. But would the sections involved be prepared to wait while the complex negotiations for such a national re-structuring were taking place? Or would they resort to competitive battles to get what they could for their own members and let the pay structure become fragmented?

Looking at possible repercussions of the new computer technology

CHAPTER TWENTY
Right-Left, Right-Left, Right-

The CPSA has always had a vigorous tradition of internal debate. I have always believed that, at the best, this has been creative – but at its lowest level it is a potent weapon of destructive tension. If we become enmeshed in hatreds and bigotries we will destroy our credibility with the public, other unions, the employer, and not least, our own members.
Bill Kendall in his last address to conference as General Secretary, 1976.

We have now become, to some extent, a trade union where the great principle of fraternity is, except among those who share beliefs, almost non-existent. I attend schools, delegations and meetings and the evidence is there for anyone to see. The boycotting of social functions designed for all to enjoy – or to pretend to enjoy – the suspicion and trap-setting – the inability even to have a drink and talk together – are very sad and very destructive of those values we are supposed to share as trade unionists.
Len Lever, President, at the 1978 conference.

Once again the warring factions which cripple our union have brought us to a crisis. The fanatics of both extremes haggle over their rights to impose their philosophy upon us. Our corporate welfare appears to be secondary to the political hunger of the self-styled crusaders of the right and would-be revolutionaries of the left.
Red Tape, November 1978.

We left the political in-fighting in the Association at the end of Chapter 12 in the middle 1960s, with the left removed from all national positions of power or influence by a moderate caucus known as The Group. A few far-away, far-left voices were still heard – those of Ron Meth and Peggy Dear in the Ministry of Housing and Local Government, for instance, and of the Christie brothers and Alex McMaster in Scotland, but one by one they were promoted away to pursue their ideals in the Society of Civil and Public Servants.

Political in-fighting in the Association is resumed

Gradually a new left emerged, not exclusively far left to begin with, certainly not exclusively Communist, but with beliefs ranging from those of the Labour Party centre to those of socialist revolutionaries. They were united – when they were united – only by opposition to The Group. The new militant spirit stirred up by Bill Kendall seemed to release many members from their former resignation. He himself had risen to the general secretaryship on the back of The Group but was among its most destructive critics. Complaints about The Group in the early stages curiously resembled the complaints about Communist domination in the immediate post-war period. It was a secret, self-perpetuating oligarchy, it was said. Anyone who opposed it was labelled as a Communist or fellow-traveller. To get on its list was the only passport to office. The Group itself, assured at that time of the backing of some of the largest branches, such as the Newcastle Central Office with 7,500 votes, the London Telephone Region with 7,500, and the London Post Office Savings Bank with 5,500, appeared complacent.

As time went on its bases were swept away. The Newcastle DHSS turned 'militant', the London Telephone Region was broken up and the Post Office Savings Bank became the National Savings Bank in red Glasgow. Battle was joined not only at national level but in every section and large branch until in the anniversary year, 1978, war was being carried on by the activists throughout the Association with unprecedented bitterness and ruthlessness. The rank-and-file, so far as one could tell, thoroughly disliked it but could not do anything about it.

The first faint hint of restiveness came within The Group itself, when a younger element consisting of Len Lever, Tommy Thomson and Ken Blinkhorn was elected to the Executive and occasionally questioned Group policies, but with little effect. In 1969 Clive Bush, who had made a name for himself with his conference speeches, became the first open opponent of The Group to be elected to the NEC – but immediately resigned. He explained his action in a letter to *Red Tape*: 'For some weeks before conference I was aware of a rumour, ostensibly fostered by the anonymous "group" which controls all CPSA elections, that I was being "officially supported". Those who know that I have fought this self-appointed body for years, seeking to inform the ordinary members of its obnoxious methods and the damaging effect on Association affairs, will understand what harm such a rumour would have done if I had taken the NEC seat.'

Bush, son of a mechanical engineer and active trade unionist at a London tyre factory, worked as a copy boy for a news agency, had three years in the merchant navy, two years national service and a miserable six months as a typewriter salesman before he entered the Civil Service in 1959 and was allocated to the Ministry of Housing and Local Government, which was later merged into the Department of the Environment. Politically roused by the well-organised far-left activities of the Ministry's CPSA branch, he became, as he later told an interviewing committee considering him for the editorship of *Red Tape*, a Marxist but not a member of any party.

During the following year Reg Williams of the DHSS, another rebel who had narrowly missed election, was 'called up' to replace a retiring NEC member, and Charlie Elliott of the Post Office, who had been elected with Group support, moved into opposition, to be followed by two other Post Office members, Billy Rashley and John Roberts. Bush was elected again in 1970 as was Mike Anderton of the DHSS, who joined the radicals. Thus in a single year the new left, or radical group, had established a nucleus of six on the NEC and had a promising base in the Post Office and DHSS.

Reg Williams, who had an eloquent and effervescent personality, came from South Wales, where he had been a chapel elder at 16½, had gone down the mines on Nationalisation Day, and led a strike of youths and joined the Young Communist League at 18. After something of a rolling-stone existence, he left the Communist Party because of Soviet intervention in Hungary and got employment with the National Assistance Board which merged into the Department of Health and Social Security. His political views were now similar to those of the Labour Party's *Tribune* group.

Elliott was a middle-of-the-road Labour supporter but not active in politics. He was a shrewd committee man and his great strength was as an operator behind the scenes. He came of a Yorkshire West Riding mining family – his father also worked on the railways and was an active trade unionist. Elliott had seven years in the Navy before entering the Civil Service in 1954.

Clive Bush was elected to the NEC and immediately resigned, later became editor of 'Red Tape'

Charlie Elliott, who switched from the New Left to be the Moderates' chairman

Reg Williams (above) of the Labour Left; several times senior Vice-President

Len Lever, who challenged a Group nominee for a vice-presidency and had two spells as President

The main force behind the new left was the Post Office Group, then in a restless state following its transfer to the public corporation and disturbed by an officer's misappropriation of its Staff Side funds and the laxity which had allowed it. Uncertain about its future, worried by its loss of influence in the CPSA, as the 1973 conference showed, it badly needed a strong new leadership. It got it in the appointment of Alistair Graham as its full-time secretary and in the election of new voluntary officers who included Elliott as Assistant Secretary. Graham was young (28 in 1970), a forceful speaker, energetic, skilful and ambitious. A Northumbrian, he was educated at Newcastle Grammar School, was articled to a solicitor, became a trainee hospital administrator and worked in the legal department of the Transport and General Workers' Union before moving to the CPSA in 1966 as an assistant secretary. He had been active in the Labour Party and in the general election of 1966 was a parliamentary candidate for the Brighton Pavilion constituency. He and Elliott worked closely together and formed a powerful partnership.

The new left not only obtained a nucleus of NEC members at the 1970 conference but also defeated one of The Group's two vice-president nominees. The Group had originally nominated Harry Gordge and Charles Garrick but Garrick had to withdraw because of illness and they decided to put forward Mary Layton instead. Miss Layton was regarded with general affection but some of the new left and a few on the right resented The Group making an arbitrary choice in this way and were doubtful whether she had the right qualities for the job. After an Executive meeting, Reg Williams and Charlie Elliott were in the bar when Len Lever came in and they asked him if he would be willing to stand for the office. Lever was a popular, outspoken, unaffected character with no sharp political axe to grind. He had been Secretary of The Group the previous year, but after some hesitation and much persuasion, he agreed. This was in March and the campaign was half-way through but both Elliott and Williams were able to get a few branches to nominate him and he was elected Junior Vice-President by 69,854 votes to 65,153 for Mary Layton. The radicals were jubilant because the result showed

The 1970 conference votes to abolish groups

that in the right circumstances The Group could be beaten. Lever was ostracised by some of The Group leaders.

A native of Ealing, Lever served in the Navy during the war, becoming a Petty Officer. Afterwards he got a job as a Clerical Officer in the Savings Bank, devoting much of his time to amateur dramatics, for which he received a number of awards. He gradually gave this up as he became increasingly involved in trade union work, turning to classical music for relaxation.

The 1970 conference carried by a substantial majority a motion saying that the existence of a group or groups in an atmosphere of secrecy hindered progress towards unity. It instructed the NEC to investigate the constitutional changes necessary either to end such secret groupings or to establish all such groupings within the framework of the constitution. Clive Bush, supporting, said that almost without exception candidates on The Group list were elected to the NEC and that smear tactics were used against other candidates. The Executive was against the motion, but Bill Kendall, who had sought and been given a free hand, declared that secret group activity did exist and effectively influenced all elections. He did not object to canvassing but believed the domination of Association affairs by one group was unhealthy. The time had come for the voluntary dissolution of all of the groups.

The Executive was apparently convinced and the following year submitted a constitutional amendment which read: 'Canvassing for nominations and votes by the circulation of lists, and the organisation or participation in the activities of unofficial committees or similar bodies which seek to influence the policies or electoral processes of the Association, shall be deemed detrimental to the interests of the Association.' This was accepted and became Rule 9.4. The Group met and formally dissolved itself but the factional struggle continued unabated.

The new left continued to make steady progress. In 1971 Lever became Senior Vice-President and Elliott failed by a small margin to join him. Bush and Williams topped the elections for the NEC in which the left increased its seats to 11. In 1972

Peter Coltman, Communist leader and chairman of the Broad Left

Len Lever was elected President without opposition and Bush became Senior Vice-President. Both retained these offices in 1973, when the left got 13 seats, or half the Executive, and in 1974 when the new left for the first time secured a majority – 16 seats to 10 for the moderates. All these NEC figures, which exclude the President and two vice-presidents, are subject to minor error because of the difficulty of being certain of individual allegiances at any particular time. Occasionally there were movements from one side to the other. Sometimes, when a member retired or was promoted, someone from an opposing group was called up to replace him.

Peter Coltman, a tall, unkempt, whiskered man who came to be accepted as leader of the Communists in the Association, was elected to the Executive in 1971 after a period on the Standing Orders Committee. The son of a Conservative joiner in Harrogate, Coltman had tried to pay his way to a science degree at Leeds University by working as a laboratory assistant but was prevented by illness from completing the course, and got employment with the Savings Bank in Harrogate. There he became secretary of the CPSA branch, which contested the local authority elections as 'Employment and Sound Economy' candidates, aiming at protecting its members' Civil Service employment within a dispersal exercise. He joined the Communist Party not long after election to the NEC.

In 1972 another new personality appeared on the scene: Mike McGrath, a member of the International Socialists, later the Socialist Workers' Party (SWP). During that year's conference he and about a dozen others, including one Communist and others on the Labour Party far left, met to discuss how to make their influence felt on Association policy. Larger meetings followed in London and in the late summer they produced their own paper which they called *Redder Tape*. McGrath was a white collar worker who for a time had a job as a building operative before getting employment in the British Museum Library. A live-minded, provocative, densely-bearded character with a sense of humour, he did not get on to the Executive (as a *Redder Tape* candidate) until 1976 and the Socialist Workers' Party never had a big following. When McGrath stood for the presidency in 1976 and 1977, he got only about 13,000 votes, whereas 100,000 were needed to win. *Redder Tape* was important as a catalyst which gave impetus to the underground factional struggles which continued in spite of Rule 9.4. The SWP frequently attracted public notice by such things as right-to-work and anti-Nazi demonstrations and CPSA notice by rank-and-file conferences which attracted its members.

In 1973 Elliott 'crossed the floor' to the moderate side, where he and Kate Losinska, a dedicated anti-Marxist, soon became the recognised leaders. He had always been anti-Communist and was worried because it seemed to him the new left was coming under Communist domination and his influence was declining. He felt he had created a monster which he could not control. He expected his Post Office colleagues to see things as he did but they did not do so.

Controversy was enlivened in this period by occasional attacks on the far left by a regular contributor to *Red Tape* writing under the name of John Kirby. Jimmy O'Dea gave him a free hand but also published many angry letters replying to his criticisms. An article which caused particular irritation was one which surveyed some of the various left-wing factions and concluded: 'The "way out" left organisations can do good in so far as they sharpen the wits of the young and bring them into active unionism. But unless youngsters grow out of these juvenile far left allegiances very quickly, they do more harm than good by diverting unions from their real function, which is *not* to foster violent political ideas but simply in the words of the CPSA constitution to "protect and promote the interests of its members".'

Mike McGrath founder of 'Redder Tape' and leader of the Socialist Workers' Party

Among the many who replied was Mike McGrath. 'As a revolutionary socialist I say that only one general solution exists to our problems – a society owned and controlled by us, the working people,' he wrote. 'We as socialists are active in our unions because we believe only working people can change this world. The Heaths and Wilsons never . . . According to John Kirby all the "way-out left" are "young". I'm 32 and I suppose could still be considered young but many in the socialist movement that I know are 50, 60 and even older. Could it be that he wishes to equate young with gullible?'

The discovery that John Kirby was the pen-name of Keith Mason, an industrial correspondent on *The Sun*, led to a motion at the 1974 conference proposing that only CPSA members should be allowed to write regularly for *Red Tape*. Jimmy O'Dea replied that this was the first time in history the proud tradition of the independence of the editor had been challenged at conference and the motion was rejected overwhelmingly, though this was the conference at which the new left first got control of the Executive.

Early in the next year Bill Kendall lost patience with the International Socialists. An NEC motion from the moderate group had expressed concern at the attempts by International Socialists to influence the policy of the Association through *Redder Tape* and by direct distribution of guidance to delegates at conference. It expressed even more concern 'at the renewed threat of more traditional Marxist influence on the thinking of NEC members and its subsequent effect upon the policy of the Association and the good name of CPSA within the trade union movement.' However, an amendment was carried by 11 votes to 6 which omitted the reference to the International Socialists and *Redder Tape* and the 'Marxist influence' but expressed concern at attempts to influence the policy of the Association through the medium of anonymous circulars.

Bill Kendall loses patience with the International Socialists

Kendall quoted the amended resolution in *Red Tape* in February 1975, adding specific criticism of the International Socialists and *Redder Tape*, and referred to Rule 9.4. 'The International Socialists,' he asserted, 'believe that the end of the capitalist system is imminent and that they are the self-appointed leadership who will drive us all into an undefined Communist society. They do not aim to change the policies of the trade union movement – they aim to destroy it, in the false belief that something of value to the working class will emerge miraculously from the ashes.' Kendall did not confine his criticisms to the International Socialists. 'An equally unpleasant and more recent manifestation has appeared,' he wrote, 'in the form of anonymous and libellous circulars emanating from a group of self-styled "moderates".'

Kendall returned to the subject two months later to reply to counter-attacks in *Socialist Worker*, the organ of the International Socialists, which he said had accused him of 'slander', 'astonishing hypocrisy', 'blatant insults', 'patent nonsense', 'smears', 'infantile jibes' and 'witch hunting'. He accepted that the Socialists and *Redder Tape* did not start the practice of electioneering and policy formation by methods contrary to the CPSA constitution, but 'they have organised so extensively and with such bitterness as to produce the sharpest of reactions and thus endanger the vital unity of the Association.' He went on to quote from an International Socialists document detailing the activities of its Civil Service faction.

Once more there were angry retorts in the letter columns. One of the more restrained came again from McGrath. '*Redder Tape* was conceived by CPSA members who were united in their *opposition* to the undercover electioneering that goes on in the Association,' he wrote. 'We wanted and want conflicts that exist in any trade union to be in the open and not discussed behind the backs of the members.' Norman Jacobs of the British Museum said he was on the editorial board of *Redder Tape* when its programme was drawn up and at that time the Board consisted of three socialist members, three communist members, two of no political party and one Labour Party member (himself).

When Lever's three years as President came to an end in 1975, the natural successor would have been Clive Bush, who had been Senior Vice-President for three years, but in the autumn of 1974 he was appointed editor of *Red Tape* in succession to Jimmy O'Dea. There was no opposition at the time but considerable sniping at him by moderates afterwards. His appointment meant that Kate Losinska, the Junior Vice-President, had a less well-known left opponent, Walter Adamson, in the contest for the presidency, and she beat him by 92,543 votes to 82,600 though the left retained a majority on the Executive. Within a year, however, she had become the centre of a major controversy which resulted in Lever taking over again in 1976 for a second three-year stint.

Losinska, of the Office of Population Censuses and Surveys branch, was born and bred in Croydon but with Irish and Scottish as well as English blood in her veins. She came of a family in which it was traditional to enter the fighting service – her father was in the army for 35 years. She entered the Civil Service in 1939 straight from school.

During the war she met and married a wounded Polish bomber pilot who later became the buying manager of the china and glass department of a big store. She was the first grandmother to become President of the Association. Never active in party politics, her sympathies were broadly Labour.

In August 1975 she attended a literary lunch given by Reader's Digest at which there was discussion of the possibility of a symposium on 'The Marxist Battle for Britain'. She gave an interview on which a 'ghosted' article was based and other contributions were obtained from Frank Chapple, leader of the electricians' union, Lord Robens, chairman of Vickers, and Brian Walden, a right-wing Labour MP. The symposium was published in February 1976.

Kate Losinska warns of the danger of a Marxist take-over and goes to law

Her main theme was the danger of a Marxist take-over in Britain. 'With their massive and covert recruitment of public service employees – nearly 10 per cent of the active membership of my union are now supporters of the militant-left – Marxists are simply following a blue-print that helped bring control in Eastern Europe,' she said. 'For were local and central government paralysed, extremists could conceivably take over the whole country.' She referred to public service strikes as warning twinges, including some in which CPSA members were involved. 'The biggest casualty of Marxist militancy has been the tradition that public servants would, whatever their grievances, carry on with their duties,' she continued in what was interpreted as an attack on the CPSA strike policy. 'Our hard-pressed security services now face many new tasks. At one time they were mainly concerned in catching traitors passing State secrets to Soviet bloc countries. Today they must also check the subtler sabotage of Trotskyists prepared to do anything to discredit the State.'

The articles by the CPSA President and other contributors were quoted in the newspapers and there was an immediate outcry in the CPSA. The NEC decided to reprimand the President, censure her conduct and issue a motion and statement to members countering allegations made in the article. Branches prepared angry motions of censure for the annual conference. Suddenly, everything of the sort was stopped. Kate Losinska went to law and obtained an injunction to prevent publication of the NEC statement and the censure motions. The Association appealed but without success. The legal judgement was based on the view that a censure would amount to a charge of misconduct and that under Association rules this could only be determined by a semi-independent tribunal.

However, when the delegates assembled at Margate for the annual conference they were allowed to debate one branch motion which expressed concern about the article but did not include the word censure. When Mrs Losinska rose to make her presidential address to the main conference, she plunged at once into a careful defence of what she had done. A small, prim figure, spectacled, thin-lipped, with red hair drawn tightly back from a high forehead, she faced the thousand delegates with courage and dignity. 'I believe that the stand I took against extremism, a personal stand, was a real issue,' she said. 'A person who has been elected to an unpaid position in a voluntary organisation has not, therefore, forfeited the right of free speech. I believe that one of the fundamental rights of an officer of a trade union is to express, as a private citizen, opinions on matters of public concern.'

Losinska referred to circulars which had been issued at a time when it was possible to affect election results. She had been stopped from issuing a circular of her own. She truly regretted any unintended offence to any section of the membership. 'I sought to reveal what I believe to be a threat to democracy,' she continued, 'and get across my unshaken belief that our union members are the

Kate Losinska, Secretary of the CPSA Moderates, addressing the 1977 Trades Union Congress

victims, and not the instigators, of minority control by politically motivated persons. I have been harassed over many weeks, but as a life-long trade unionist and a socialist I have fought to uphold principles which I hold dear, principles that demand a duty to myself, the membership of the CPSA and this country to defend our heritage of free speech.'

Kate Losinska already knew that she had been ousted from the Presidency. 'I shall still fight on for the right to express my views and your right to express your views and I shall stand again for the presidency,' she declared.

Bill Kendall put the Executive's point of view. The issue, he said, had developed into a struggle to preserve for members, for branches, for the Executive Committee, the right to disapprove and if necessary dissociate themselves from actions of elected representatives and to do so without resorting to legal machinery and without using the Association's elaborate disciplinary machinery. 'It's the Executive Committee that's been gagged, its branches that have been gagged in this thing. We have had pages and pages and pages in the national press, but nobody willing to present our case . . . I personally very much regret that the law has been prompted to intrude into our internal affairs, but then I'm old-fashioned enough to believe that in the rough and tumble of trade union life, you have to expect a few knocks, especially when you chance your arm and it does not pay off. And I'm old-fashioned enough to believe that people who choose to seek high office and the plaudits of their colleagues should also be prepared to accept the reprimands and, yes, the censures without running for the protection of the law. I'm old-fashioned enough to believe that the traditions of this Association and the rights of its members are worth fighting to preserve. Since its beginning censure motions as a form of reprimand have been part of the tradition of the Association, and the ability to air grievances and call their leaders to account in whatever terms they wish, has been a fundamental right of members.'

No quarter was given by either side in the debate that followed until it was abruptly ended by a motion for 'next business' which the vast majority thought a merciful release. Though Losinska lost the presidency by 20,000 votes, she came top in the Executive ballot, in which the moderates gained some ground.

At the same conference the delegates enthusiastically endorsed the unanimous recommendation of the NEC that Ken Thomas should succeed Bill Kendall as the Association General Secretary. Kendall, with only a couple of years left before he reached the CPSA retiring age of 55, had accepted an invitation to become Secretary General of the National Staff Side in June of the following year, 1976.

The choice of Thomas's successor as Deputy General Secretary was a more contentious matter. The previous year there had been a factional struggle over the appointment to the new position of Assistant General Secretary, a job created partly to provide a senior officer as secretary of the Post Office group. The Selection Committee had decided by 6 votes to 5 to recommend Alistair Graham for the job in preference to the most senior assistant secretary, R W Footman, with the left voting for Graham and support for Footman coming from the President and Mrs Losinska and the three senior officers, Kendall, Thomas and Baker. The full Executive endorsed the recommendation by 17 votes to 9 with one abstention. Footman appealed to the 1975 conference on the grounds that 'along with many other issues since conference 1974 a majority politically-inspired block vote operated on the NEC' and was responsible for the Selection Committee recommendation. Kendall asked for a free hand (to support Footman) but the NEC refused and the conference rejected a motion to allow him to speak. The choice of Graham was endorsed by 113,298 votes to 89,161.

Losinska loses the presidency

Press interference in the Association's internal struggles, usually on the side of the moderates, was common, generally resented and, in 1976, costly. An article in the *Daily Express* of February 6 described Alistair Graham as a Communist sympathiser and Peter Thomason as another young extreme left sympathiser. The article alleged that it was the intention of the leftists in the CPSA to 'thwart the will of Parliament and control the running of the country.' Graham and Thomason initiated libel actions against Beaverbrook Newspapers, proprietors of the *Daily Express*, which were settled out of court by the payment of £500 damages and costs to each and the publication of a retraction. *Red Tape* produced a picture of the two men handing over their cheques to the CPSA Fighting Fund.

In 1976 Graham was up for the Deputy General Secretary job with an NEC recommendation. There was an appeal from John Raywood, an officer with longer experience supported by the moderate group, but this time senior officers were in favour of Graham. One delegate wondered why they had changed round. Len Lever said what had changed his mind during the past year was Alistair's first-class leadership as he had seen it in action. The Executive choice was endorsed by 138,460 votes to 73,283.

To fill Graham's place as Assistant General Secretary, the NEC chose Peter Thomason. Again Raywood was the choice of the moderates and appealed to the 1977 Conference against the NEC recommendation. The resulting series of decisions turned the conference, according to *Red Tape*, into 'one of the most exciting and controversial ever seen with constitutional problems, heart-searching by delegates, challenging points of order and at times near uproar.'

It all began quietly. Ken Thomas moved a motion endorsing Thomason's appointment to the job which he had actually been doing since July 1 the previous year. Then the two candidates put their cases. Both were comparatively young men – Thomason 39 and Raywood 36 but with longer national CPSA service. Thomason had made his name as Secretary of the DHSS during a long period of struggle. Raywood had had wide experience including an important part in the MLSA and COA mergers and the reorganisation which followed the hivings-off from the Department of Employment. Each put his case quietly and competently. The NEC recommendation in favour of Thomason was defeated by 121,132 votes to 97,197 on the Wednesday morning. On Wednesday afternoon Raywood's appeal was also defeated – by 110,839 votes to 91,768.

Bitter struggles for senior office

Amid the general consternation, it was assumed that the question would be referred back to the NEC but the senior officers met and decided there should be another vote the next day. On Thursday morning Len Lever, the President, announced he would first take a motion on the agenda which rejected both the NEC recommendation and the appeal and instructed the NEC to re-advertise the post. If that were rejected he would take a straight vote between the two candidates. Its rejection, it was argued, would in effect be a rejection of the previous day's rejections. There was a lot of excitement but the motion was debated and rejected. There was then a straight vote between the two candidates which resulted in a victory for Raywood by 82,432 votes to 74,237.

After many points of order and protests Len Lever succeeded in declaring Raywood appointed, and legal advice later approved his rulings. Since the war there had been almost regular appeals against NEC recommendations for senior office but this was the only one ever to succeed. Numerous theories have been advanced as to how it all happened.

Yet another decision of the 1976 conference was to abolish Rule 9.4 which banned group activities. Since they were all working underground, and not far

The factional press (right)

Kevin Roddy, leader of the Labour Militants

underground at that, there seemed no point in continuing it. The following autumn the moderates produced their own paper, *Daylight* (the organ of the National Moderate Group) and in January 1977 the various left factions, conscious that the moderates were making inroads into their positions, co-operated to publish *Broadside* (the organ of the Broad Left). From then on the rival lists of candidates were published for all to see. The Broad Left also started calling six-monthly conferences of representatives of left groups, the first at Manchester in March 1977, electing its candidates for the following year's elections in the autumn. But it did not hold together very well.

The *Redder Tape* group had not been able to agree with the others about a Presidential candidate in 1976 or 1977. The others supported Lever, on the grounds that anyone was better than Losinska, but *Redder Tape* argued that it was dishonest to support one moderate to keep another off and put up McGrath both times. The left vote was thus divided but McGrath did not get enough support to affect the issue. Again in 1978, when the Broad Left conference voted to put up Coltman against Lever, the militants, a comparatively new arrival on the scene under the leadership of Kevin Roddy, of the Newcastle DHSS, apparently voted for Lever. Roddy, who came from Washington, Co Durham, was the son of a Co-operative Society butcher who had been a Labour councillor. He went into the Service straight from school and became active in the Association as a Labour Party member before he was 20. He was Secretary of the DHSS Newcastle branch in 1974, a NEC member in 1976 and DHSS Section Organiser the following year.

The most controversial policies advocated by the Broad Left generally were the election of full-time Association officers, a break with Whitleyism, an end to Pay Research and affiliation to the Labour Party. The Communist Party, with its strong organisation, aimed at getting control of the Association. The Socialist Workers' Party laid greater emphasis on building up rank-and-file support. The militants, working within the Labour Party, were particularly anxious to get the CPSA into the party. Other smaller factions each had their own special objectives.

However, the moderates regained control of the Executive in 1977 with a majority of 15–11. They had a troubled year. They took over from the previous Executive plans for a special Rules Revision Conference, the first for many years, and added proposals of their own. The most important was to introduce an individual postal ballot for elections in place of the existing system under which branches cast block votes at the annual conference. The moderates were convinced that a substantial majority of members were against the far left but from apathy or because of left-wing tactics did not make their views felt. Postal ballots might, therefore, result in a lasting moderate majority on the NEC.

To prepare the ground the NEC decided, against strong left-wing opposition, to conduct a referendum which the President, Len Lever, pointed out was a consultative exercise to test the views of the membership on a matter of great importance. Changes in the electoral procedure could only be brought about by a two-thirds majority vote at conference. Less than half the members voted in the referendum, in which 74,640 declared themselves in favour of individual balloting and 22,606 against. In the event, the whole conference, held at Southport in November, proved a fiasco, 'a constant and undisguised political dogfight' as *Red Tape* put it. Branches were invited to submit amendments to a proposed new Rule Book, and 1,898 amendments were received, but neither side was able to obtain a two-thirds majority for any important (and therefore controversial) change. The motion to introduce individual membership ballots for national CPSA elections did not even get a simple majority, though moderate speakers made much play with the referendum figures. A little useful tidying up was all that was achieved.

Inter-faction trouble also arose out of a lock-out of members in the Gibraltar branch which lasted from October 1976, to May 1977. At the end the NEC threatened a national one-day strike to bring pressure on the Ministry of Defence but called it off when it received the new offer which led to an agreement. On the day the strike was to have taken place, a number of left-wingers, who thought the Association should have held out for better terms, arrived at the Nightingale Lane offices and asked for Ken Thomas to receive a deputation. When he refused, 20 or 30 of them took part in a sit-in in the front hall which lasted from early afternoon to about 9.30 p.m. They also took over the switchboard, but later explained that that was only to send a telegram to Gibraltar.

The police were sent for and one stayed for a long time keeping an eye on the sitting men and women (one with a baby in a carry-cot). The staff were sent home and later the chief officers followed, leaving Tony Baker to look after the place. Mick Duggan, a well-known left-winger, said at the Rules Revision Conference that he and his branch were proud of having taken part in the 'occupation', but the Association of Professional, Executive, Clerical and Computer Staff (APEX), which organised the Association's employees, made a protest because of the effect on the staff. The NEC considered for a year whether to take any disciplinary action and then decided to drop the matter, but submitted a motion to the 1978 conference saying that such events were to be deplored and instructing the NEC not to hesitate to take disciplinary action if there was any repetition of such an incident. This was overwhelmingly carried.

Terry Adams, centre of a factional controversy

Early in October 1977, the NEC decided not to recommend confirmation of the appointment of Terry Adams as an assistant secretary made by the left-wing Executive the previous year. Adams, who had served six years as Director of Research, had been appointed under the normal arrangement for a year's probation.

The initial reason given for the refusal to confirm his appointment was his handling of the dispute in Gibraltar, for which he was the assistant secretary responsible, but Mrs Losinska also said that his association with *Militant*, the paper of a Labour Party Marxist group, manifestly inhibited him from performing his duties as a full-time officer.

Ken Thomas, the General Secretary, opposed the NEC decision, saying that Adams had satisfactorily served his probationary period and pointing out that no directive existed which would enable a political judgement on a headquarters officer to be made and Alistair Graham also gave him strong support. Adams himself appealed against the recommendation, defending his record and arguing that the attack on him was political. He said he agreed with the views of *Militant* but there was not a shred of evidence that his political views had in any way, or at any time, undermined his effectiveness as an official of the union. Len Lever ruled that, as the NEC could only make a recommendation, Adams should retain his job until the 1978 conference decided the matter.

The affair caused a storm in the Association. An effective 'Terry Adams Defence' campaign was organised by Roddy and other sympathisers, and in March, after hearing further reports on Adams' record, the moderates gave way and the NEC unanimously reversed its recommendation. The 1978 conference severely censured it. The episode must have contributed to the heaviest ever defeat of the moderates in that year's elections, which reduced their membership of the NEC to

Pickets at a CPSA Executive meeting. The General Secretary lights his pipe

six. The left also made capital out of the fact that the moderate group had received financial assistance for the production of *Daylight* from Truemid, an organisation set up by anti-Communist union leaders and business men to fight Communism.

The new left-wing Executive soon ran into trouble itself, however. At its August meeting it adopted a resolution restricting the representation of full-time officers on the Selection Committees for assistant secretaries and Negotiation Officer (HEO) posts to the General Secretary and Deputy General Secretary. This would have meant exclusion from the committees of John Raywood and Tony Baker, both moderates, but was objected to by the full-time officers on the broad principle that it involved down-grading their status in relation to elected members. APEX, which represented officers as well as staff, strongly opposed the proposal but the NEC nevertheless persisted. After calling a full meeting of members, during which the Balham offices were closed, APEX decided to picket a meeting of the NEC the next morning. The Executive was presented with the unaccustomed sight of the Association's head-quarters employees, from Senior Officers to typists and clerks, waiting outside the Nightingale Lane offices to picket them when they arrived, and some engaged in angry exchanges, to the delight of the media. After some hours delay the Executive met and decided to hold over its decision for a ruling by the 1979 conference.

The most controversial issue in the long struggle between the moderates and the left was still to come. When the voting figures at the 1978 conference for the two vice-presidents were examined, it was discovered that some branches had voted for candidates other than those they had nominated, which was a breach of rule. So the presiding officer (the Association's Chartered Accountant) was asked to conduct an investigation. The voting had been:

Breaches of rule in the election of vice-presidents

Reg Williams	132,811	Elected
Peter Coltman	97,838	
Kate Losinska	96,671	Not Elected
Charlie Elliott	53,944	

No one supposed that the position of Reg Williams or Charlie Elliott would be affected by the breaches of rule but the votes of Coltman and Losinska were sufficiently close to raise doubts. The inquiry showed that 20 branches had voted against their nominations and five others, all of which had nominated Coltman and Williams, had not voted at all. If all these were adjusted to comply with the nominations, then Losinska's vote would be raised to 97,167 but Coltman's would be little changed at 97,789 so that he would still have won.

But it was questioned whether the votes of the five branches which made nominations but took no part in the ballot should be counted. Len Lever ruled they should not – and there were 801 of them for Coltman. This meant that Coltman's adjusted vote was 96,988 while Losinska's remained at 97,167 – and she had won. Lever accordingly declared Losinska elected instead of Coltman.

Lever explained his ruling this way. He agreed it was possible to argue that the rule meant every branch that nominated must vote for its candidate. In other words failure to vote was itself a breach of the rules. To interpret the rule that way would, however, create a complete inconsistency because the rules made it quite clear that not every branch (all of which were entitled to nominate) would be allocated a seat at conference and thereby a right to vote. They could not insist on every branch voting for its nominees and then deny them the right to vote. Nor would it be humanly possible to insist that every branch represented at conference had to vote if it had nominated. Delegates naturally should do everything possible to vote but accidents could happen to prevent this.

Lever's ruling had a second consequence. When it was thought at the conference that Coltman had been elected a vice-president his name was deleted, according to normal practice, from the ballot paper for election to the NEC. He had therefore been denied the rightful opportunity to stand for election to the NEC. Lever felt he must declare the NEC elections at the conference void and ordered a new ballot. A puzzling fact was that though Losinska had drawn attention to apparent discrepancies in June, Lever did not announce his ruling until the middle of October. At one stage Losinska had hinted at the possibility of legal action. After the ruling Coltman informed Lever formally that he would ask for an injunction to compel him to reverse it, but did not proceed with his application.

Once the ruling was made, Lever appealed to the 26 'erroneously elected' members of the Executive to serve in a caretaker capacity but the majority refused.

For two months the CPSA has no Executive

For two months the Association had to do without an Executive and the President, vice-presidents and senior officers took over, issuing bulletins to members to keep them informed.

There followed a period of hectic electioneering, at the end of which the moderates got back by a majority of 16 to 10 with the known Communists on the 'erroneously elected' Executive, including Coltman, completely eliminated. The latest see-saw of fortune was attributed partly to the fact that the number of votes cast was higher than in any previous election, partly to the fact that the elections were the sole purpose of the meetings at which the votes were cast, and partly to the issue of election addresses by candidates for the first time.

However, the Broad Left autumn meeting had decided by a small majority to nominate Coltman, its chairman, rather than Reg Williams, for the presidency in 1979, though Reg Williams had topped the voting for vice-presidents for three years in succession. Williams was attempting to form a new middle group, the Labour Left, which issued a paper under that title in August, and he decided to stand for the presidency in spite of the Broad Left decision. The Association emerged from its 75th anniversary year with all sides preparing to renew their internal battles in 1979.

Elections to the CPSA National Executive Committee
May 1968–December 1978

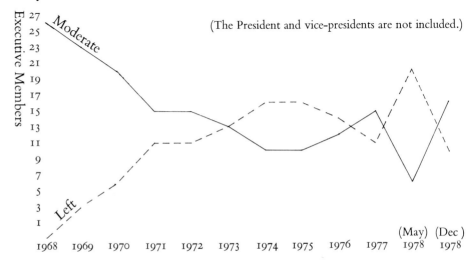

(The President and vice-presidents are not included.)

CHAPTER TWENTY-ONE
Ready for a Rough Future

Our membership is realising that 1979 will be, in many senses, a crucial year for the Association. We believe that members are fully aware of the likelihood of some kind of showdown with the Government and the Civil Service Department over the coming months. Without wishing to over-dramatise the situation, the last few years have built up a growing log-jam of frustrations and legitimate demands for change which cannot be contained indefinitely by this Government or its successor.

November 1978

L. Lever (President)
K. R. Thomas (General Secretary)

Those words from the foreword to the 1978 annual report indicated, in the 75th anniversary of the Association, an approaching climax to the most difficult years for trade unions, particularly those in the public service, since the early 1930s. The Government, faced with price increases of nearly 35 per cent between January 1974, and January 1975, concentrated on anti-inflation policies which resulted in falling living standards and rising unemployment. For four years in succession, restrictions on pay were reinforced by expenditure cuts and the imposition of departmental cash limits. By the end of 1978, annual inflation had been reduced to 8 per cent but, as under previous incomes policies, the public services bore the brunt of the sacrifices involved. A fourth year of Government pay restriction seemed to the CPSA and other public service unions intolerable. Partly as a result of this experience and partly of longer term trends, the basic principles of Whitleyism were coming under question. Arbitration could no longer be relied on. Strains were appearing on the Staff Side. Attempts to bring the Civil Service into the labour relations age of the closed shop and industrial democracy were making no progress. The silicon chip, the full implications of which were still difficult to assess, was casting its first shadows over the future.

The basic principles of Whitleyism are questioned

It was not only the limitations on basic pay increases that caused frustration. Improvements in hours and leave, shortening of incremental scales and a score of other adjustments were ruled out because their cost would have to be deducted from the amount to be allowed under the pay limits. A few gains were made, after several years of negotiation, in 1978. Members' working lives were made easier by an agreement in September on new heating and lighting standards. Revised agreements were made for catering, amenity and recreation room facilities.

At the end of a long struggle, some progress was made on 'open reporting' – the right of a Civil Servant to see the annual report on him by his immediate supervisor – for which the CPSA had been campaigning for years. The chance of promotion depended to a large extent on these reports, and with the growth in the number of young Clerical Officers, competition for promotion was greater than ever. Promotion procedures were revised in 1972 and appraisal interviews, at which applicants could be given some information about their reports, were encouraged, but there was no right to see the reports.

With the support of the Society, whose members write the reports, the CPSA started a campaign for Clerical Officers to ask to see their reports and for Society members to reveal them on receiving such a request. New negotiations followed with Departmental Establishment officers, according to Alistair Graham, insisting through the CSD that to allow civil servants to see their annual reports in cold, stark print, without accompanying soothing explanations provided at job appraisal reviews, could destroy motivation. 'The joint SCPS/CPSA campaign could have smashed them to smithereens,' he wrote, 'if more SCPS members had had the courage to show their staff the reports and more of our members had wanted to see them. However only tiny proportions of our members asked to see their reports – well below 10 per cent – and many supervisors were frightened off by management's instructions to mark each report that it had been shown to staff.'

The outcome was an agreement in March 1978 that a civil servant could be told all that was in his report, except the part dealing with his long-term potential, and must be told the markings relating to overall performance and promotability if he asked, and if he disagreed on any point he could have his disagreement recorded in his own words. A large majority at the CPSA annual conference accepted the agreement as a step forward.

Restrictions on the political rights of civil servants

Restrictions on the political rights of civil servants, which had been a source of grievance among members, certainly since the days of the MacDonnell Royal Commission and no doubt earlier, were discussed again. The rules laid down in 1953, resulting from the Masterman report, were still far from satisfying the CPSA and other associations. They divided civil servants into three groups: a free category, including industrial and non-office staff, such as messengers, who could engage in national or local political activities; an intermediate category comprising clerical staff, typists and similar grades, who were elegible to engage in local and most national political activities if they got permission first; and a restricted category, including the Executive Officer grade and above, which could not engage in national politics but might get permission for local activities. The Staff Side constantly pressed for greater freedoms and in 1976 the Armitage Committee was appointed to go into the matter.

The Committee reported in the spring of 1978, recommending the transfer of some 175,000 Executive Officers and other senior grades to the intermediate category, the use of block permission for political activity for as many as possible in that category and the creation of an appeal body for those aggrieved by departmental decisions. All this was welcome but the Committee also included, in a list of sorts of staff who could not expect to get permission for national political activities, those whose duties brought them face-to-face with the public – for instance thousands of CPSA members employed in social security and employment offices and so on. The CPSA opposed this vigorously and got the support not only of the Staff Side but also of the TUC.

Relations between the CPSA and the new Labour Government of 1974 began badly. When Labour was hoping to strengthen its position in an autumn election, the CPSA was the only sizeable union to vote against the 'social contract' between the Government and the TUC which was one of the strongest planks in the Party's election platform. The contract was a bargain under which the TUC advised unions not to try to do more than keep pace with price increases in their wage settlements and the Government promised a number of measures to strengthen the position of the unions. Kendall explained that the CPSA doubted the Government's ability, as distinct from its willingness, to deliver its side of the bargain. But the persistence of the CPSA in voting against the 'social contract' made it unpopular with the Labour Party and leaders of other unions, most of whom had yielded to pressure for unity behind the contract.

So far as pay was concerned, there was a brief halcyon period between the Heath restrictions and those of Denis Healey. The pay increases obtained in the last six months of the Tory regime were followed nearly every month by 'threshold' increases related to the cost of living and then by the Pay Research exercise of 1975 which provided 30 to 45 per cent increases for executive and clerical grades, 30 to 50 per cent for typists and secretaries, 29 to 46 per cent for machine grades and 41 to 59 per cent for teleprinter grades.

Healey's budget of 1975, imposing substantial expenditure cuts in public services, marked the end of the honeymoon. In July the Government, after consultation with the TUC, introduced the first stage of its voluntary incomes policy with a White Paper, *Attack on Inflation*, which proposed a £6 limit on pay

Members lobby the CPSA Executive, urging it to oppose the Government's White Paper

increases for 12 months from August 1 and suspended the Civil Service Pay Agreement negotiated the previous year. Wage-related payments such as those for overtime and shift work were not to be increased and any improvements in non-wage benefits, such as annual leave, were to be set against the £6 limit. The CPSA Executive issued a statement opposing the White Paper policy. Since there was no commitment on the part of the Government to move to radical policies, it said, there could be no belief that the proposals were simply to meet a temporary situation. They had to be regarded 'as a serious threat to the social fabric of the nation.' The CPSA voted against the Government-TUC proposals at the 1975 Trades Union Congress but they were approved by 7 million votes to 3 million. Kendall accepted that the CPSA had no choice but to abide by the majority TUC decision and vainly pressed for a special Congress early the following year.

While the 1976 Association conference was sitting in May, it was announced that the Government and the TUC General Council had reached agreement on a second stage of incomes policy and that it would be put before a special Congress on June 16. This gave the NEC time to ballot members beforehand on the proposals, which it did with a strong recommendation to oppose them. But nearly three-quarters of the members, 81,983 to 26,148, were in favour of the deal. The CPSA was obliged to do a U-turn and vote for the new Government-TUC policy at the special Congress. *Red Tape* hastened to argue that this did not prove a lack of awareness of membership feeling on the part of the NEC, but did prove the need for members to attend branch meetings and exercise their votes, not as an afterthought on some particular issue but consistently and enthusiastically. *Red Tape* also forcibly condemned the attempt by forces of reaction 'to use recent events as a basis for peddling the old chestnut about postal balloting.'

It was at this embarrassing moment in the Association's history that Ken Thomas took over the general secretaryship from Bill Kendall. Thomas, born in Penarth in 1927, was the son of a master baker and flour chemist for Spillers who was an influential local Tory. Thomas became a Labour supporter in his youth, after reading the collected works of Bernard Shaw and much else, and his allegiance never wavered. Even after he became Deputy General Secretary he was a member of the General Management Committee of the Lewisham Party, where he had three years on the Council. He was intended for university when he left school but was attracted to journalism and instead got a job as a copy boy on the *South Wales Echo* and *Western Mail*, where war-time shortages of staff enabled him to try his hand at reviews and much else, acting as general dogsbody from morning until night. When he rebelled against the hours, friends of the family got him into the Welsh Board of Health, where he immediately joined the small CSCA branch which had already produced Bill Ellerby and Len Wines. He became branch secretary in a year and came to London in 1950 doing almost full-time union work. Five years later he was appointed a full-time CPSA officer with an NEC majority of two, provided by about half the moderates and the two or three remaining left-wingers. With his mobile features, wavy hair and vigorous Welsh oratory, the small man, dragging along one leg which had been hurt in an accident at school, soon became a well-known and popular figure who earned respect by his command of every detail of pay and pension negotiation. He had worked closely with Kendall and continued CPSA policy with no obvious break.

Since a majority of members had now voted in favour of the Government-TUC incomes policy, the CPSA had of necessity to concentrate its fire on the Government's expenditure cuts which were becoming an increasing threat to employment in the public services. Announcement of new cuts in the Public

Ken Thomas becomes General Secretary at an embarrassing moment for the CPSA leadership

Expenditure White Paper in February 1976 had been followed by emergency cuts later in the year and by the introduction of 'cash limits' which tied each department to a maximum expenditure based on Government estimates for the following 12 months. If for some reason one of its services exceeded the limits, then another had to be reduced. Ken Thomas seconded a motion condemning the cuts at the Trades Union Congress in September, warning that thousands of his members' jobs were now in jeopardy. To satisfy the demands of overseas bankers, it appeared they would need to return to 19th-century economics and social conditions, he said. The most disturbing fact was that the public, including some trade unionists, was beginning to regard public expenditure as the root cause of the country's economic ills. 'What cherished part of the trade union movement's social programme is to be felled next?' he demanded.

Thomas explained in *Red Tape* that the campaign against public expenditure cuts would develop along two distinct strands – opposition to the philosophy of cutting expenditure as a solution to the country's economic problems and Departmental resistance to cutbacks in Civil Service manpower. On the one hand, the CPSA joined in a mass lobby of Parliament on November 17 and on the other hand, sections were given authority from the same date to ban overtime which could be replaced by additional jobs. The Department of Employment Section initiated an effective ban on the collection of statistics but the NEC ordered its calling off when management threatened to suspend members supporting the ban.

A Hyde Park demonstration against government expenditure cuts

It was severely censured by the 1977 conference for doing so in spite of Peter Coltman's defence that support at the Department of Employment was running out and there was lack of support from the rest of the Association. A controversial aspect of the campaign against the cuts was reflected in a motion from a Ministry of Defence branch expressing grave concern at continuing cuts in the defence forces. Conflicting principles were involved here and there were fierce attacks on the motion by those who advocated reducing armaments, but it was carried by 117,493 to 85,471.

The campaign against the cuts and cash limits was continuing at the end of 1978. It was effective in a limited number of branches but it was not always clear whether a ban would result in saving jobs and the loss of overtime pay was unpopular. A national steering committee of public sector unions, which co-ordinated the campaign, tried to stimulate it by an autumn offensive in 1977, beginning with a week of action in mid-November. November was chosen because the International Monetary Fund team would be in London going through the nation's books and making up their minds on the economic policies to be followed by the British Government. There was a lobby of Parliament, a meeting in Central Hall and regional and local activity.

The Department of Employment Section strongly resisted a plan to introduce fortnightly instead of weekly signing on at unemployment benefit offices which was calculated, if introduced nationally, to reduce staff by about 1,000. Pilot schemes were started and there was a promise of no redundancy. In March 1978, the Section was refused permission to take industrial action in support of its opposition but the annual conference censured the Executive for not giving the Section wholehearted support. The Section then called a week's strike at five selected offices in July and the following month asked for permission to call rolling two-week strikes at benefit offices, five at a time. The National Disputes Committee, however, took the view that it would be wrong to spend large sums of the Fighting Fund on further action for doubtful returns when it knew it would need every pound it had in the fund to fight the Government in early 1979 for the implementation of Pay Research settlements in full.

One Government action which particularly infuriated the unions was the

Public Sector union leaders meet in 1978 to organise further opposition to the cuts. Ken Thomas is second from left

refusal to allocate additional resources for the implementation of the Health and Safety at Work Act, 1974, which provided for the appointment of safety representatives and safety committees. This meant that the additional cost could only be met by savings elsewhere. Len Murray, the TUC General Secretary, wrote about this to the Lord Privy Seal, Fred Peart, but without result. Over the two years of campaigning against the cuts it was reckoned there were 20 or 30 instances of CPSA action which resulted in raising complements.

Meanwhile, resistance to incomes policy had been resumed in the summer of 1977, when the TUC withdrew its support and advocated 'an orderly return to free collective bargaining'. The Government tried on its own to enforce a Stage III policy which said that the general level of pay settlements should be moderate enough to secure that the national earnings increase would be no more than 10 per cent. By July, the unions' attitude had become clear and the Staff Side met the Prime Minister to put the case for a restoration of the 1974 pay agreement in 1978. The Prime Minister replied that Pay Research could not be restored until there had been changes in the agreement to meet political and press criticisms which had been mounting since the 1975 settlement, which gave increases averaging 30 per cent. The main criticisms were directed at a system under which civil servants (the Official Side) negotiated with civil servants (the Staff Side) on the basis of facts obtained by civil servants (in the Pay Research Unit), with ministers ultimately responsible but the outside world knowing little of what was going on. The Whitley Council thought these criticisms were based on inadequate understanding of the procedures but accepted the need for public confidence in the system and agreed to the creation of an independent Pay Research Unit Board, the director and some of the staff of which need not have Civil Service experience, which was intended to encourage openness about the process.

A new meeting with the Prime Minister was arranged for November 9, but before that a series of events led to the first of a number of disputes which threatened the unity of the Staff Side in this period. The Society of Civil and Public Servants, now rivalling the CPSA in militancy, pressed for a half-day strike on November 8. The other unions thought a strike immediately before the meeting with Callaghan would be unhelpful and decided to co-operate in a Week of Action

Civil Service Association leaders arrive at No 10 for the November 9 meeting with Jim Callaghan. Bill Kendall is in the centre, and Ken Thomas is looking at the doorway, but there is no one there from the Society

CPSA pickets at Somerset House campaigning for the restoration of pay research

beginning on November 28 if the Prime Minister's response was unsatisfactory. Ken Thomas tried hard to secure unity but the Society went ahead with its unilateral action, and accompanied it with a number of circulars reflecting on the other unions. They retorted by excluding the Society from the meeting with Callaghan on the grounds that it had publicly presented a picture which showed it to be in total disagreement with the National Staff Side.

However, the Prime Minister declined to restore the Pay Research procedure before 1979 and the Week of Action took place, somewhat hampered in the CPSA by the absence of many activists during the preceding week at the Rules Revision Conference. The branches had been left to decide for themselves what action to take, so long as it did not involve strikes of longer than a day, and various forms of protest were adopted including many meetings, one at the Central Hall, and some during working hours, where possible co-ordinated by the Staff Side. At the request of the Staff Side, a meeting of the full National Whitley Council was held, the first for 27 years, to impress upon the Official Side the dangers of the situation.

The 1978 annual conference censured the NEC for lack of leadership. The scattered protests had produced many problems and attracted little attention in the national papers but, as Thomas pointed out, it had achieved greater coverage in the local media than ever before. Members of Parliament from all over the country had had impressed on them the case for the restoration of the pay agreement.

The CPSA put in a claim for 14 to 20 per cent increases based on estimates of what had happened outside, rather as a step towards the big effort to come in 1979 than with any hope of getting it, and had to settle within the 10 per cent limit. In July 1978, when a new Government White Paper, *Winning the Battle Against Inflation*, proposed a fourth-stage pay limit of 5 per cent, the Civil Service unions could see no prospect of immediate implementation of whatever resulted from the 1979 Pay Research. It seemed the best they could expect was its introduction by

The lobby of the Trades Union Congress at Brighton

stages over two years or so on the lines of recent police and fire brigades' settlements. The Staff Side accepted a motion from the Society and the CPSA calling for co-ordination of contingency planning of any necessary industrial action in 1979. The Staff Side recommended that each union should decide, in a situation affecting all unions, what form of action they would be prepared to take and, if selective strike action was one of the choices, where it would get a response from members, what effect on government business it would have, what financial help could be given to unions which required it, what machinery would be needed centrally and what autonomy unions would pass on to it. With or without the others, the CPSA prepared to fight.

At the 1978 Trades Union Congress in Brighton the Association sought the understanding and support of the other unions. It was a foregone conclusion that the Congress would reject the Government's 5 per cent policy but Ken Thomas took advantage of the debate to summarise the Civil Service position: 'Let me say what we want in the Civil Service. It can hardly be called unreasonable. We want the same rate as comparable workers outside the Service – no more, no less – and we are prepared to argue our case on facts which are completely impartially collected. But we want it in full: no intervention, no phasing, no fiddling.' The NEC organised a lobby of the Congress, bringing in members on the day of the economic debate and arming them with placards and leaflets.

From mid-October to mid-December, a crucial period of preparation for the struggle, the CPSA was without an Executive for reasons explained in the previous chapter. Preparations for battle were therefore in the hands of the President, vice-presidents and senior officers, who reported on their stewardship to the first meeting of the newly-elected Executive on December 18. They had issued leaflets, campaign badges and stickers to members. A series of pamphlets had been prepared. Senior officers had visited a number of branches thought particularly suitable for selective strikes to assess the likelihood of support, the number of members who would be involved, what management reaction might be, whether there were alternative ways of doing the work, how quickly a stoppage would become effective and whether the support of another Association would be necessary.

Co-operation by the other associations was uncertain, not so much because of differences about the need for industrial action, if the 1979 Pay Research settlement was not fully implemented, as about its timing. Most of the others argued that they should await the outcome of negotiations on the PRU report. The CPSA said they had to avoid being boxed in by the Government so that April 1, the operative date for their pay increase, was not so hard on their heels that they would have no room to take industrial action without having to worry about the operative date. But it seemed almost certain that the Society would act with the CPSA. Local authority and health service unions had already decided to take industrial action in the latter part of January, and it was evident there would be the biggest resistance ever in the public service.

The senior CPSA officers in their branch visits had found that before members started selective strikes they would need tangible proof that the whole membership was behind them. The NEC therefore decided there would be a consultative exercise in January in which all branches would be asked to endorse the programme and that any selective action would be preceded by a one-day national strike. There was also to be a total overtime ban. The committee devoted much attention to the mechanics of organising the dispute. A motion was carried declaring that the new (moderate) Executive would vigorously continue the campaign against the 5 per cent policy and take whatever steps were necessary to safeguard the interests of its members. It was also agreed that in drawing up the programme of selective action priority should be given to areas which would have maximum impact upon big business and Government rather than impose hardships on the unemployed, the sick and the elderly.

Preparing for industrial action in 1979

The day after the NEC meeting a letter was sent to the CSD asking for permission for the branch consultative meetings to be held in official time. When this was refused, branches were recommended to hold their meetings in official time without CSD permission. 'It is always a daunting task to fight a Government, which is why such a fight should only be entered after due care and consideration,' said a brief for speakers at the branch meetings. 'But we believe that if the case is good and the strategy sound the Government can be made to modify its inflexible attitude.'

Doubts about the relevance of the old Whitleyism to the strike policy age were growing in strength. The events of Edward Heath's regime provoked a 1973 instruction to the NEC to review the Whitley procedure with a view to obtaining an alternative negotiating system. The Executive, however, reported that the problem was not so much one of replacing one system by another, or of furnishing an alternative, but of evolution to meet developing and changing needs. In the 1960s the system began to show signs of not meeting the challenge of an era in which Governments began more and more to enter the arena and to interfere with negotiating processes. Confidence in arbitration, 'one of the pillars on which the system rested', had been eroded by incomes policies. Whitleyism flourished when industrial action by civil servants was generally regarded, even by civil servants themselves, as virtually out of the question, but this attitude of mind no longer applied. 'But a system which has operated for so long and been exported so widely must have had considerable merits to commend it,' the report continued, 'and it is entirely conceivable that the method of consultation and negotiation which succeeds

Whitleyism will contain many of the features of it. It is possible that what is called for is evolution rather than revolution, but whatever is devised must be equal to the challenge of the harsh economic conflicts from which the Civil Service is no longer partly isolated.' An NEC motion pursuing this line of thought, carried at the 1976 conference, instructed the Executive to enter into discussions with other Staff Side unions to devise an up-to-date Code of Practice which would include a *status quo* clause and disagreements procedure.

In the next year or two the Government's commitment to legislation on industrial democracy and the appointment of the Bullock Committee, to consider how best worker representation on boards of companies could be achieved, gave a new impetus to the discussions. Bullock was concerned with private industry but while the committee was sitting the Government conducted parallel studies in the public sector. In the Civil Service the Whitley Council set up a joint committee 'to review the existing industrial relations procedures and practices and the scope for developing them to extend industrial democracy within the limits imposed by the need to preserve the overriding prerogatives of ministers and the requirements of the public interest.' Earlier Staff Side proposals to extend the scope of arbitration and make changes in its machinery were referred to the new committee.

By the end of 1976 the Staff Side had prepared a policy document for consideration by the constituent unions. Main proposals included prior consultation on estimates, cash limits, new legislation and location of work in so far as they affected the interests of staff; greater provision of information of all kinds; a standstill arrangement pending the resolution of a dispute (the *status quo*); a joint disputes procedure; revised arrangements for conciliation and arbitration, and experiments in representation on management bodies. The CPSA thought the Government must have been taken aback by the comprehensiveness of the proposals since for a long time they produced no reaction at all.

Plans to moderate the Whitley system

The 1977 conference carried a resolution welcoming the widespread desire for more influence for trade unionists over management decisions but rejecting the idea of workers' participation, as commonly understood, in the Civil Service. It advocated a *status quo* clause in all future agreements. Another motion called for dismissal notices to be held in abeyance until the result of an appeal was made known. However, the Bullock Report had aroused such a hubbub of controversy that the Government adopted a go-slow policy on discussions and legislation became more and more unlikely during the lifetime of the Parliament. It was not until September 1978 that the Official Side was ready to meet the unions to begin discussions on the proposals made two years earlier.

Ken Thomas told the Staff Side that the *status quo* was seen by CPSA members as the keystone of any new structure and most of the others members agreed. The thinking behind this was that circumstances had been changed by the formal adoption of a strike policy by some Associations and a readiness to take industrial action by others. While the strike policy had been thought of mainly as a means of resistance to national government infringements of the Pay Agreement, it had affected relations at all levels. Two long stoppages in 1977, those of Air Traffic Control Assistants and members in Gibraltar, had demonstrated the readiness and ability of the CPSA to give backing to comparatively small number of members, at high cost in strike pay, and to achieve results. But apart from that the Association's disputes committee received two or three local requests every week for authority to take industrial action of one sort or another. This was attributed largely to the slow, bureaucratic procedure provided by the outdated Whitley machinery and to the management practice of imposing a change by administrative

Nina Williams, CPSA
member of the Post
Office Board

action where agreement could not be reached. It was argued that such problems could be resolved by a *status quo* arrangement that unacceptable changes should not be made until they had been considered by new disputes machinery at all levels leading to arbitration where necessary. It would be possible to refer local, regional or departmental disputes to the National level.

The CPSA gave a much lower priority to trade union representation on management bodies, which the Staff Side had recommended on an experimental basis but was rejected by the 1977 conference resolution. No one thought Civil Service unions could be represented on the ultimate controlling bodies, the Cabinet and Parliament, but it would be possible to try representation on such boards as those controlling the British Museum or even the Inland Revenue Department. Outside the Civil Service an experiment in trade union representation was introduced in the Post Office and the first CPSA member of the Post Office Board, Nina Williams, was welcomed at the 1978 conference.

However, dissatisfaction with the lack of constructive reaction by the Official Side to the proposals for reform, accentuated by its refusal to take a disputed London Weighting claim to arbitration, and divisions on the Staff Side, meant that at the end of 1978 the CPSA had less confidence in Whitleyism than at any time since the Second World War.

Negotiations on a claim for the closed shop were no less frustrating. A resolution favouring it was adopted at the 1968 conference but in a *Red Tape* article later in the year Bill Kendall held out little hope of early progress. Some staff associations were against it. 'A reasonable number of Civil Service unions will have to pledge support before there can be a realistic approach to the employing authority,' he wrote. 'Because we are talking about a closed shop in public employment there are also massive political considerations which put the issue outside normal Service collective bargaining machinery.' After the coming of a Conservative Government in 1970 the idea lay dormant – indeed in 1973 a Conference motion instructing the NEC to resume its efforts was defeated.

In 1974, with Labour back and legislative obstacles to be removed, the conference again approved a closed shop resolution. House of Lords amendments to Government legislation delayed matters, however, and it was not until 1977 that the CPSA presented a claim, the Staff Side having decided that individual unions should negotiate 100 per cent union membership agreements independently. The Inland Revenue Staff Association and the Civil Service Union were to follow the CPSA. White-collar closed shops were spreading through the public corporations, including the Post Office. There was still vigorous opposition from a minority in the CPSA, however. A motion at the 1977 conference endorsing the claim was carried by 128,175 to 56,749, with the opponents vainly demanding a referendum.

The CSD reply to the claim infuriated the associations. The Government, it said, was concerned to ensure that a union membership agreement should not create obligations for civil servants which could risk conflicting with the duty of loyalty to the elected government. Safeguards were therefore proposed which included a ballot of all existing staff, whether union members or not, before an agreement was made; the provision of an option, as an alternative to union membership, of paying the equivalent of union dues to charity; and a grade cut-off point at about the Clerical Officer level. Non-members of unions among existing staff would be excluded.

The Staff Side and the three unions submitting claims were unanimous in rejecting these terms. Ken Thomas, at the 1978 conference, said he felt deeply ashamed that such proposals had emerged from the Labour Government. They were nothing to do with trade unionism but were positively anti-trade union. With a general election in the offing and opinion polls forecasting a Conservative victory there seemed little chance of a negotiated closed shop agreement in the near future.

As the CPSA moved to the end of its 75th anniversary year it faced two groups of major problems, the first in relations with the Government, the second in relations among its own members. The Civil Service associations welcomed and preserved the Whitley system because it offered a means of dealing with an omnipotent employer which could have fair results. The Priestley Commission gave it the chance of practical implementation through fair comparison, which could have taken pay out of politics. But one Government after another broke away from the principle, to which it had agreed, 'in the national interest'.

The CPSA, like public service unions in many industrial countries in the 1960s and 1970s, turned to militant action as the only alternative, and in the autumn of 1978 surveyed its experience of nearly 10 years of strike policy. Industrial action to change a Government's political course is unlikely to be successful, said the review, thinking of the campaign against public expenditure cuts, and all out action by a very large group of members could rarely be contemplated. On the other hand, small-scale industrial action on local issues had proved invaluable. Strikes by small groups in a very large union, such as those of the Gibraltar members and the

Reg Williams and other CPSA members on their way to No 10 Downing Street to deliver a letter explaining the position of the association's locked-out members in Gibraltar

Lobby of the TUC in support of the Air Traffic Control Assistants. Len Lever is fourth from left

Air Traffic Control Assistants in 1977, could be effective but were costly so long as the strikers received full net pay. In both cases the Strike Fund came near to insolvency. The cost of the ATCA strike was £423,886 and of the Gibraltar lock-out £266,970.

The problem in these disputes, as in others where members adopted action short of a strike, was employer retaliation, usually in the form of suspending members, which extended the stoppage and raised the cost. In Gibraltar the members were locked out after taking guerilla action. In the ATCA dispute the Association had to call out all members of the grade after a few had been suspended for blacking work from the computer system.

There had been successful actions short of a strike not mentioned in the review, for instance the DHSS overtime bans in 1972 and 1974. Another example was a campaign which started in 1973 against the employment of typists from fee-charging employment agencies, for which a young female assistant secretary, Diana Warwick, the first woman since Margaret Leaver to hold the position, had immediate responsibility. It included refusals to work with agency staff, blacking of their work, bans on overtime, a petition to the Prime Minister, leaflet campaigns and a rally and, with support from other unions, resulted in a big reduction in the number of agency girls employed in the Service and a CSD circular to establishment officers aimed at making a continued reduction a matter of urgency.

The final option, according to the review, was selective strikes where small groups of key staff stopped work for what might be a long period on behalf of the whole membership. The union could either call selective strikes which did not allow management retaliation or, if the strategy was blown off course, reduce

Diana Warwick, who led the campaign against the employment of typists from fee-charging agencies in the Civil Service

strike pay. In spite of the heavy costs of 1977, the Strike Fund had more than £1 million available to finance the national dispute expected in 1979.

Ever since the days 75 years earlier, when the Association consisted of a few hundred badly-paid clerks, it had shown exceptional energy and determination and those qualities were still apparent among the young men and women of 1978. Loyal and unselfish work was being done by a host of branch workers, but there was an excessive rate of turnover among officials and activists. It has been estimated that usually about a third of the delegates at an annual conference were attending for the first time.

The union had a democratic and open constitution. It had at last a strong financial base. But some delegates seemed ready to plunge into action without care in counting the cost, one of the essentials for a fighting union. If the sections were to indulge in a competitive scramble for extra pay; if the factions continued their bitter struggle for domination, with many executive meetings reduced to a long succession of recorded block votes, all going one way one year and the other way the next; if the union could not achieve unity and stability and continuity of purpose among its voluntary leaders, it could be seriously weakened in spite of the efforts of the full-time officers. A new voting system might well help towards stability. But what the union probably needed most of all, by a restructuring of the clerical classes or by a merger with the Society, was to stop or reduce the constant drain away of many of its most able and experienced members through promotion.

Appendices

The Growth of the CPSA

A MEMBERSHIP

Year	Members	Year	Members
1903	383	1941	100,000 approx
1904	554	1942	129,005
1905	820	1943	135,000 approx
1906	945	1944	–
1907	–	1945	–
1908	1,230	1946	139,000 approx
1909	1,286	1947	149,117
1910	1,704	1948	153,292
1911	1,814	1949	144,126
1912	2,223	1950	134,557
1913	2,404	1951	147,005
1914	2,837	1952	149,590
1915	2,672	1953	147,830
1916	1,449	1954	144,268
1917	609	1955	146,847
1918	623	1956	148,809
1919	3,500	1957	141,996
1920	5,368	1958	138,155
1921	–	1959	141,239
1922	16,500	1960	140,293
1923	18,219	1961	142,730
1924	20,012	1962	144,944
1925	20,468	1963	143,151
1926	19,123	1964	146,324
1927	20,555	1965	145,775
1928	22,941	1966	151,935
1929	26,350	1967	160,569
1930	29,278	1968	173,822
1931	28,920	1969	181,067
1932	29,911	1970	184,935
1933	31,972	1971	188,085
1934	35,359	1972	189,209
1935	43,231	1973	215,702
1936	47,364	1974	215,144
1937	57,628	1975	224,918
1938	65,394	1976	230,905
1939	–	1977	226,370
1940	85,000 approx	1978	224,772

B MERGERS

1909

ASSISTANT CLERKS ASSOCIATION

1920

Change of name to
CLERICAL OFFICERS ASSOCIATION

Association of Post Office Engineering Clerical Assistants (1916)
Association of Writing Assistants
Telephone Provincial Clerical and Contract Officers Association (District Manager's Office)

1921

Civil Service Typists
Association of Supplementary Clerks (Public Records Office)
Survey Staff Clerks' Association (Board of Trade)
Association of Audit Clerks (National Insurance Audit Department)
Association of Valuation Office Male Clerks and Draughtsmen★
Association of Women Clerks and Secretaries (Civil Service Branch)

1922

Change of name to
CIVIL SERVICE CLERICAL ASSOCIATION
Civil Service Union (1919), (Admiralty and Outports Clerical Association, 1906)

1923

Association of Civil Clerks (War Department)
Association of Established Supervising Clerical Staff (War Department)
War Department Members of the National Union of Clerks
War Department Writers' Association

1926

Admiralty Pensioner Clerks Section of the Workers' Union

1933

District Probate Registry Clerks Association
Inland Revenue Stamping Department Association

1934

Sorting Assistants' Association

1969

Change of name to
CIVIL AND PUBLIC SERVICES ASSOCIATION

1973

Ministry of Labour Staff Association (1912)

1974

Court Officers' Association (1881)

To eliminate confusion, founding dates have only been included for major organisations.

★ Later withdrew. Affiliated to the Inland Revenue Staff Federation in 1937.

Association Officials

A PRESIDENTS

Assistant Clerks Association
1903–1906	H W J Holt	
1906–1908	J G Walker	*Customs*
1908–1911	P Tait	*Post Office Savings Bank*
1911–1912	P R Brame	*Board of Education*
1912–1913	D Milne	*Patent Office*
1913–1914	A E Bateman	*Inland Revenue, Secretary's Office*
1914–1915	W R Dayton	*Post Office, Secretary's Office*
1915–1917	S B Hocking	*Admiralty*
1917–1918	R E Dick	*Customs and Excise, Statistical Office*
1918–1920	J McGilvray	*Customs and Excise*

Clerical Officers Association
1920	J McGilvray	*Customs and Excise*
1921	W Thomas	*Post Office, Manchester*

Civil Service Clerical Association
1922–1925	W Thomas	*Post Office, Nottingham*
1925–1937	R Wyld	*Post Office, London Telephone Service*
1937–1939	Miss M Jackson	*Post Office, London Engineering Department*
1939–1941	H Broadhead	*Post Office, Manchester*
1941–1942	Miss M Jackson	*Post Office, London Engineering Department*
1942–1944	E W McMillan	*Post Office, London Telecommunications Region*
1944–1946	W P James	*War Transport Headquarters*
1946–1947	E W McMillan	*Post Office, London Telecommunications Region*
1947–1948	E J Hicks (Acting)	*Air Ministry, Kingsway*
1948–1950	W E Leftly	*Ministry of Pensions Headquarters*
1950–1952	F J Houghton	*Customs and Excise, London Port*
1952–1954	G W Cargill	*Post Office, Glasgow*
1954–1956	Miss F O Bonsor	*Post Office Savings Bank*
1956–1963	T E Lillywhite	*Post Office Savings Bank*
1963–1966	J Bryce	*Post Office, London Telecommunications Region*
1966–1969	C Garrick	*Army Department, Leeds*

Civil and Public Services Association
1969–1972	Miss F O Bonsor	*Post Office Savings Bank, London*
1972–1975	L Lever	*Post Office Savings Bank, London*
1975–1976	Mrs K M Losinska	*Office of Population Censuses and Surveys*
1976–	L Lever	*Post Office Savings Bank, London*

B THE ASSOCIATION'S SECRETARIES

Honorary Secretaries

1903–1906	J Maxwell
1906–1907	R McC Beamish
1907–1909	H W Luker
1909–1910	C Edwards
1910–1913	L E de St. Päer
1913–1916	D Milne
1916–1919	W J Brown

Full-time General Secretaries

1919–1942	W J Brown
1942–1955	L C White
1955–1963	G F Green
1963–1967	L A Wines
1967–1976	W L Kendall
1976–	K R Thomas

C GENERAL TREASURERS

1920–1921	S D Cox
1921–1936	S Slocombe
1936–1947	C Holock
1947–1963	A I McPherson
1963–1973	A R Gerrard
1973–	A J Baker

D 'RED TAPE' EDITORS

1911–1919	F W Saunderson
1919–1939	W B Bird
1939–1948	L Harrison
1948–1956	W J F Thompson
1956–1974	T J O'Dea
1974–	C J Bush

The Direct Democracy of the Civil and Public Services Association

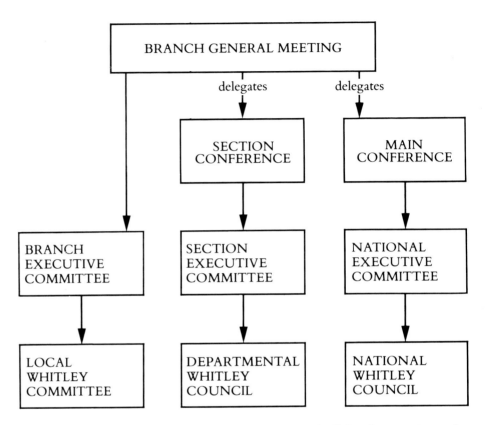

This diagram shows the steps through which CPSA Civil Service members who attend branch meetings exercise control of their representatives up to the joint Whitley bodies at three levels. In some departments with regional controllers there are in addition regional committees which negotiate on regional Whitley Councils. On the other hand, sections do not exist in small Civil Service departments. Branches in public services outside the Civil Service follow the same pattern in so far as it is practicable.

The basic structure comprises three independent lines of control based on the branch without any formal connection between branch, section and national executive committees. Outside the main structure, however, there are area co-ordinating committees, which bring together representatives of different departments in localities for specific organisational purposes, and Northern and Southern assemblies, which provide a meeting ground for representatives of non-section branches.

Author's Acknowledgements

Greg Challis

My overriding debt is to Greg Challis who gave me invaluable help in assembling facts and generally acted as my guide to the mysteries of the Civil Service and its unions and as my counsellor and friend. He read and commented on my manuscript from beginning to end. Jimmy O'Dea helped me to find my way through the *Red Tape*s of the post-war period and also read my drafts of Parts Three and Four. Both Challis and O'Dea had been near to the heart of things and were full of illuminating reminiscences. Two former general secretaries who gave me help were George Green and Bill Kendall. Among those who searched far back in their memories were Stanley Mayne, a leading figure in the Association between the wars; Charlie Inskip, who used to do the conference report in that period; Jean Cormack, Bill Brown's secretary, and Min Jackson, the first female President. Other past presidents who talked to me were Bill Hicks, Flo Bonsor, Joe Bryce and Charles Garrick.

Gerry Gerrard and George and Muriel Jamieson had a look at Chapters 12 and 13 and offered sometimes incompatible observations. Mrs Jamieson also advised me on the equal pay chapter. I did not show Chapter 20 to anyone still active in the Association as I thought whatever I wrote was bound to provoke criticisms from all sides and it was better that others should not be even faintly involved. Mrs Losinska, Elliott, Coltman, Williams, McGrath, Roddy and others all talked to me, I think, fairly frankly, considering they were engaged in war. Help also came from present and former officials of other unions, such as the Lords Houghton and Crook, and of the Staff Side, the Treasury and Civil Service Department.

I am grateful to the NEC and senior officers for commissioning me to write the history and for that priceless gift to an author – complete freedom to get on with it in my own way and to see everything I wanted to see. Tony Baker's patience about my ever-receding completion date, and my excessive wordage, was monumental. Practically every officer or member I approached, past or present, voluntary or professional, went out of his way to help. In a hectic period of the CPSA's life, the President and vice-presidents, General Secretary, Deputy General Secretary, Assistant General Secretary and General Treasurer found time to answer my questions. Peter Smith and his colleagues in the Research Department also assisted. So did Clive Bush, editor of *Red Tape*. None can be blamed for the result. To all of them, those I have named and those I have not, I offer sincere thanks.

Among books which have been of special help are *So Far . . .*, W J Brown's autobiography; *Clerical Unions in the Civil Service* by B V (Betty) Humphreys (1958); *Staff Relations in the Civil Service: Fifty Years of Whitleyism* by Henry Parris (1973) and, of course, the fiftieth anniversary history of the Association, *Yours for Action* by Bernard Newman (1953). To these I should add a draft history of the CSCA by Stanley Mayne, commissioned by the Finance and Organisation Committee and full of information about current problems for members, particularly young members, which he completed on the eve of the Second World War and which was never published. He included much of it in a series of articles for *Red Tape* after the war. *Red Tape* published another series of historical articles, by Derek Robinson, starting in August 1960 and largely based on Betty Humphreys' book. I found the CPSA Compendium a useful storehouse of facts.

Red Tape, from its beginnings a paragon among union journals, gave life – for me at least – to the otherwise bald and unconvincing narrative.

Appendix

Publisher's Acknowledgements

The Civil and Public Services Association would like to thank the individuals and organisations listed below for their kind permission to reproduce the following photographs in this book.

Associated Photo Services: page 119.
Averys: page 102 (bottom).
Barratts Photo Press: pages 32, 45.
BBC Hulton Picture Library: pages 19, 30, 42–43, 51, 56, 71.
Cyril Bernard: page 180.
Eddie Caswell: page 150.
Howard Coster: pages 76, 80, 81, 82 (centre), 83.
David A Hart: page 223.
F A Fyfe: page 106.
London News Agency: pages 54 (top), 63.
Charles Love Photographic: page 162.
Pat Mantle: pages 6–7, 165, 175 (top), 178, 179 (top), 193, 196, 207, 208, 213, 214.
Manx Press Pictures: pages 175 (bottom), 187 (top).
Derek Pratt: pages 12–13.
Press Association: pages 131, 197.
J W Sills: page 138.
H L Smerdon: page 90.
Sport & General: page 129.
The Star (by permission of Associated Newspapers Group Limited): page 100.
Sunbeam Photo Ltd: pages 102 (top), 112, 189.
John Topham Picture Library: pages 41, 92–93, 115, 122, 134, 137, 159, 184.
Unity Studio: page 95.
Universal Lens Craft: page 128 (bottom).
Wakefield Express: page 155.
Brian Worth: page 175 (centre).

Index

Biographical
Subject

Biographical Index

Numbers in heavy type refer to illustrations.

Subject Index